The Abridgement

of the

Book of Am Tuat

Solving the Mystery
of
the Hall of Records
and
the Sphinx Connection

Using Ancient Egyptian Texts, Astronomy,
and the Edgar Cayce Readings

John Bunker

Karen Pressler

THE ABRIDGEMENT OF THE BOOK OF AM TUAT
Copyright ©2014 by John M. Bunker & Karen L. Pressler

ISBN: 978-0-9669774-7-9

Printed in 2015

BUNKER PRESSLER BOOKS

"Two and a Guide"

Cover Illustration Credits

The image of the tomb painting comes from the tomb of Amenhotep II, fifth division of the Amduat, photographed by Francis Dzikowski, c Theban Mapping Project.

The image of the Khafra pyramid and the Sphinx was taken by Apples and Oranges and is used with permission according to the Creative Commons liscence agreement at http://creativecommons.org/licenses/by-sa/3.0/legalcode.

Questions regarding this book can be addressed to:

BUNKER PRESSLER BOOKS

8829 Heffelfinger Rd.
Churubusco, IN 46723

Bunker.Pressler@gmail.com

http://sites.google.com/site/edgarcayceandthehallofrecords/

In Honor of Sir Norman Lockyer

"Lockyer was not too bold, as is usually said; he was not bold enough. Had he lived in the time of Lepsius and Brugsch, he might have found more courage. He would have recognized planetary gods in the documents, had he not been bemused by the current verbiage about cult practices, which is making Egyptian history ever less interesting. The time has come to reopen the case, to honor Lockyer as a pioneer, and to carry on in his spirit, with securer data."

Giorgio de Santillana, from the preface to the 1964 edition of Norman Lockyer's *The Dawn of Astronomy*

"The best way to learn about something is to write a book about it."

Martin Gardner
(1914-2010)

Table of Contents

INTRODUCTORY MATERIALS I
   INTRODUCTION 3
   BELZONI'S ACCOUNT OF HIS DISCOVERY OF THE TOMB OF SETI I 7
      Belzoni's Account of His Discovery of the Tomb of Seti I 9
   AN OVERVIEW OF THE TRANSLITERATION 40
      Understanding the Text 49

ABRIDGEMENT OF THE AM TUAT 71
TEXT, INTERLINEAR TRANSLATION, AND TRANSLITERSTION 71
      The Text and Translation 72
   THE CONTINUATION OF THE ABRIDGEMENT OF THE AM TUAT 101
      Paul Bucher 103
      The Text and Translation 107

FURTHER EXPLANATORY MATERIALS 137
   DISCUSSION OF THE FOURTH DIVISION OF AM TUAT 139
      Alpha Centauri 140
      Stars Mark the Location of the Hall of Records 141
   The Upper Register 142
      The Narrow Line Across the Very Top 142
         Narrow Line – Right Side 143
         Narrow Line – Left Side 145
      Upper Register – Part 1 - Text 148
         Arura 149
         The Serpent Aligned with the Flat Top of the Pyramidal Mound 151
      Upper Register – Part 2 - Text 153
      Upper Register – Part 2 - Text 153
      Upper Register – Part 1 & 2 – The Figures 154
      Upper Register – Part 4 157
      Upper Register – Part 5 159
   The Middle Register 165
      Middle Register – Part 1 166
      Middle Register – Part 2 167
      Middle Register – Part 3 172
   Lower Register 174
      Lower Register – Part 1 176
         The Multifaceted Design: Encrypted Meaning 180
      Lower Register – Part 2 184
      Lower Register – Part 3 187
      Lower Register – Part 4 189
   DISCUSSION OF THE FIFTH DIVISION OF AM TUAT 190
   The Shabaka Stone 193
   The Symbology of the Fifth Divison 195

  Meridians 196
 The Pyramid is Aligned with Specific Star Constellations 198
 Seker and the Trapezoidal Mound 200
THE EDGAR CAYCE FACTOR 204
 An Illustrated Look at Some of the Highlights from the Cayce Readings 204
  The Hall of Records lies just beyond the Sphinx. 204
  It is along the causeway that leads from the sphinx to the pyramid, in a pyramid of its own. 205
  The Hall of Records is still covered. 206
  It is built upon a mound 207
  The position of the Hall of Records lies as the line of light falls between the paws of the Sphinx. 208
  The Readings for Miss 993 209
 The Location of the Tomb of Osiris 211
  Ancient Texts 211
   The Ancient Egyptian Coffin Texts 212
  Edgar Cayce Readings 214
  Egyptian Illustrations 216
   The Serpent Guardian of Osiris 217
   The Serpent Aligned with the Apex of the Pyramid 218
   The Pyramidion of Amenhotep-Huy 219
 The Location of the Hall of Records 220
  Ancient Illustration and the Edgar Cayce Readings 220
  Ancient Egyptian Artistic License 222
CONCLUSION 225
 Who will open the Hall of Records? 226

APPENDICES 229
 Appendix 1: Sphinx Chronology 230
 Appendix 2: The Pyramid and the Positions of the Stars 232
  The Throne of Osiris 240
 Appendix 3: Three Measurements in the Text of Am Tuat: 248
 Appendix 4: The Significance of 220 250
 Appendix 5: 300 Degrees – the 20th Hour 253
 Appendix 6: The Sealed Room - The Hall of Records 254

BIBLIOGRAPHY 257
INDEX 260

INTRODUCTORY MATERIALS

INTRODUCTION

This is an original new translation and study of the abridgement of the Am Tuat (otherwise known as the short form) from the tomb of Seti I. It seems like a different book than traditional interpretations have suggested. The title itself reveals how we should regard the rest of the book. "*Am*" means "that which is in" and "*Tuat*" means "the other world" (or, the abode of the dead) and refers to a place in the sky, an area of the stars in the heavens. So if we restate the title in English, using this understanding, the title becomes: *That which is in the Stars*. If this is correct, then what it means is that everything in the book of Am Tuat needs to be taken in the context of astronomy for it to make sense.

The book of Am Tuat records its own name in the second hour, taken here from the tomb of Tuthmosis III:

Akhm	m	seshem	pen	net	em	sesh	em	a	neth	Tuat	her
fly		canal	guide	this	which	in	book	of	praises	of Other World	above

Fly canal guide which is in this Book of Praises of the Other World Above

The book of Am Tuat is identified as *The Book of Praises of the Other World Above*. The stars are the map that was left for us to follow. Astronomy is the knowledge of the One God. It is our hope that someone will soon turn the search for the Hall of Records toward the place that map leads us. All evidence points to an entrance on the northeast corner of the middle pyramid at Giza, just above the construction change.

The first translators of the book of Am Tuat were not astronomers, and thus they did not recognize or connect the ideas in the book with the science of astronomy. While it remains true that the book of Am Tuat is more of a religious text than a scientific text, it does contain some science. Astronomy clearly infused all areas of life in the ancient world, and it appears to have held religious significance for the ancient people who originally compiled the book. But over time the true meaning was confused or forgotten. For many generations that followed, faithful priests kept the ancient records intact and, even though they may not have been able to completely understand them, these texts were considered to be Holy Writ.

---

[1] Budge, EHD, 136A, *akhm*: to fly (?) to glide about (?)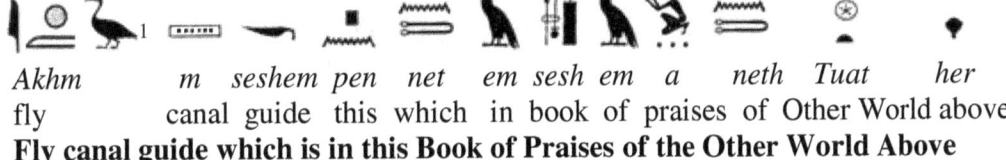

The ancient Egyptians used words like *gods*, *circles*, *hidden path*, *images of gods*, *to go down,* and *to rise like the sun* (among others) as astronomical terms to identify planets, obits, the ecliptic, constellations, declination, ascension, etc. By the time the book of Am Tuat was being used for tomb paintings in dynastic Egypt, astronomy was already ancient.

After translating and studying the ancient Egyptian texts for nearly 20 years, some ideas have emerged. You will see these key ideas throughout the abridged Am Tuat in this translation:

- There was a huge trapezoidal mound that the texts record as the Earth of Seker (fifth division). The top of this mound was a square area, described as being 100x100 Egyptian land-cubits. The throne of Osiris (his resting place) was upon the Earth of Seker.

- In reference to the 'place of Osiris,' the texts recorded the move-ments of stars. In the first division of the book of Am Tuat, the opening scene is the beginning of the night sky. At that time Gemini, was visible and Leo would follow shortly thereafter. Nearby, just below and east of Leo, the serpent constellation of Hydra began to make its appearance about 9:45 PM at the position of 120°. The first star of Hydra rises at this particular location on September 21st in 10,390 BC.

- At midnight, Gemini, Orion, and Hydra were visible. (beginning of the fourth division). The transit time of Hydra is given as 14 hours, shown by 14 heads, circles, and stars. But only the first 1/3 of Hydra was visible rising, and in this position it looked as if it was standing. The fifth division records that although the god of evil stands, he does not rise up from the earth.

- The fourth division explains that the serpent travels in a canal in the Tuat to a position above the Earth of Seker, accompanied by the god Af (the double man headed sphinxes of the fifth division) then goes away.

- Other information from the text explains that the serpent god and the guardian lion gods protect the 'sky-house of Osiris'. The texts even record the appearance of the star Sirius, which appears in the southern sky. This briefly occurs from 12:50 to 1:50 AM. and may be the first recorded appearance of Sirius.

Regarding the pyramid of Khafra:

- According to the Edgar Cayce readings, the Atlanteans first constructed this monument in remote times. (see readings 993-1 and 993-3). Thereafter, a portion of the continent was submerged under water for 250,000 years. Gradually it resurfaced. (see reading 341-09). When the first people again entered into this area (the Nile region) they began to excavate the ruins of the former civilization. (see reading 5748-6) They built a temple upon the mound.

- This can be compared with the *Mythical Origin of the Egyptian Temple*, written by E.A.E. Reymond, PhD. She translated the building texts from the ancient temple at Edfu, Egypt. Basically, the same information is recorded there.

- Comparison with information written by Mark Lehner in *The Complete Pyramids* gives further clarification. He notes that there is an obvious change in construction in upper ¼ of the Khafra pyramid from that of the bottom ¾ of the pyramid. This indicates that the top was added at a later date.

- In 1894 Norman Lockyer published *The Dawn of Astronomy*, in which he makes the statement that a complete difference in civilization is required to explain the difference in the construction at Giza (equinoctial orientation) compared with the majority of the Egyptian architectural orientation (solsticial orientation).[2]

This, in a nutshell, explains some of the basic ideas that will help you navigate the minds and writings of our ancient ancestors.

In order to fully understand the magnitude of what the ancient texts are telling us, we have found that three factors are absolutely required:

1. One must study the ancient Egyptian language in order to be able to formulate a basic concept of the meanings of the words.

2. One must study astronomy in order to be able to relate to the perspective from which the great religious texts were written.

3. One must study the psychic readings of Edgar Cayce to find the keys that unlock mysteries of our ancient Egyptian heritage.[3]

If any one of these factors is not considered, it is impossible to navigate the complexities of learning to understand a culture so very far removed form the one we know today. This may

---

[2] Lockyer, *Dawn of Astronomy*, pages 83-85.
[3] The readings of Edgar Cayce are discussed more fully on page 204.

be what Edgar Cayce reading #5750-1 was trying to tell us when speaking of "the three places where the records are one."

We have primarily used Sir Wallis Budge's 2-volume *Egyptian Hieroglyphic Dictionary* (abbreviated in the footnotes as EHD) for the translations. We have used Skyglobe astronomical software to study the views of the sky from Cairo during the ancient time periods. And we have used the *Complete Edgar Cayce Readings on CD-ROM* (abbreviated ECRS in the footnotes) for our study of the readings.

We hope this study will provide convincing proof of both the location of the tomb of Osiris and the location of the much sought after Hall of Records, as well as providing the most comprehensive translation of the abridgement of the book of Am Tuat from the tomb of Seti I ever completed.

John Bunker
Karen Pressler

October 2014

BELZONI'S ACCOUNT OF HIS DISCOVERY OF THE TOMB OF SETI I

The tomb of Seti I was first discovered in 1817 by Giovanni Belzoni, an Italian explorer and collector of antiquities. (His own fascinating account of this discovery follows on page 9)

Giovanni Battista Belzoni
(1778 –1823)

Eugène Lefébure
(1838 – 1908)

Decades later, in 1883, French Egyp-tologist Eugène Lefébure recorded hieroglyphic inscriptions from within the tomb, including those presented in this book.

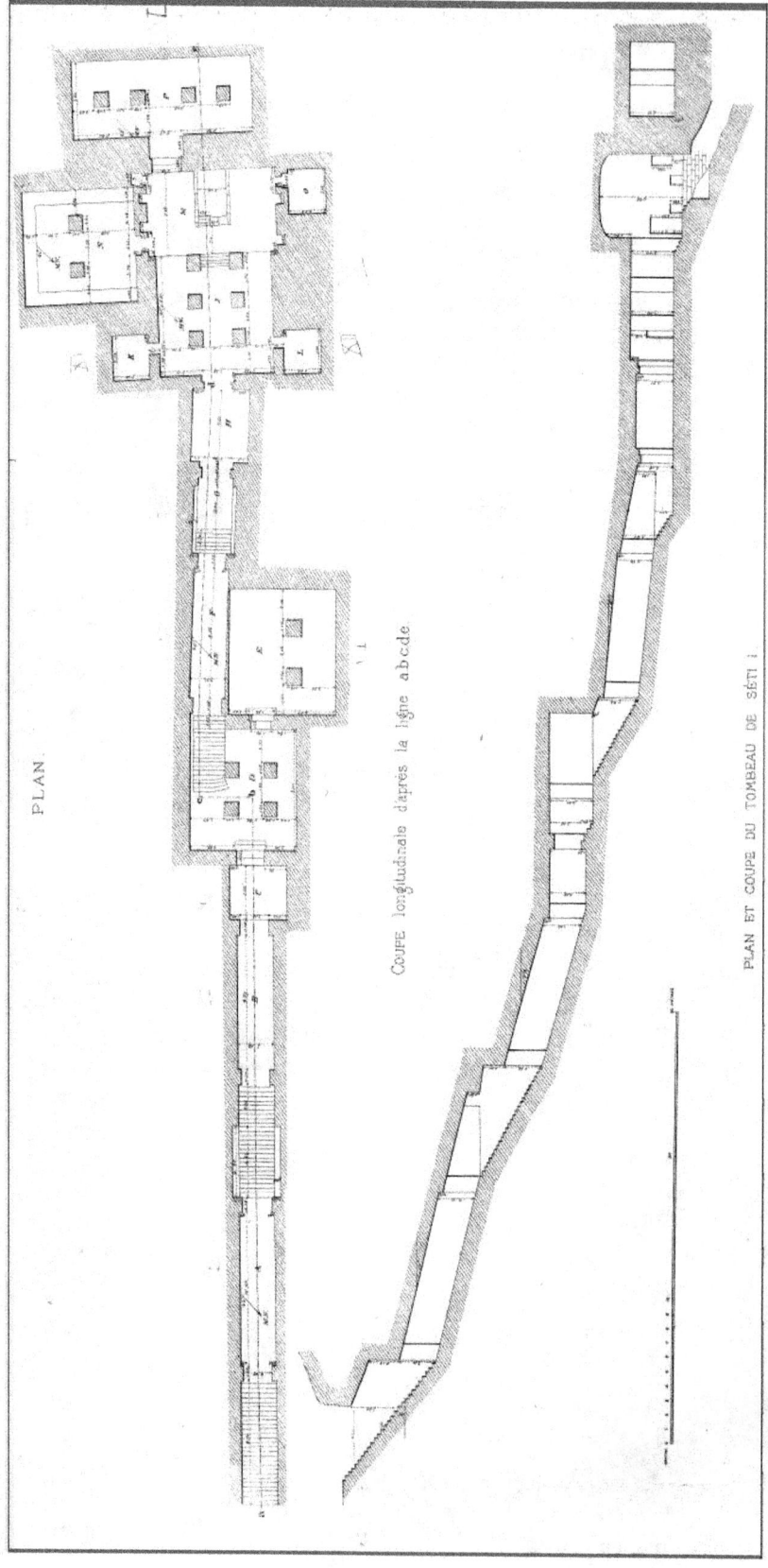

The plan of the tomb of Seti I from Eugène Lefébure's *Mémoires publiés par les membres de la Mission archéologique française au Caire, 1882–1884.*

Belzoni's Account of His Discovery of the Tomb of Seti I [4]

On the 16th (of October [1817]), I recommenced my excavations in the Valley of Beban el Malook, and pointed out the fortunate spot, which has paid me for all the trouble I took in my researches. I may call this a fortunate day, one of the best perhaps of my life; I do not mean to say, that fortune has made me rich, for I do not consider all rich men fortunate; but she has given me that satisfaction, that extreme pleasure, which wealth cannot purchase; the pleasure of discovering what has been long sought in vain, and of presenting the world with a new and perfect monument of Egyptian antiquity, which can be recorded as superior to any other in point of grandeur, style, and preservation, appearing as if just finished on the day we entered it; and what I found in it will show its great superiority to all others. Not fifteen yards from the last tomb I described, I caused the earth to be opened at the foot of a steep hill, and under a torrent, which, when it rains, pours a great quantity of water over the very spot I have caused to be dug. No one could imagine, that the ancient Egyptians would make the entrance into such an immense and superb excavation just under a torrent of water; but I had strong reasons to suppose, that there was a tomb in that place, from indications I had observed in my pursuit. The Fellahs who were accustomed to dig were all of the opinion, that there was nothing in that spot, as the situation of this tomb differed from that of any other. I continued the work, however, and the next day, the 17th, in the evening we perceived the part of the rock that was cut, and formed the entrance. On the 18th, early in the morning, the task was resumed, and about noon the workmen reached the entrance, which was eighteen feet below the surface of the ground. The appearance indicated, that the tomb was of the first rate; but still I did not expect to find such a one as it really proved to be. The Fellahs advanced till they saw that it was probably a large tomb, when they protested they could go no further, the tomb was so much choked up with large stones, which they could not get out of the passage. I descended, examined the place, pointed out to them where they might dig, and in an hour there was room enough for me to enter through a passage that the earth had left under the ceiling of the first corridor, which is 36 ft. 2 in. long, and 8 ft. 8 in. wide, and, when cleared of the ruins, 6 ft. 9 in. high. I perceived immediately by the painting on the ceiling, and by the hieroglyphics in basso relievo, which were to be seen where the earth did not reach, that this was the entrance into a large and magnificent tomb. At the end of this corridor I came to a staircase 23 ft. long, and of the same breadth as the corridor. The door at the bottom is 12 ft. high. From the foot of the staircase I entered another corridor, 37 ft. 3 in. long, and of the same width and height as the other, each side sculptured with hieroglyphics in basso relievo, and painted. The ceiling also is finely painted, and in pretty good preservation. The more I saw, the more I was eager to see, such being the nature of man; but I was checked in my anxiety at this time, for at the end of this passage I reached a large pit, which intercepted my progress. This pit is 30 ft. deep, and 14 ft. by 12 ft. 3 in. wide. The upper part of the pit is adorned with figures, from the wall of the passage up to the ceiling. The passages from the entrance all the way to this pit have an inclination

---

[4] Budge, E. A. Wallis. 1906. *The Egyptian Heaven and Hell*. Chicago: Open Court Pub. Co.

downward of an angle of eighteen degrees. On the opposite side of the pit facing the entrance I perceived a small aperture 2 ft. wide and 2 ft. 6 in. high, and at the bottom of the wall a quantity of rubbish. A rope fastened to a piece of wood, that was laid across the passage against the projections which formed a kind of door, appears to have been used by the ancients for descending into the pit; and from the small aperture at the opposite side hung another, which reached the bottom, no doubt for the purpose of ascending. We could clearly perceive, that the water, which entered the passages from the torrents of rain ran into this pit, and the wood and rope fastened to it crumbled to dust on touching them. At the bottom of the pit were several pieces of wood, placed against the side of it, so as to assist the person who was to ascend by the rope into the aperture. I saw the impossibility of proceeding at the moment. Mr. Beechey, who that day came from Luxor, entered the tomb, but was also disappointed.

The next day, the 19th, by means of a long beam we succeeded in sending a man up into the aperture, and having contrived to make a bridge of two beams, we crossed the pit. The little aperture we found to be an opening forced through a wall, that had entirely closed the entrance, which was as large as the corridor. The Egyptians had closely shut it up, plastered the wall over, and painted it like the rest of the sides of the pit, so that but for the aperture, it would have been impossible to suppose, that there was any further proceeding; and anyone would conclude, that the tomb ended with the pit. The rope in the inside of the wall did not fall to dust, but remained pretty strong, the water not having reached it at all; and the wood to which it was attached was in good preservation. It was owing to this method of keeping the damp out of the inner parts of the tomb, that they are so well preserved. I observed some cavities at the bottom of the well, but found nothing in them, nor any communication from the bottom to any other place; therefore we could not doubt their being made to receive the waters from the rain, which happens occasionally in this mountain. The valley is so much raised by the rubbish, which the water carries down from the upper parts, that the entrance into these tombs is become much lower than the torrents; in consequence, the water finds its way into the tombs, some of which are entirely choked up with earth.

When we had passed through the little aperture we found ourselves in a beautiful hall, 27 ft. 6 in. by 25 ft. 10 in., in which were four pillars 3 ft. square. I shall not give any description of the painting, till I have described the whole of the chambers. At the end of this room, which I call the entrance-hall, and opposite the aperture, is a large door, from which three steps lead down into a chamber with two pillars. This is 28 ft. 2 in. by 25 ft. 6 in. The pillars are 3 ft. 10 in. square. I gave it the name of the drawing-room; for it is covered with figures, which though only outlined, are so fine and perfect, that you would think they had been drawn only the day before. Returning into the entrance-hall, we saw on the left of the aperture a large staircase, which descended into a corridor. It is 13 ft. 4 in. long, 7 ft. 6 in. wide, and has 18 steps. At the bottom we entered a beautiful corridor, 36 ft. 6 in. by 6 ft. 11 in. We perceived that the paintings became more perfect as we advanced farther into the interior. They retained their gloss, or a kind of varnish over the colours, which had a beautiful effect. The figures are painted on a white ground. At the end of this corridor we descended ten steps, which I call the small stairs, into another, 17 ft. 2 in. by 10 ft. 5 in. From this we entered a small chamber, 20 ft. 4 in. by 13 ft. 8 in., to which I gave the name of the Room of Beauties; for it is adorned with the most beautiful figures in basso relievo, like all the rest, and painted. When standing in the centre of this chamber the traveler is surrounded by an assembly of Egyptian gods and goddesses. Proceeding farther, we entered a large hall, 27 ft. 9 in. by 26 ft. 10 in. In this hall are two rows of square pillars, three on each side of the entrance, forming a line with the corridors.

At each side of this hall is a small chamber; that on the right is 10 ft. 5 in. by 8 ft. 8 in., that on the left 10 ft. 5 in. by 8 ft. 9½ in. This hall I termed the Hall of Pillars; the little room on the right, Isis' Room, as in it a large cow is painted, of which I shall give a description hereafter; that on the left, the Room of Mysteries, from the mysterious figures it exhibits.

At the end of this hall we entered a large saloon, with an arched roof or ceiling, which is separated from the Hall of Pillars only by a step so that the two may be reckoned one. The saloon is 31 ft. 10 in. by 27 ft. On the right is a small chamber without anything in it, roughly cut, as if unfinished, and without painting; on the left we entered a chamber with two square pillars, 25 ft. 8 in. by 22 ft. 10 in. This I called the Sideboard Room, as it has a projection of 3 ft. in form of a sideboard all round, which was perhaps intended to contain the articles necessary for the funeral ceremony. The pillars are 3 ft. 4 in. square, and the whole beautifully painted as the rest. At the same end of the room, and facing the Hall of Pillars, we entered by a large door into another chamber with four pillars, one of which is fallen down. This chamber is 43 ft. 4 in. by 17 ft. 6 in.; the pillars 3 ft. 7 in. square. It is covered with white plaster, where the rock did not cut smoothly, but there is no painting on it. I named it the Bull's, or Apis' Room, as we found the carcass of a bull in it, embalmed with asphaltum; and also, scattered in various places, an immense quantity of small wooden figures of mummies 6 or 8 in. long, and covered with asphaltum to preserve them. There were some other figures of fine earth, baked, coloured blue, and strongly varnished. On each side of the two little rooms were wooden statues standing erect, 4 ft. high, with a circular hollow inside, as if to contain a roll of papyrus, which I have no doubt they did. We found likewise fragments of other statues of wood and of composition. But the description of what we found in the center of the saloon, and which I have reserved till this place, merits the most particular attention, not having its equal in the world, and being such as we had no idea could exist. It is a sarcophagus of the finest oriental alabaster, 9 ft. 5 in. long, and 3 ft. 7 in. wide. Its thickness is only 2 in., and it is transparent, when a light is placed in the inside of it. It is minutely sculptured within and without with several hundred figures, which do not exceed 2 in. in height, and represent, as I suppose, the whole of the funeral procession and ceremonies relating to the deceased, united with several emblems, &c. I cannot give an adequate idea of this beautiful and invaluable piece of antiquity, and can only say, that nothing has been brought into Europe from Egypt that can be compared with it. The cover was not there; it had been taken out, and broken into several pieces, which we found in digging before the first entrance.

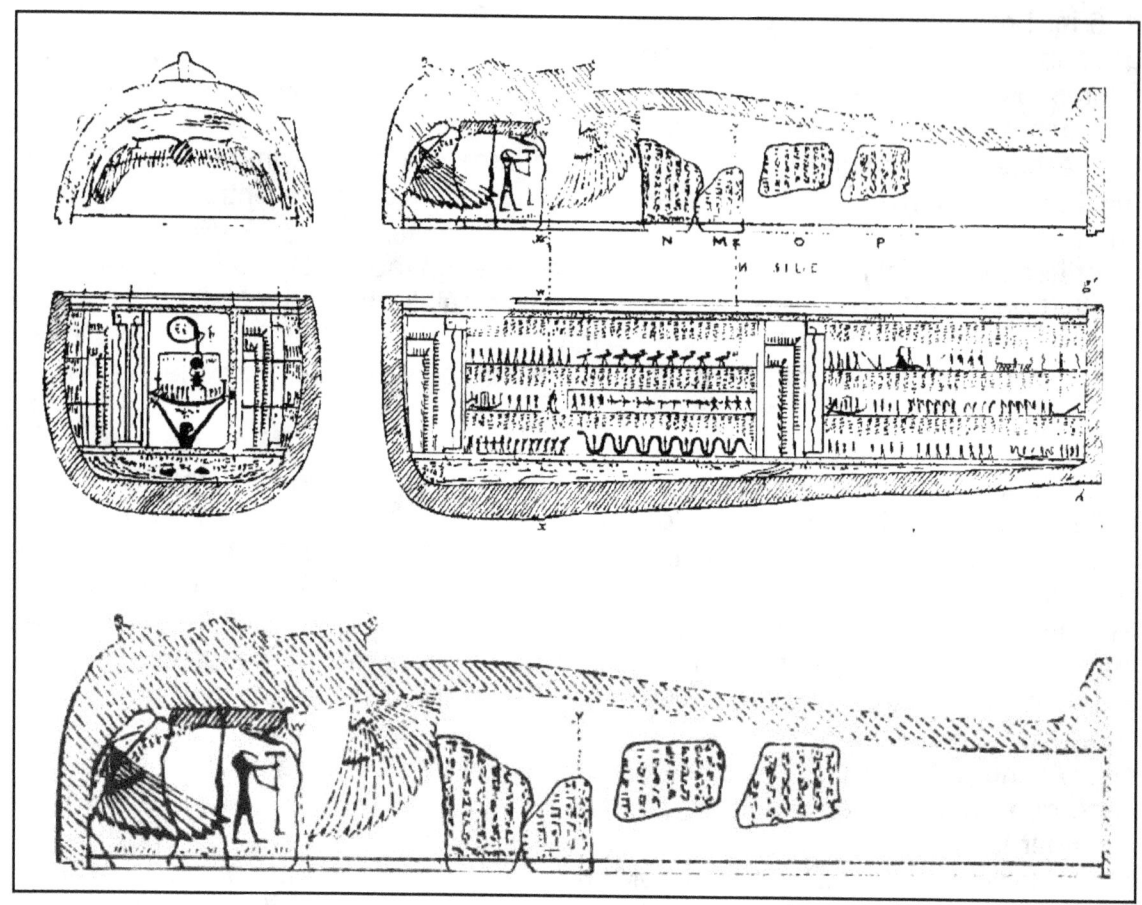

"The tomb faces north-east and the direction of the whole runs straight south-west."[5]

Thoth, the god of measurement, writing, and astronomy, can be seen here using a star with which to measure.

---

[5] Quote from Belzoni narrative (see page 15)

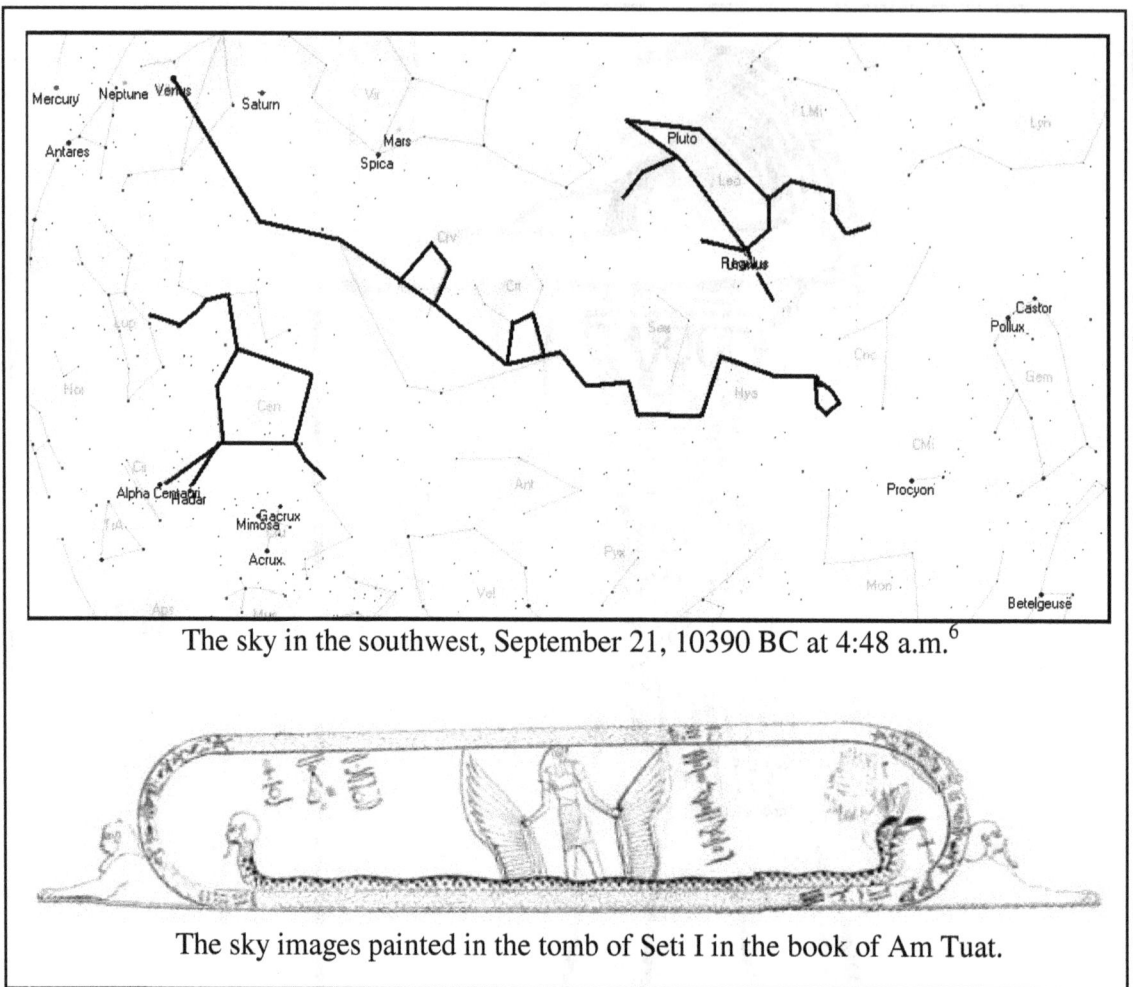

The sky in the southwest, September 21, 10390 BC at 4:48 a.m.[6]

The sky images painted in the tomb of Seti I in the book of Am Tuat.

The sarcophagus was over a staircase in the centre of the saloon, which communicated with a subterraneous passage, leading downwards, 300 ft. in length. At the end of this passage we found a great quantity of bats' dung, which choked it up, so that we could go no farther without digging. It was nearly filled up too by the falling in of the upper part. One hundred feet from the entrance is a staircase in good preservation; but the rock below changes its substance, from a beautiful solid calcareous stone, becoming a kind of black rotten slate, which crumbles into dust only by touching. This subterraneous passage proceeds in a south-west direction through the mountain. I measured the distance from the entrance, and also the rocks above, and found that the passage reaches nearly halfway through the mountain to the upper part of the valley. I have reasons to suppose, that this passage was used to come into the tomb by another entrance; but this could not be after the death of the person who was buried there, for at the bottom of the stairs just under the sarcophagus a wall was built, which entirely closed the communication between the tomb and the subterraneous passage. Some large blocks of stone were placed under the sarcophagus horizontally, level with the pavement of the saloon, that no

---

[6] Illustration from Skyglobe.

one might perceive any stairs or subterranean passage was there. The doorway of the sideboard room had been walled up, and forced open, as we found the stones with which it was shut, and the mortar in the jambs. The staircase of the entrance-hall had been walled up also at the bottom, and the space filled, with rubbish, and the floor covered with large blocks of stone, so as to deceive any one who should force the fallen wall near the pit, and make him suppose, that the tomb ended with the entrance-hall and the drawing-room. I am inclined to believe, that whoever forced all these passages must have had some spies with them, who were well acquainted with the tomb throughout. The tomb faces the north-east, and the direction of the whole runs straight south-west.

To give an accurate description of the various representations within this tomb, would be a work above my capacity. I shall therefore only endeavor to describe the most remarkable that are to be seen in the various parts of it. From these the reader may form some idea of this magnificent excavation.

The entrance into the tomb is at the foot of a high hill, with a pretty steep ascent. The first thing the traveler comes to is a staircase cut out of the rock, which descends to the tomb. The entrance is by a door of the same height as the first passage. I beg my kind reader to observe, that all the figures and hieroglyphics of every description are sculptured in basso-relievo, and painted over, except in the outlined chamber, which was only prepared for the sculptor. This room gives the best ideas that have yet been discovered of the original process of Egyptian sculpture. The wall was previously made as smooth as possible, and where there were flaws in the rocks, the vacuum was filled up with cement, which, when hard, was cut along with the rest of the rock. Where a figure or any thing else was required to be formed, after the wall was prepared, the sculptor appears to have made his first sketches of what was intended to be cut out. When the sketches were finished in red lines by the first artist, another more skilful corrected the errors, if any, and his lines were made in black, to be distinguished from those which were imperfect. When the figures were thus prepared, the sculptor proceeded to cut out the stone all round the figure, which remained in basso-relievo, some to the height of half an inch, and some much less, according to the size of the figure. For instance, if a figure were as large as life, its elevation was generally half an inch; if the figure were not more than six inches in length, its projection would not exceed the thickness of a dollar, or perhaps less. The angles of the figures were all smoothly rounded, which makes them appear less prominent than they really are. The parts of the stone that were to be taken off all round the figure did not extend much farther, as the wall is thickly covered with figures and hieroglyphics, and I believe there is not a space on those walls more than a foot square without some figure or hieroglyphic. The garments, and various parts of the limbs, were marked by a narrow line, not deeper than the thickness of a half-crown, but so exact, that it produced the intended effect.

When the figures were completed and made smooth by the sculptor, they received a coat of whitewash all over. This white is so beautiful and clear, that our best and whitest paper appeared yellowish when compared with it. The painter came next, and finished the figure. It would seem as if they were unacquainted with any color to imitate the naked parts, since red is adopted as a standing color for all that meant flesh. There are some exceptions indeed; for in certain instances, when they intended to represent a fair lady, by way of distinguishing her complexion from that of the men, they put on a yellow color to represent her flesh; yet it cannot be supposed, that they did not know how to reduce their red paints to a flesh color, for on some occasions, where the red flesh is supposed to be seen through a thin veil, the tints are nearly of the natural color, if we suppose the Egyptians to have been of the same hue as their successors, the present Copts, some of whom are nearly as fair as the Europeans. Their garments were generally white, and their ornaments formed the most difficult part, when the artists had to employ red in the distribution of the four colors, in which they were very successful. When the figures were finished, they appear to have laid on a coat of varnish; though it may be questioned, whether the varnish were thus applied, or incorporated with the color. The fact is, that nowhere else except in this tomb is the varnish to be observed, as no place in Egypt can boast of such preservation, nor can the true customs of the Egyptians be seen any where else with greater accuracy.

With the assistance of Mr. Ricci, I have made drawings of all the figures, hieroglyphics, emblems, ornaments, &c. that are to be seen in this tomb; and by great perseverance I have taken impressions of every thing in wax: to accomplish the work has been a laborious task, that occupied me more than twelve months.

The drawings show the respective places of the figures, so that if a building were erected exactly on the same plan, and of the same size, the figures might be placed in their situations precisely as in the original, and thus produce in Europe a tomb, in every point equal to that in Thebes, which I hope to execute if possible.

Immediately within the entrance into the first passage, on the left hand, are two figures as large as life, one of which appears to be the hero entering into the tomb. He is received by a deity with a hawk's head, on which are the globe and serpent. Both figures are surrounded by hieroglyphics; and farther on, near the ground, is a crocodile very neatly sculptured.

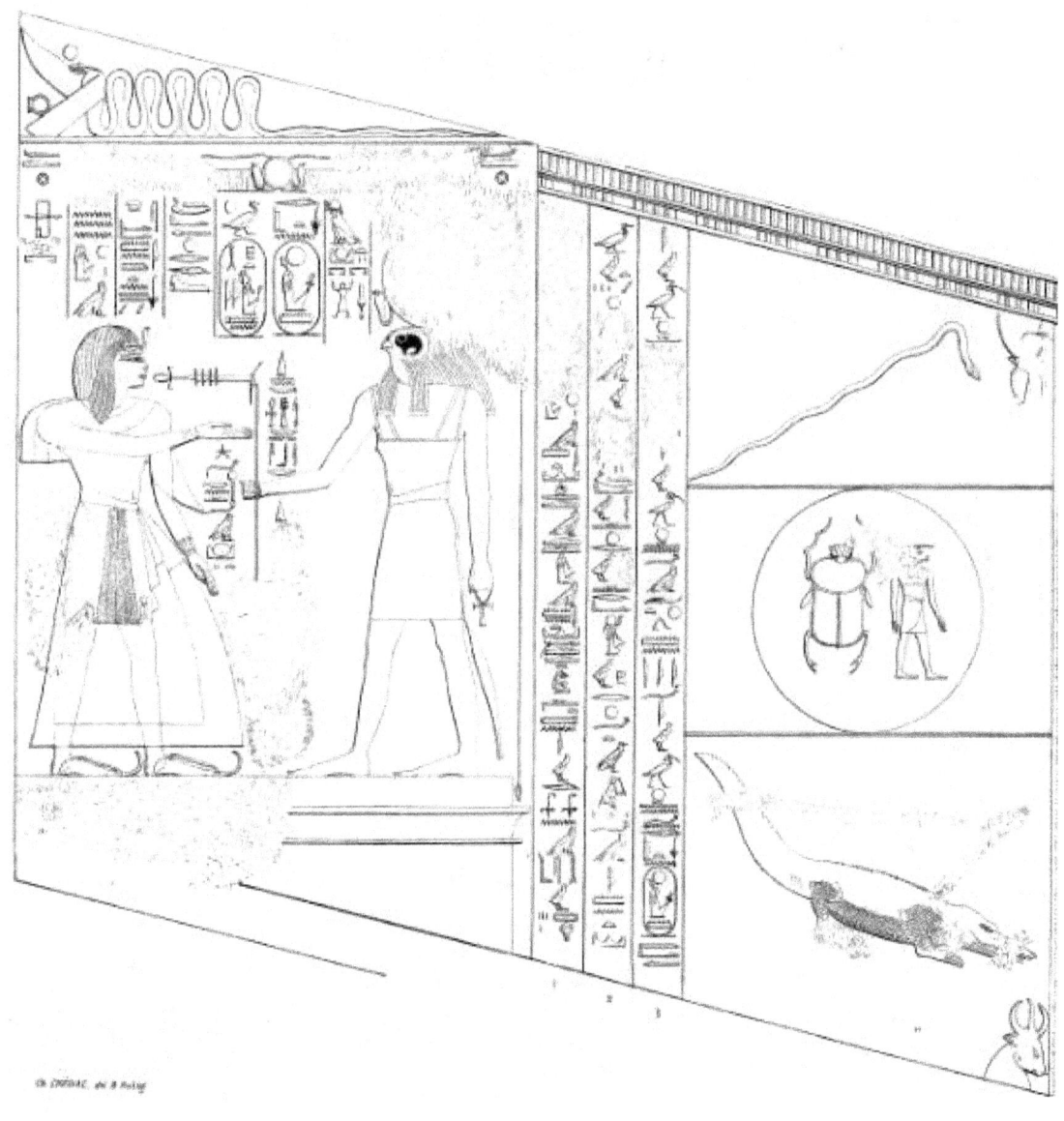

[7]

---

[7] This illustration from Lefébure, 1886, plate IV

The walls on both sides of this passage are covered with hieroglyphics, which are separated by lines from the top to the bottom, at the distance of five or six inches from one another. Within these lines the hieroglyphics form their sentences; and it is plainly to be seen, that the Egyptians read from the top to the bottom, and then recommenced at the top. The ceiling of this first passage is painted with the figure of the eagles, as in Plate 2.

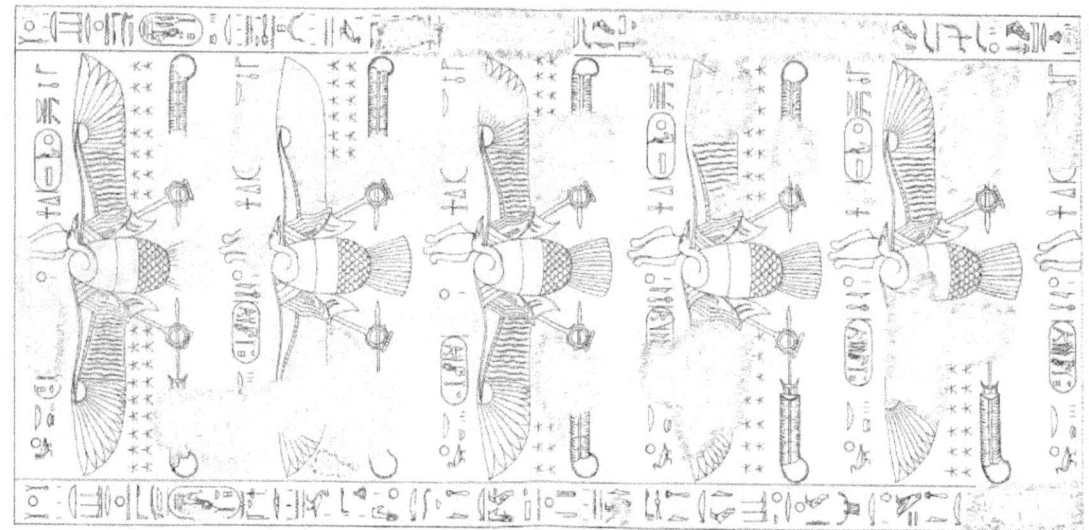

---

[8] This illustration from Lefébure, 1886, Plate III, which corresponds with Belzoni Plate 2.

Beyond the first passage is a staircase with a niche on each side, adorned with curious figures with human bodies and the heads of various animals, &c. At each side of the door at the bottom of the stairs is a female figure kneeling, with her hands over a globe. Above each of these figures is the fox, which, according to the Egyptian custom, is always placed to watch the doors of sepulchers.

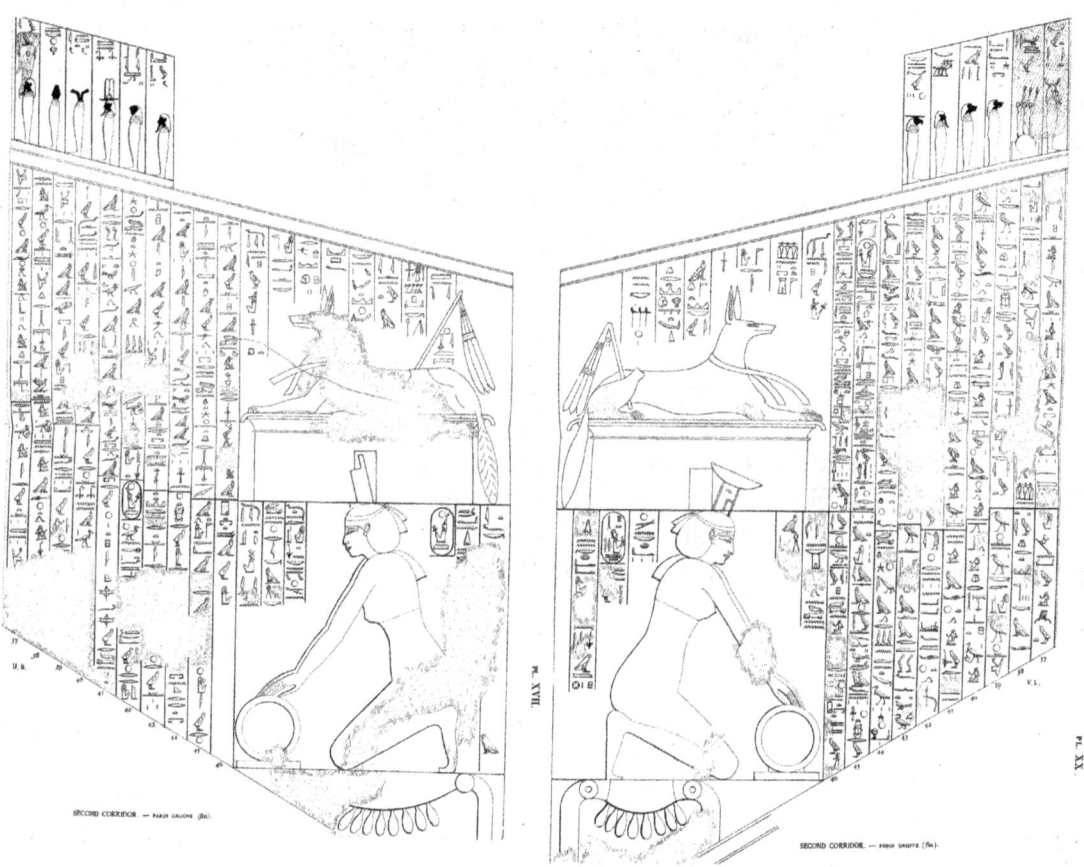

On the front space over the door are the names of the hero and his son, or his father, at each side of which is a figure with its wings spread over the names to protect them, as is seen in Plate 9. The names are distinguished by being enclosed in two oval niches. In that of Nichao is a sitting figure, known to be a male by the beard. He has on his head the usual corn measure, and the two feathers; on his knees the sickle and the flail; over his head is a crescent with the horns upward; above which is what is presumed to be a faggot of various pieces of wood bound together, and by its side a group twisted in a serpentine form. Behind the figure are what are thought by some to be two knives, by others feathers; but as the feathers are of a different form, I for my part think they are sacrificing knives, which may have served as emblems of the priesthood, for we know, that the heroes or kings of Egypt were initiated into the sacred rites of the gods. Below the figure is a frame of two lines drawn parallel to each other, and connected by similar lines, beneath which is the emblem of moving water.

In the next oval on the right is a sitting female figure with a band round the head fastening a feather, and on her knees she holds the keys of the Nile. Above the head is the globe, and beneath the figure the form of a tower, as it is supposed to represent strength. The faces of both figures are painted blue, which is the color of the face of the great God of the creation. On each of the oval frames there is the globe and feathers, and beneath it two hieroglyphics not unlike two overflowing basins, as they are under the two protecting figures at each side of the oval frame.

THE DISCOVERY OF THE TOMB OF SETI I

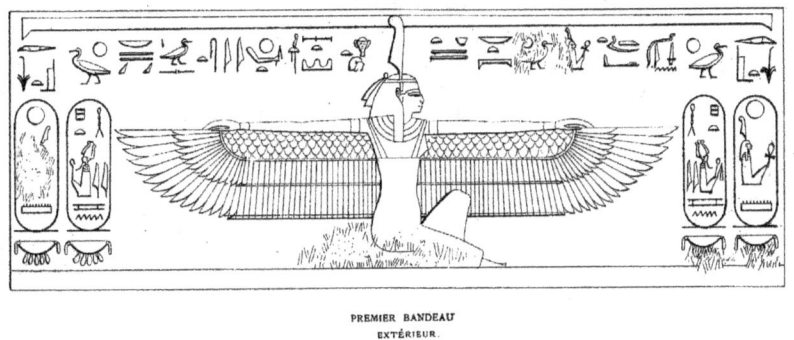

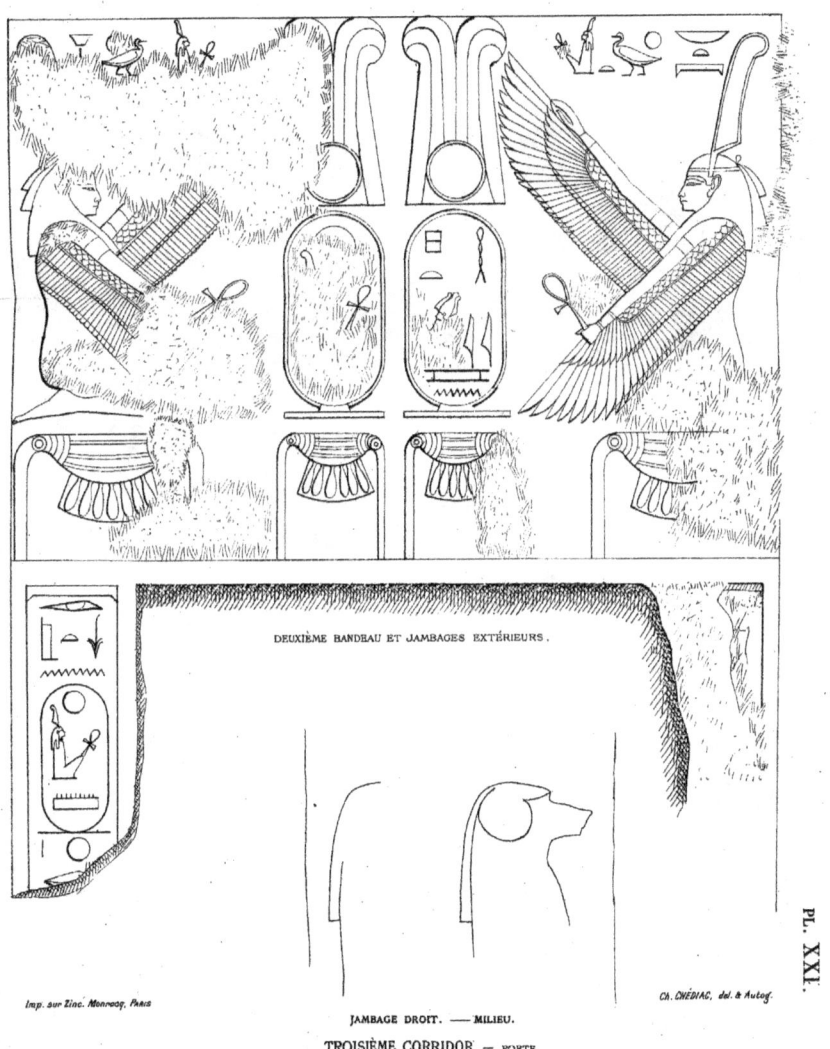

---

[9] This illustration from Lefébure, 1886, plate XXI, which corresponds with Belzoni Plate 9.

Next is the second passage, on the right hand side of which are some funeral processions, apparently in the action of taking the sarcophagus down into the tomb, the usual boat, which carries the male and female figures upon it, and in the center the boat with the head of the ram drawn by a party of men.

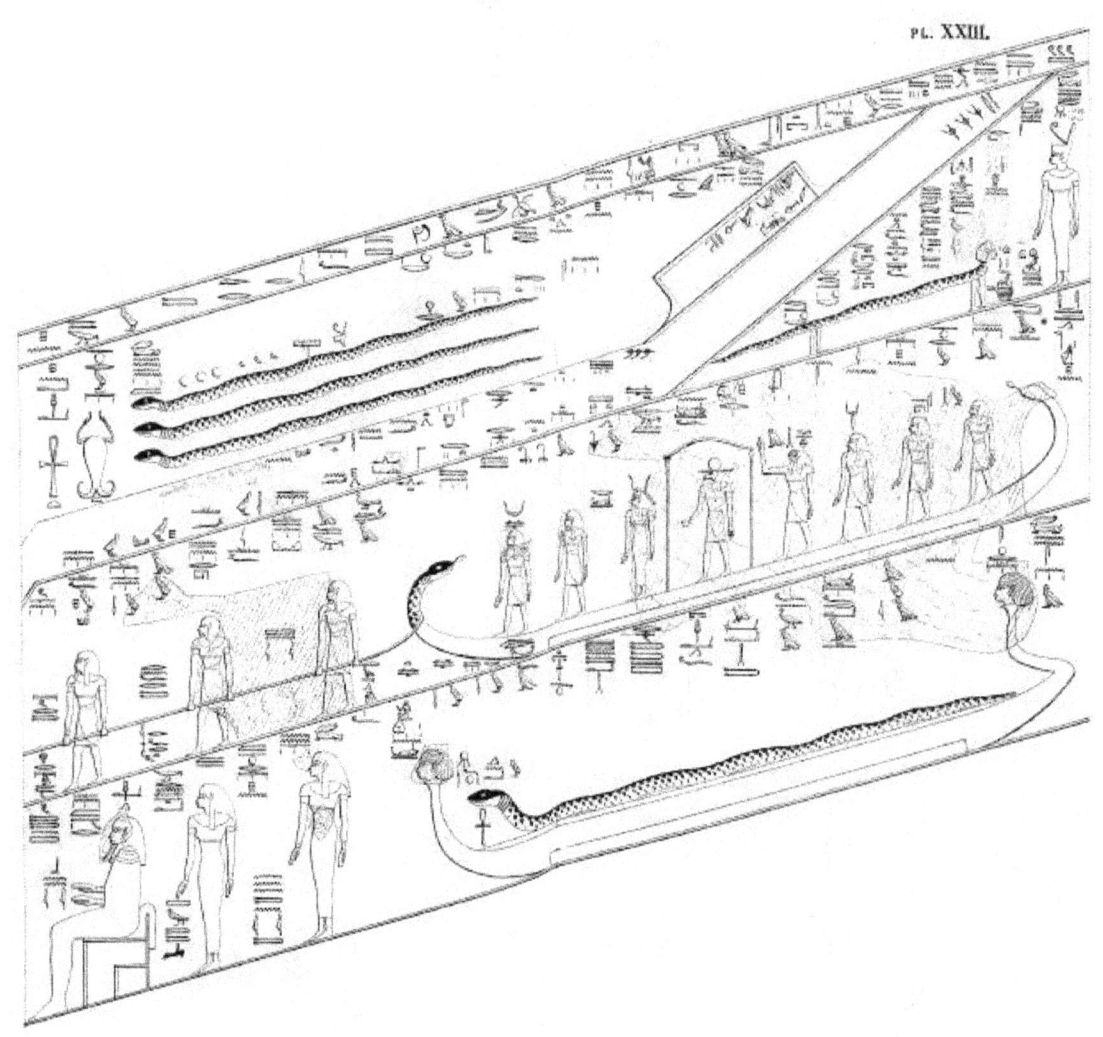

The wall on the left is likewise covered with similar processions. Among them is the scarabaeus, or beetle, elevated in the air, and supported by two hawks, which hold the cords drawn by various figures; and many other emblems and symbolical devices. The figures on the wall of the well are nearly as large as life. They appear to represent several deities; some receiving offerings from people of various classes.

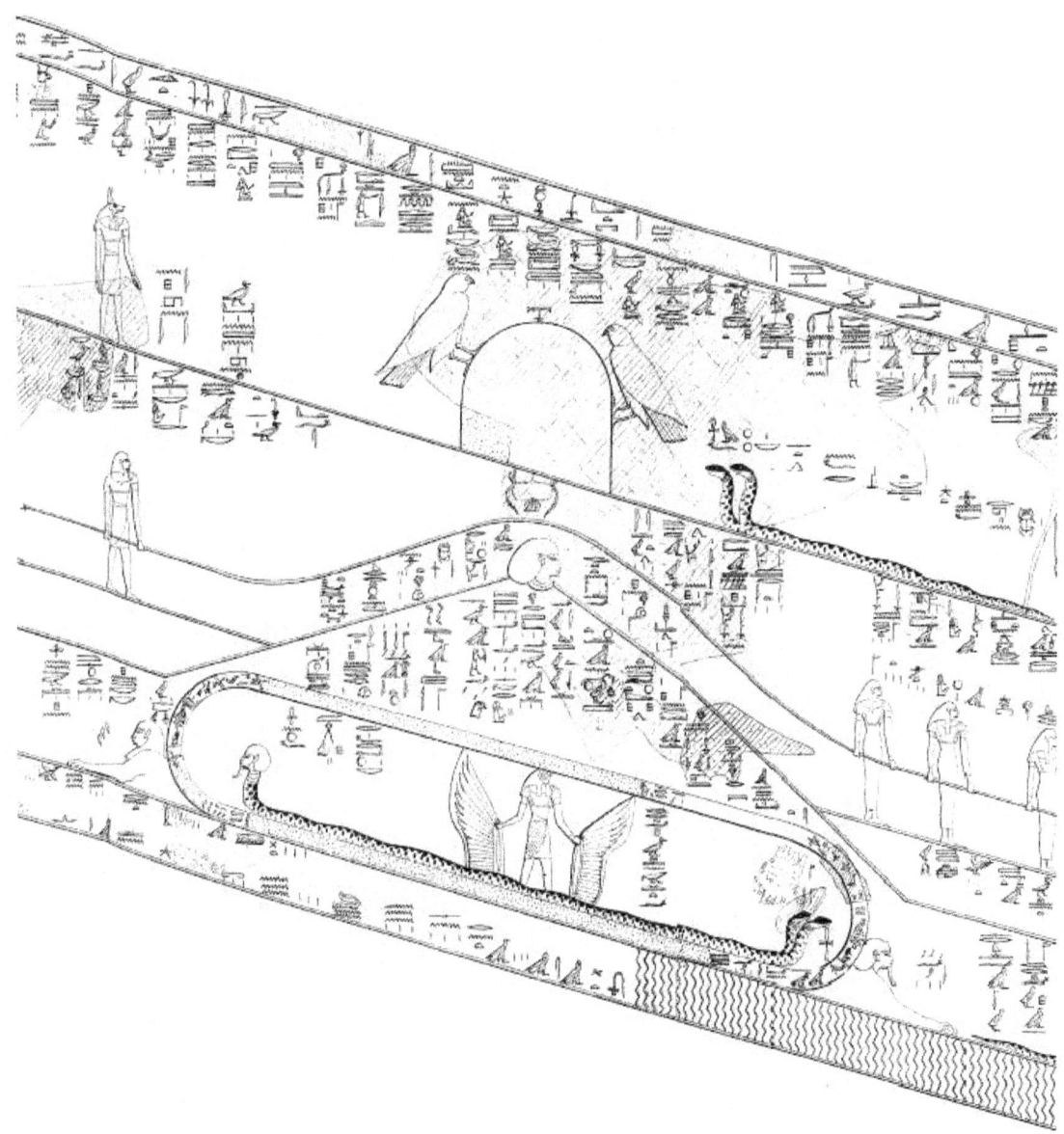

24　　　　　　　　　　INTRODUCTORY MATERIALS

Next is the first hall, which has four pillars in the center, at each side of which are two figures, generally a male and a female deity.

---

[10] This is a sample of the pillars described by Belzoni, as illustrated by Lefébure.

On the right hand-side wall there are three tiers of figures one above the other, which is the general system almost all over the tomb. In the upper tier are a number of men pulling a chain attached to a standing mummy, which is apparently unmoved by their efforts.

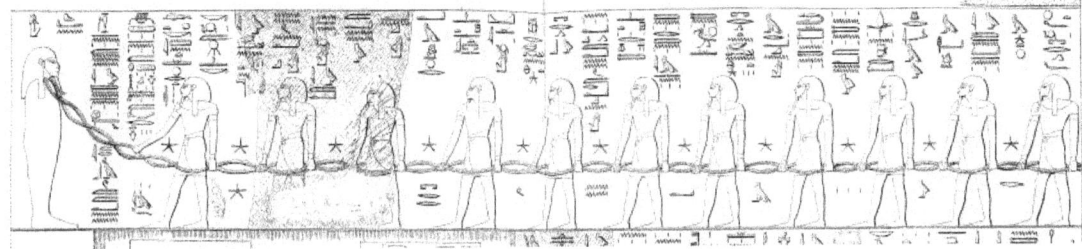

The two beneath consist of funeral processions, and a row of mummies lying on frames horizontally on the ground.

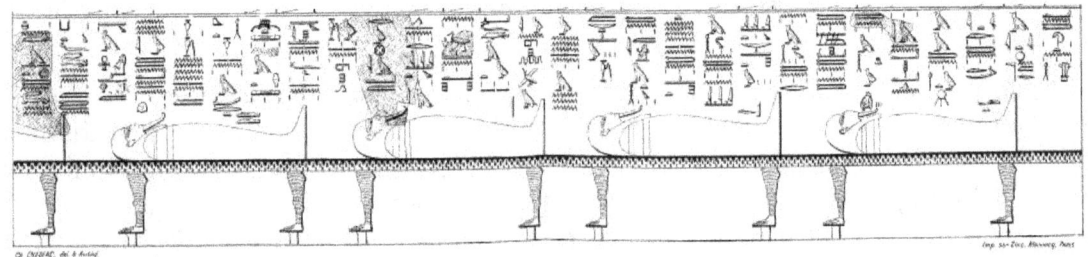

On the left is a military and mysterious procession, consisting of a great number of figures all looking toward a man who is much superior to them in size, and faces them. At the end of this procession are three different sorts of people, from other nations, evidently Jews, Ethiopians, and Persians.

Behind them are some Egyptians without their ornaments, as if they were captives rescued and returning to their country, followed by a hawk-headed figure, I suppose their protecting deity.

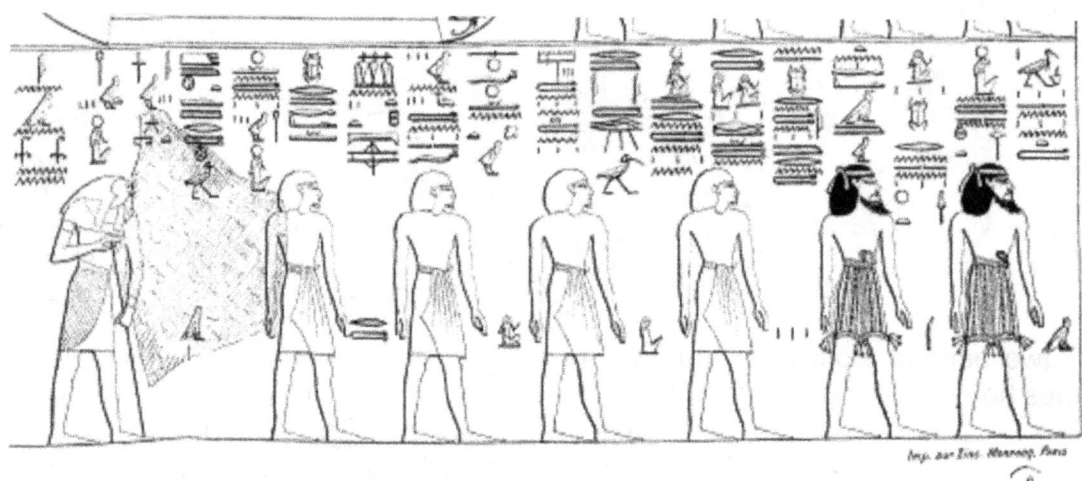

I have the satisfaction of announcing to the reader, that, according to Dr. Young's late discovery of a great number of hieroglyphics, he found the names of Nichao and Psammethis his son, inserted in the drawings I have taken of this tomb. It is the first time that hieroglyphics have been explained with such accuracy, which proves the doctor's system beyond doubt to be the right key for reading this unknown language; and it is to be hoped, that he will succeed in completing his arduous and difficult undertaking, as it would give to the world the history of one of the most primitive nations, of which we are now totally ignorant. Nichao conquered Jerusalem and Babylon, and his son Psammethis made war against the Ethiopians. What can be more clear than the above procession? The people of the three nations are distinctly seen. The Persian, the Jews, and the Ethiopians, come in, followed by some captive Egyptians, as if returning into their country, guarded by a protecting deity. The reason why the Egyptians must be presumed to have been captives is, their being divested of all the ornaments, which served to decorate and distinguish them from one another. The Jews are clearly distinguished by their physiognomy and complexion, the Ethiopians by their color and ornaments, and the Persians by their well-known dress, as they are so often seen in the battles with the Egyptians.

Belzoni's Plate 19

In the front of this hall, facing the entrance, is one of the finest compositions that ever was made by the Egyptians, for nothing like it can be seen in any part of Egypt. It consists of four figures as large as life. The god Osiris sitting on his throne, receiving the homages of a hero, who is introduced by a hawk-headed deity. Behind the throne is a female figure as if in attendance on the great god. The whole group is surrounded by hieroglyphics, and inclosed in a frame richly adorned with symbolical figures. The winged globe is above, with the wings spread over all, and a line of serpents crowns the whole. The figures and paintings are in such perfect preservation, that they give the most correct idea of their ornaments and decorations (See plate 19).

Straight forward is the entrance into another chamber with two pillars. The wall of this place is outlined, ready for the sculptor to cut out his figure. It is here that we may plainly see the manner, in which the artist prepared the figure on the wall ready to be cut; and it is almost impossible to give a description of the various figures, which adorn the walls and pillars of this chamber. There are great varieties of symbolical figures of men, women, and animals, apparently intending to represent the different exploits of the hero, to whom the tomb was dedicated.

On going out of this chamber into the first hall is a staircase, which leads into a lower passage, the entrance into which is decorated with two figures, on each side, a male and a female, as large as life. The female appears to represent Isis, having, as usual, the horns and globe on her head. She seems ready to receive the hero, who is about to enter the regions of immortality. The garments of this figure are so well preserved, that nothing which has yet been brought before the public can give a more correct idea of Egyptian customs. The figure of the hero is covered with a veil, or transparent linen, folded over his shoulder, and covering his whole body, which gives him a very graceful appearance. Isis is apparently covered with a net, every mesh of which contains some hieroglyphic, serving to embellish the dress of the goddess. The necklace, bracelets, belt, and other ornaments, are so well arranged, that they produce the most pleasing effect, particularly by the artificial lights, all being intended to conduce to this purpose.

On the wall to the left, on entering this passage, is a sitting figure of the size of life: it is the hero himself on his throne, having the sceptre in his right hand, while the left is stretched over an altar, on which are twenty divisions, as will be seen, in Plate I. A plate in the form of an Egyptian temple is hung to his neck by a string. It contains an obelisk and two deities—one on each side of it. Plates of this kind have been much sought after, as they appear to have been the decoration or breastplate of the kings of Egypt. Few have been found, and I have seen only two, —one is in the British Museum, and the other I was fortunate enough to procure from an Arab, who discovered it in one of the tombs of the kings in Beban el Malook. It is of black basalt, much larger and superior in workmanship to the other, which proves, that they were of various sizes, and more or less finished. It has the scarabaeus or beetle in alto relievo on a small boat with a deity on each side of it, and on the reverse is the usual inscription. Over the head of this figure is the eagle with extended wings, as if protecting the king.

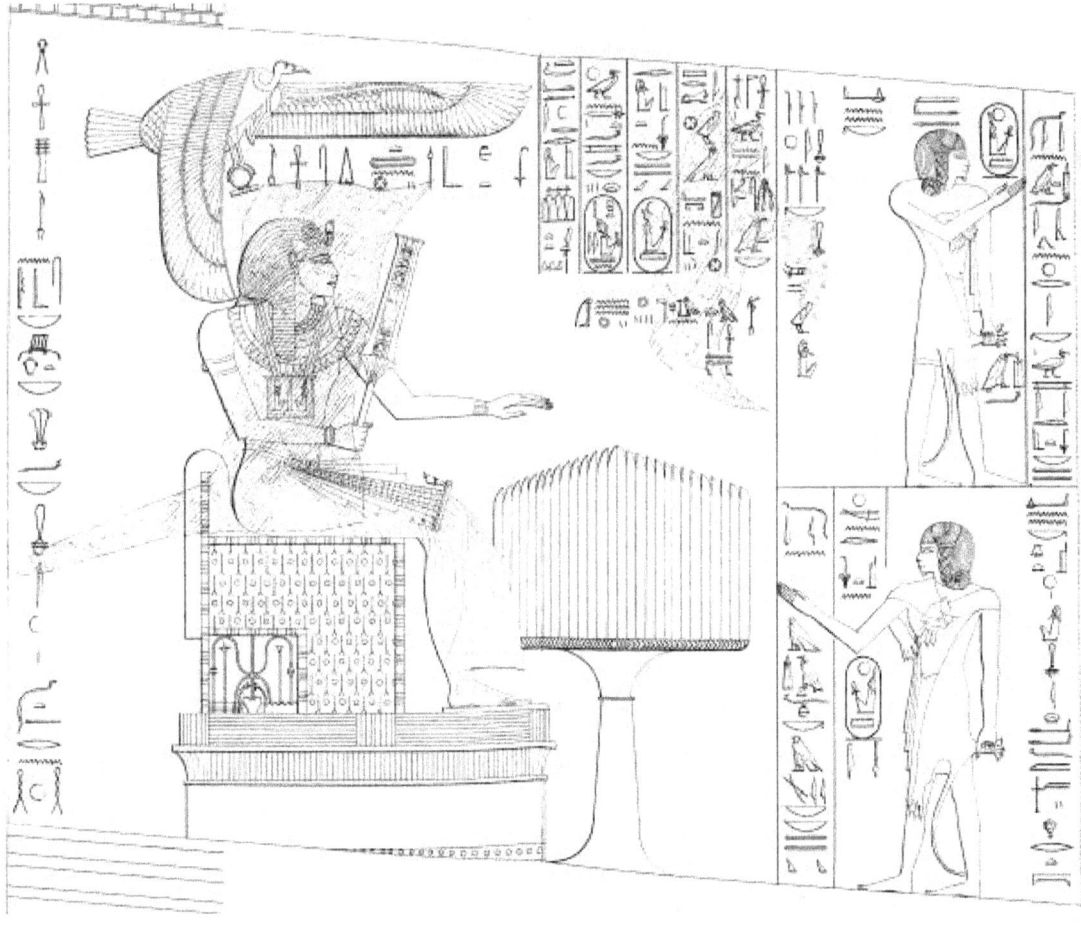

On the upper part of each side of the walls of the passage is the history of the hero divided into several small compartments nearly two feet square, containing groups of figures eighteen inches high. The hero is to be seen every where standing on a heap of corn, receiving offerings from his soldiers or companions in war.

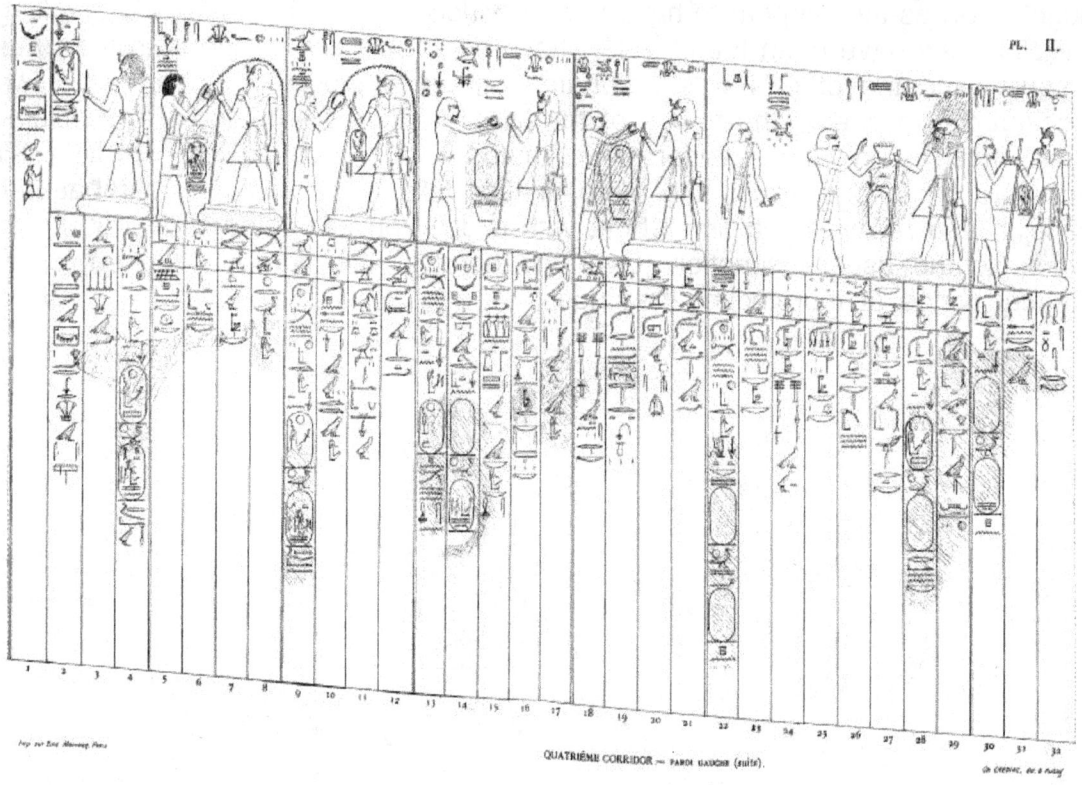

Farther on is a small staircase leading into a short passage, where the procession still continues, and the sacrifice of a bull is to be seen.

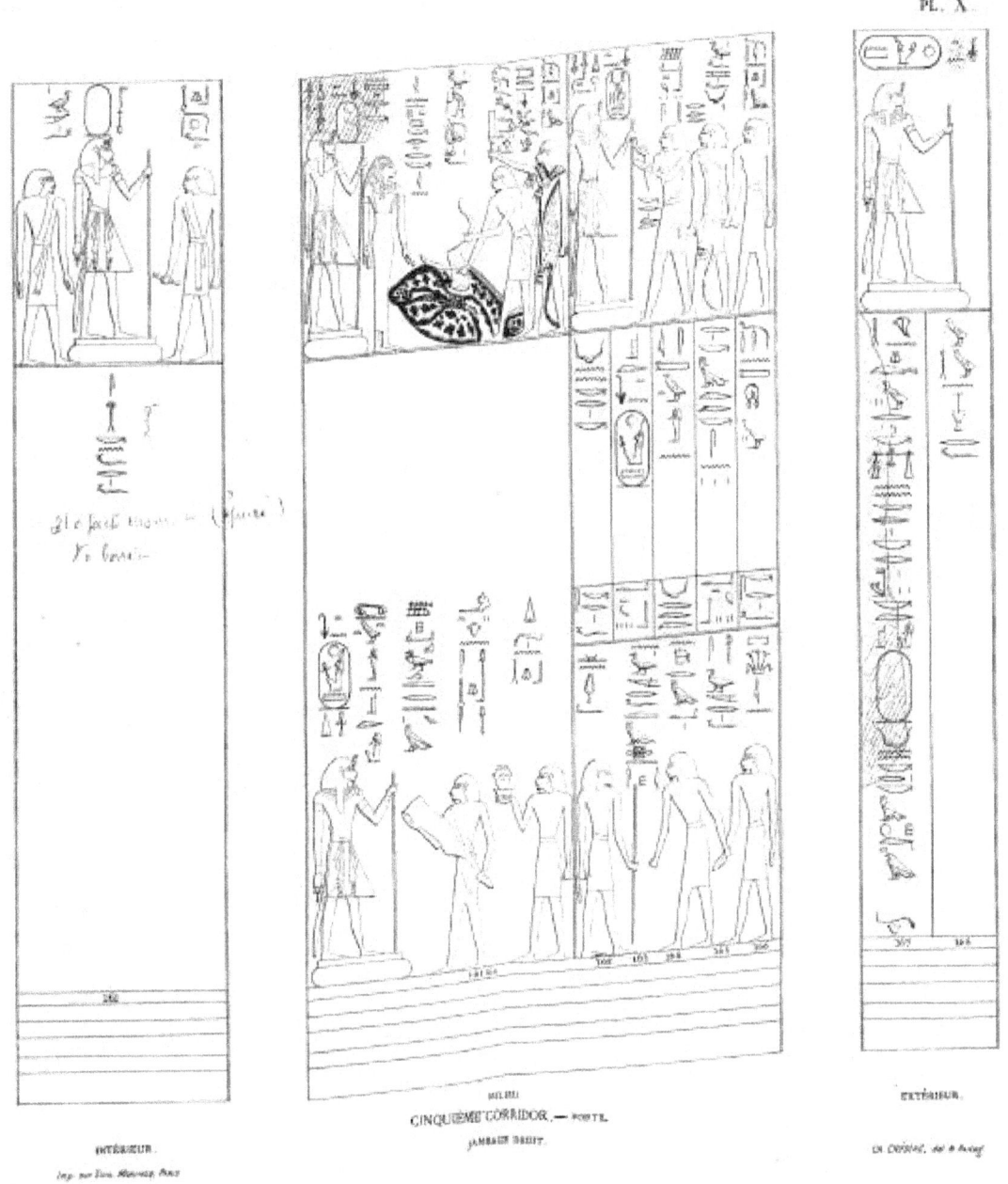

The walls of both passages are covered with hieroglyphics in separate divisions. From this short passage there is an entrance into another much wider than the rest. The charming sight of this place made us give it the name of the Room of the Beauties. All the figures are in such perfection, that the smallest part of their ornaments can be clearly distinguished. The sides of the doors are most beautifully adorned with female deities, surrounded with hieroglyphics, and the lotus is to be seen both in bud and in full bloom, with the serpent on a half globe over it.

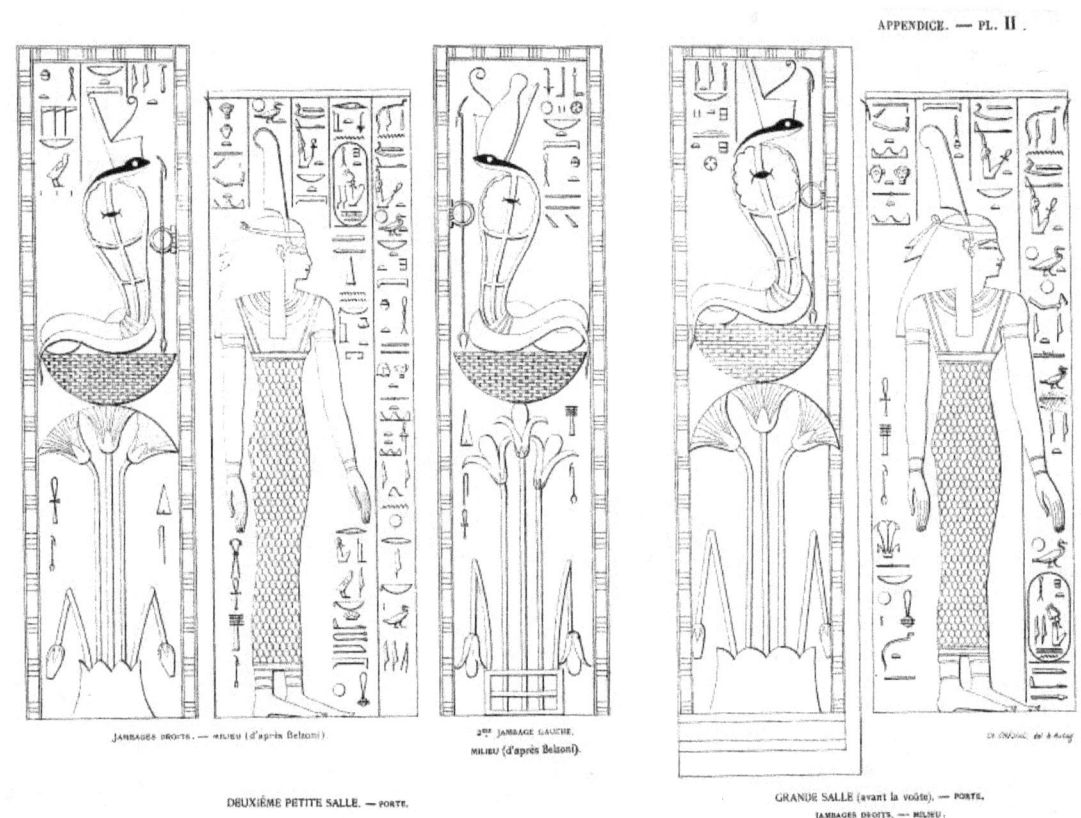

Farther on is the great hall with six pillars, containing on each side of it, two figures as large as life.

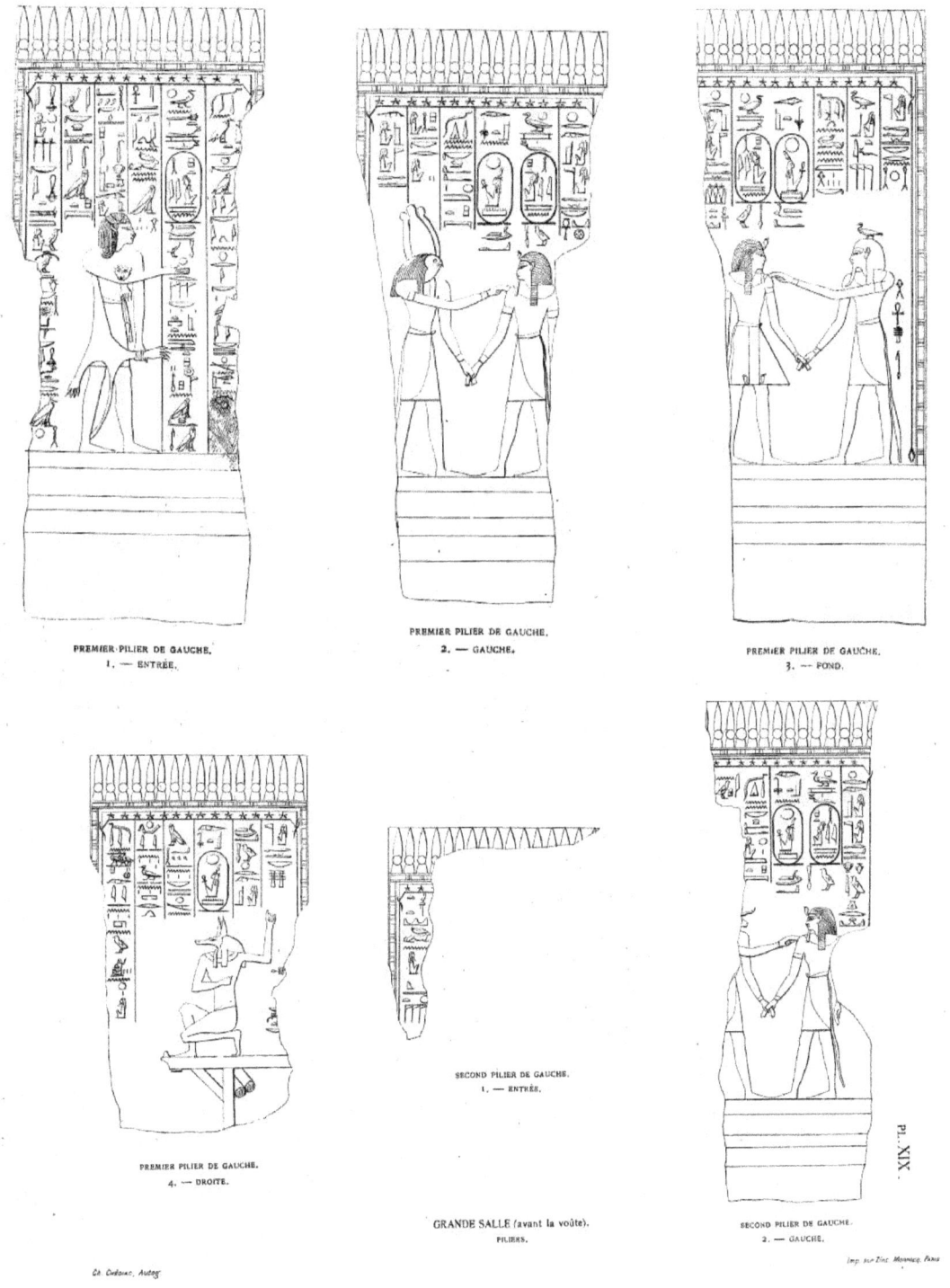

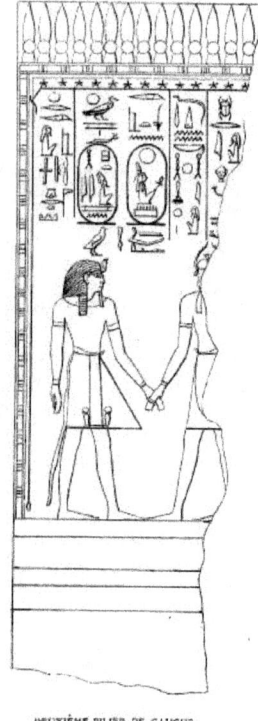
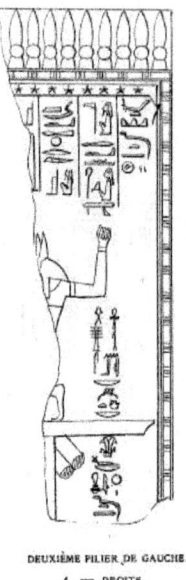
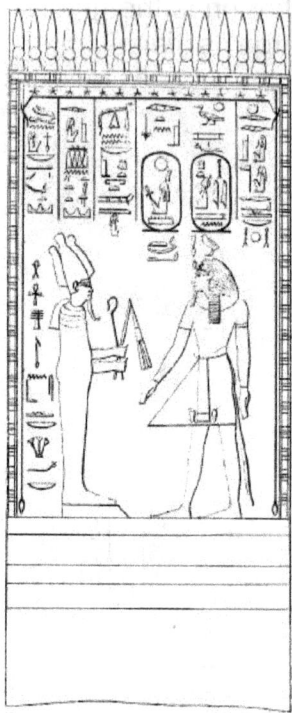

DEUXIÈME PILIER DE GAUCHE.
3. — FOND.

DEUXIÈME PILIER DE GAUCHE.
4. — DROITE.

TROISIÈME PILIER DE GAUCHE.
1. — ENTRÉE.

TROISIÈME PILIER DE GAUCHE.
2. — GAUCHE.

TROISIÈME PILIER DE GAUCHE.
3. — FOND.

TROISIÈME PILIER DE GAUCHE.
4. — DROITE.

Ch. CHÉDIAC, del. à Autog.

GRANDE SALLE (avant la voûte). — PILIERS (suite).

Imp. sur Zinc. Monrocq, Paris

PL. XX.

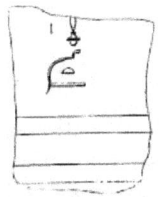

Fragment isolé qui se trouve
entre le 3ᵉ pilier de gauche et le
3ᵉ pilier de droite.

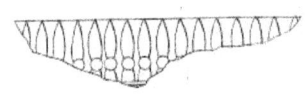

PREMIER PILIER DE DROITE.
2. — GAUCHE.

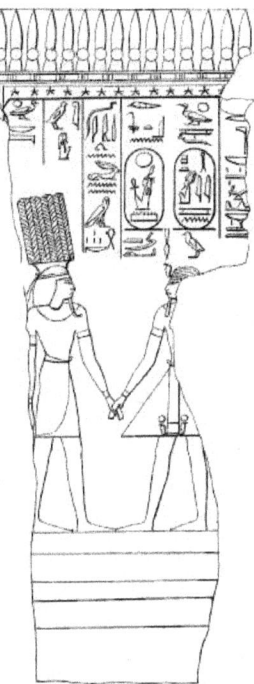

PREMIER PILIER DE DROITE.
3. — FOND.

PREMIER PILIER DE DROITE.
2. — GAUCHE.
Fragment détaché
appuyé contre cette face du pilier.

PREMIER PILIER DE DROITE.
1. — ENTRÉE.

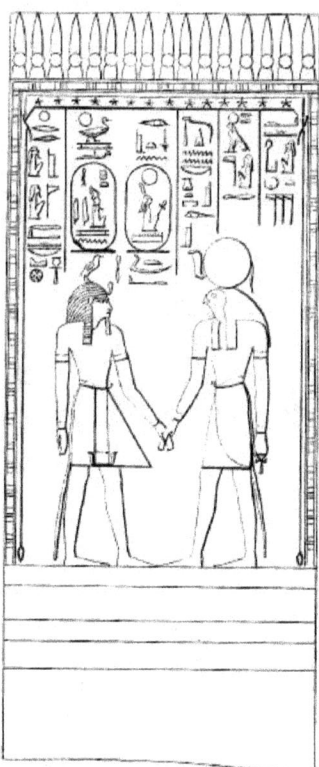

TROISIÈME PILIER DE DROITE.
1. — ENTRÉE.

TROISIÈME PILIER DE DROITE.
2. — GAUCHE.

The walls are adorned with the procession and other symbolical figures. Over the door, in the inside, is the figure of a female with extended wings. At each side of this hall is a small cell; that on the left containing various mummies and other figures, and that on the right a cow of half the natural size with a number of figures under it, which form a very curious group.

The Discovery of the Tomb of Seti I

GRANDE SALLE (avant la voûte). — COTÉ DROIT.
CHAMBRE ANNEXE. — PAROI DU FOND.

The walls also are covered with hieroglyphics. In the large hall close to the door are a number of men carrying a long slender pole, at each end of which is a cow's head, and on the pole two bulls.

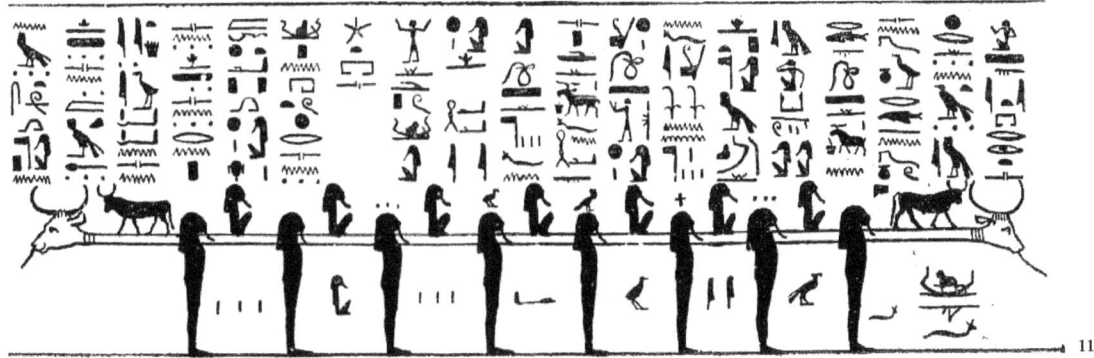

[11]

---

[11] This image comes from Budge, *Egyptian Heaven and Hell*, Volume II, page 104.

Still farther, the hall opens into the large vaulted chamber. It would be impossible to give any description of the numerous figures, which adorn the wall of this place. It was here that the body of the king was deposited, as I found in its centre the beautiful sarcophagus. This is sculptured within and without with small figures in intaglio, coloured with a dark blue, and, when a light is put into the inside of it, it is quite transparent. The ceiling of the vault itself is painted blue, with a procession of figures and other groups relating to the zodiac.

The next is a chamber with a projection like a side-board. It. has two square pillars with two figures on every side. The walls in every part of this chamber are also beautifully adorned with symbolical figures, which represents a compartment over the door within the chamber. It is useless to proceed any further in the description of this heavenly place, as I can assure the reader he can form but a very faint idea of it from the trifling account my pen is able to give; should I be so fortunate, however, as to succeed in erecting an exact model of this tomb in Europe, the beholder will acknowledge the impossibility of doing it justice in a description.

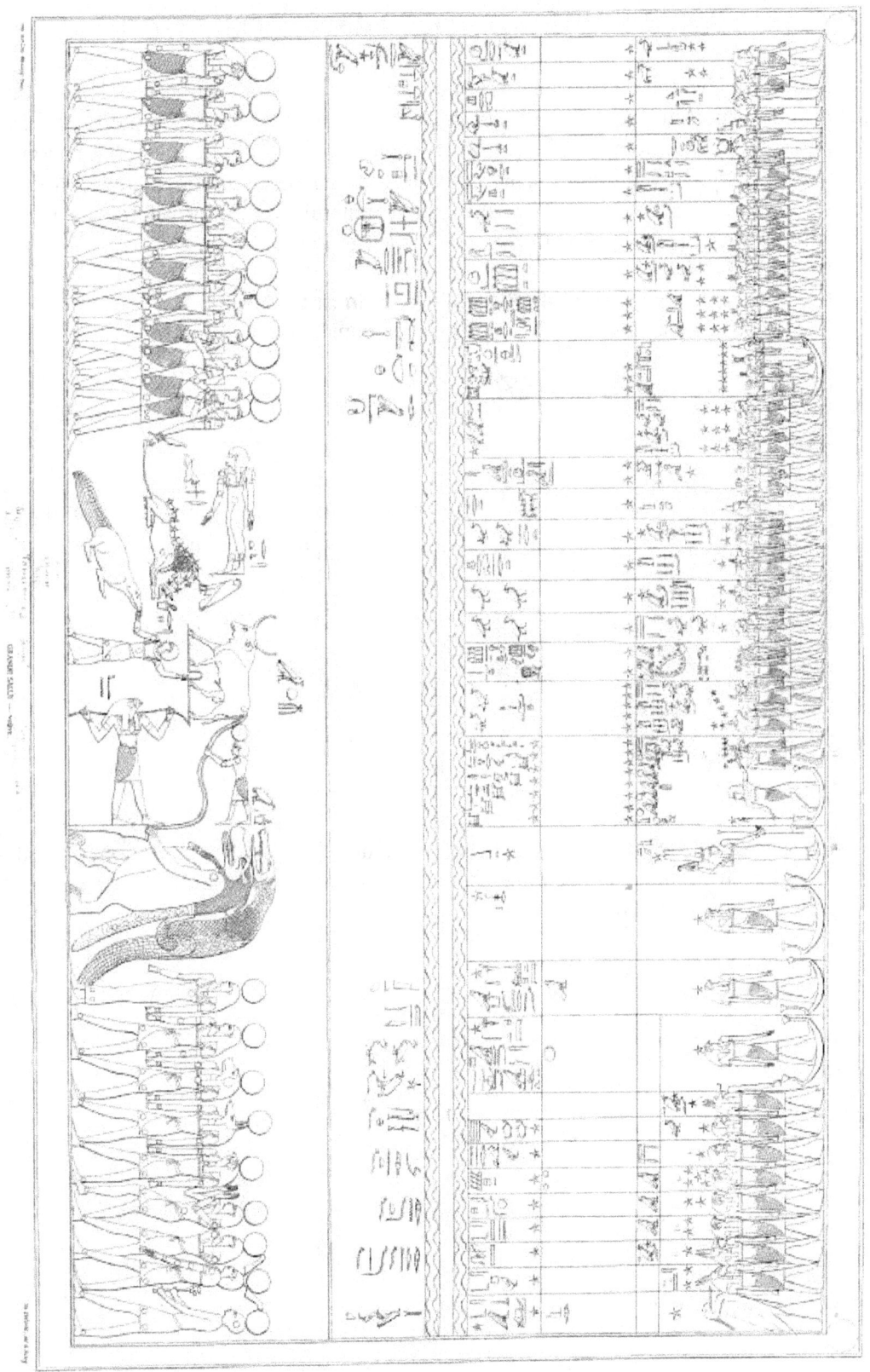

AN OVERVIEW OF THE TRANSLITERATION

In this section we give the basic transliteration of the abridgement of the Am Tuat within the context of the entire Am Tuat from the tomb of Seti I. It provides an uninterrupted flow of the words the ancient authors were trying to convey. This is followed by a discussion of the transliteration, section by section. This can serve as an introduction to the concepts and phraseology that occur in these texts, and give a general orientation of the locations and relationships of the various parts of the text.

[Our insertions are bold in brackets]
Names as given in the hieroglyphic translation are in *italics*.

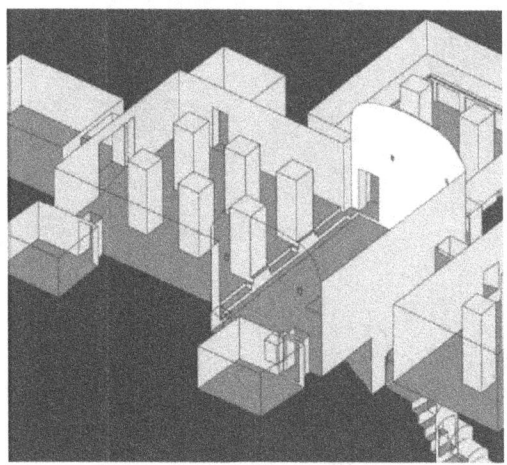

The Am Tuat begins on the wall of the burial chamber highlighted in white.

The outlined text in the next image is one segment of a very long section of text (213 columns), wrapping around several walls (not all shown here). These 213 columns constitute the abridged version of the Am Tuat.

The transliteration of this section follows:

> The utter darkness of the night is ended every day with the appearance of this god [**the constellation of Hydra**] as he enters the horizon at the point of 120°, as if from an invisible gateway; moving through the sky like he is traveling above, through an unseen canal. He travels in through the gateway of the horizon, his appearance is as the other world gods. *The Tuat of the Celestial Water of the Sun God* is the name of this province of the beginning of the sky of the Tuat. To measure the land of his region's entrance, those gods who are therein follow him up to his domain.
>
> Recite the words and see the designs of the gods who enter into the Tuat province. Come and see them together with this image of a god,[12] at the hidden house[13] in the morning. Know it by means of these guides together with the image of the great god himself. His spirit comes, dweller on earth, regularly and always. His spirit comes in the motionless Tuat. The *Goddess of the First Hour of the Night*[14] is the name of the hour beginning this night sky, guiding this great god in the gateway. Therein he rests.

---

[12] The constellations Hydra, Centaurus, and Leo taken together may represent Seker

[13] Hidden house = Pyramid

[14] Dusk or civil dusk is the time at which the sun is 6° below the horizon in the evening. At this time objects are distinguishable but there is no longer enough light to perform any outdoor activities. The first star visible on the horizon was Bellatrix, on September 21st, 10390 BC. This star is in the constellation of Gemini.

If you follow this great god in the great river that flows in the Tuat canal, in this length of 480 in this domain, the image at 120° is to be spread out.[15] *Divine Souls, Gods, and Other Beings of the Tuat* are the names of the gods who are in this domain. Make known their names. He is with them to measure land for him, this great god regions entrance place, in their domain, the great river that flows in the Tuat where the "Enemy God"[16] stands. He travels therein. Follow this great god.

He enters in the earth and his soul opens a way out to the Tuat to lead gods with side-locks. He travels above to swallow the sun god.[17] Follow with the two Goddesses of Truth[18] to measure land. He is bright and shining. He eats bread. To be removed, the earth gives him a towing rope for his boat. A form of the sun god comes - these images, the divine souls, gods, and other beings of the Tuat - in writings, in their images. They are hidden in a hidden door. The first hidden writings place is the hill cemetery. Make an offering to them, dweller on earth. They shine in their names. Praise them dweller on earth.

Their unit of measure is infinite time. Know these words, spokesman, gods, and other beings of the Tuat, of this god, spokesman of words of this great god, to ascend with gods and other beings of the Tuat, to shine in him, dweller on earth, in regular continuity forever. The name of the hour of night guiding this great god in this domain is *Knowledge of the Watercourse Protected by the Star God.* Follow in peace, by the majesty of this great god in this domain.

The Harvest gods paddle by this god in the celestial water. The canal of Osiris is 480 in length in the domain, to be spread out 120°. This great god is bright and shining. Follow the words, which are herein, to the place of Osiris' entrance. Make haste, he is in their regions, the entrance domain of these

---

[15] This is illustrated in the 4th and 5th Divisions connected, as can be seen below:

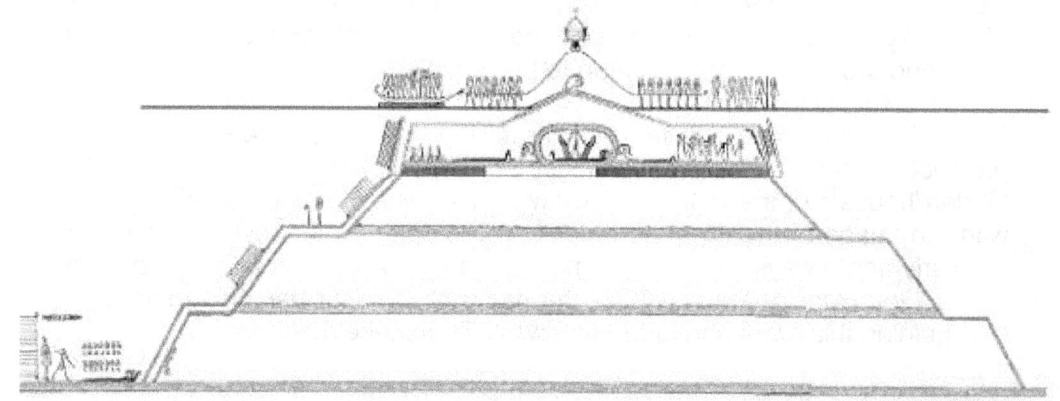

[16] *Apep*, the Egyptian serpent god was viewed as the greatest enemy of Ra, and thus was given the title "Enemy."
[17] In the ancient Egyptian legend of the battle between the evil serpent god Apep and the sun god Ra, it was believed that Apep waited at Bakhu - the mountain of the horizon - to swallow the barque of Ra.
[18] Constellation Gemini

divine souls. *Secret Gods* is the name of the gods who are in this domain. Know them by their names, dweller on earth.

He comes to go up to his entrance place under Osiris within. Give this in his domain of the celestial waters' domain, his entrance, this lord of celestial water. *One God Existent Largeness*[19] is the name of this domain. Come see the image; these images of the secret of the divine souls. Secrets of this image are not in writings, but are hidden in the Tuat, the first writings. Come know the entrance of the abode of the dead. They travel from above. They lead him in to roar. They do not travel in his entrance, their furnaces.[20] Come know them together with places this soul hides his entrance above with the Sun god.

Come know them with divine spirit power; his two legs are at the entrance. He does not enter in the place of destruction. He comes forth to shine in his images. Praise his winds, his great hour.[21] The name of the hour guiding this god is *Earth Division*. Souls at peace follow in tow by the majesty of this great god in the secret circle of the abode of the dead. See the designs of the gods to come, conducted in with his voice. They do not see him. The name of this circle is *Living One*. *Images House* is the name of the door of this circle, this hidden corridor through which boats are towed.

Come know the images of the gods in these secret paths of the Memphite necropolis.[22] Behold these paths, among these large stones, the great house hidden doors which are in the earth. Seker over his sand to eat bread at the entrance of evil, the living gods in the great house of the creator of heaven and earth, come to know they give the paths of Amen[23] of the other world.

See the Images of the Gods in the Great House is the name of the hour of night guiding this great god. Great powers, star passages through which boats are towed for this great god in roads above. Houses of the Tuat with half of the sky circle hidden, of Sekri over his sand, not seen nor perceived, guiding this secret in the earth under. This god Af, the two man-headed sphinxes, comes. The gods who are in this god hear their voice; the sun god calls out. *The Entrance Time of This God* is the name of the door to this place. *Stand Mighty Gods* is the name of the circle of this god. The hidden hill cemetery roads, secrets of the abode of the dead, the doors of the hidden house. *The Holy Place of Sekri, the Two Man Headed Sphinxes, the Flesh of the Body in His Image Above* is the name of the gods who are in this circle. The divine souls who are in door images, they who are in the hours, their images, their secrets, not known, not seen nor perceived; these images of the gods of Horus himself. Come see this image together with images of gods. This is not in writings; it is the secret of the Tuat over the South hidden house. Come to know them.

---

[19] This name refers to the domain of the stars.
[20] Budge, EHD, 465, *Hatu* : ovens, furnaces. This may refer to the sunrise, when the appearance of the fire of the sun destroys the constellations..
[21] The dawn in Egypt was accompanied by wind.
[22] The Giza plateau was part of the Memphite necropolis.
[23] the god of the solar disk

In peace his soul rests in his offerings. Khemit[24] does not cut to pieces Sekri's dead bodies. He passes away over them in peace. Come to make an offering to these gods, dweller on earth. The name of the hour of night guiding this great god in the circle is this guide *The Star of the Goddess of the Temple*. Rest by the majesty of this great god of deep celestial water. The gods and other beings of the Tuat become bright. His words to the gods therein become bright. His power is their divine offerings; this is their entrance place. He travels about, equipped in a bright and shining boat, in their regions in their entrance. Offerings they give him in their celestial waters. Of their celestial waters entrance they travel in the Tuat daily.

The name of the door to this place is *Sothis Pierces the Hidden House Road of Ament*. This great god navigates the celestial water to conduct entrance in his boat. See the designs of the gods and other beings of the Tuat to unite within. Know their names together within images, their hours, their hidden course of events, and unknown images of gods. This is the secret in the Tuat. For mankind, the goddess[25] comes.

See these images of gods in these writings, altogether hidden in this house of the Tuat, come over the southern hidden house. To know, unite lengths in the Tuat. Satisfy him with offerings. Gods who are therein follow. Osiris come truth in his bright cycle of time. His people upon earth bright and shining recite the words of this god, and give with divine offerings to the gods and other beings of the Tuat. He stands among them, see their powers, they in their domains the length of the horizons. They are Kheper in their shining brightness, this great god. *Metch-t-nebt-Tuat*[26] is the name of this domain. *Road of the Ship of the Sun-God* is the name of this hour of night guiding this great god in this domain, to lead to the land about the house. At the house the star comes to rest by this great god in the sky house of Osiris.[27] Recite words by majesty of this great god, entrance this sky house, these great gods who are in.

This ends the portion of the text that constitutes the abridgement of the Am Tuat. The remainder of this wall is transliterated here for context, but is not examined further within this book.

---

[24] Budge, EHD, 574B *Khemit*: a goddess of destruction.
[25] Nut, the sky goddess.
[26] Budge, EHD, 337A, *Metch-t-nebt-Tuat*: the name of the 6th division of the Tuat
[27] This refers to the top of the pyramid of Khafra, see further discussion in the section "The Location of the Tomb of Osiris" on page 211.

An Overview of the Transliteration

The writings and drawings of the hidden positions of the souls, gods, shadows, spirits, forms beginning daily the hidden star in hidden horizon ends utter darkness, the star horizon, the abode of the dead.

Writings and drawings of the hidden positions of the souls, gods, shadows, spirits, forms, hidden star in horizon, the abode of the dead ends darkness.

Scientific knowledge to know dekans, to know them, to know their spirits in their circle.

Scientific knowledge to know the divine souls, gods, and other beings of the Tuat; to know their spirits in their circle.

Scientific knowledge to know the divine secret souls of Egypt; to know of the gods in their hours; to know he calls out to them.

Scientific knowledge to know the secrets, to know between their hour-gods,
to know he calls out to them,
to know the stars paths, the great god travels over them;
to know the stars journey and their gods,
to know those who sing praises and destroyers,
to know the doors and the paths; the great god travels over them;
to know the hours journeys and their gods,
to know those who sing praise to the gods and the destroyers come and go in this god in the hidden gateway belonging to the horizon. The god stands near canal region 120° above this, comes to this gateway belonging to the star-gods. He travels the celestial water, the river that flows in the Tuat. Gods

enter in the hidden gateway belonging to the horizon. The god stands near the canal region 120º to come forth the ship of the gods and other beings of the Tuat, he travels in to follow the river that flows in the Tuat.

The gods enter in the gateway of the abode of the dead of this horizon. The god stands at the entrance of the territory at the canal belonging to 120º and arrives to come forth. The boat of the gods, and other beings of the Tuat, he travels in to follow into the river that flows in the Tuat.

The names of nine baboon gods who are the door openers for the great soul. (9)

The names of goddesses whose stars are in the earth. (12)

The names of the star-gods. (9)

The names of the goddesses who guide the great god. (12)

An Overview of the Transliteration

47

The twin goddesses of truth are not in the boat of the setting sun.[28] The journey to the gateway of this place belongs to 220 degrees[29]. He travels behind in the celestial water. The great entrance belongs to the celestial water at 300 degrees[30] in this birth place of the entrance of the gods who are following him, who are behind in the celestial water of the Sun god, the name of this domain, the image of the double fire god is the name of the image of the domain of this great god, recite the words, see the designs that are in the Tuat, near the gateway of the domain, this god travels over them in ram[31] form to come into being, to follow he travels in this gateway, the dead follow but do not come forth. His power is to ascend the entrance of this gateway above him. Recite the words.

---

[28] Tuthmosis III reads: The double goddesses of truth tow this god in the boat of the setting sun. A boat procession of the gateway of this place, this canal 120º he travels in celestial water to follow into the river that flows in the Tuat canal, long ropes in this place to command.

[29] See Appendix 4 on page 250 for more information about journey to the gateway and the number 220.

[30] 20th hour - in other words, the hour beginning at 8:00 PM and ending at 8:59 PM. See Appendix 5 (page 253) for the full explanation.

[31] the entrance or birth of Leo into the horizon

Double Goddess of Truth, opener of the ways of knowledge, the goddess of the ship of the Sky-god. Praise the Double Goddess, the lookout in front of the ship. The murderer. The first of those in Amenti.[32] The age of the lioness-headed goddess.

Their great tablet, their great illumination; to speak the command of the Sun god, tablet of the words of the Sun god; to speak the command of Tem, the tablet of the words of Tem; to speak the command of Kheper, the tablet of the words of Kheper; to speak the command of Osiris, the tablet of the words of Osiris. The stars travel and divide the earth. The star travels the hours.

The names of gods who are singers of sun god as he enters into the Tuat. (9)

The names of goddesses who give light in the darkness of the Tuat. (12)

The names of nine star-gods of the nine gods. (9)

The names of the goddesses the guides of the great god. (12)

---

[32] The Shabaka Stone records the murder of Osiris (see page 193).

If you search the Edgar Cayce readings[33], you find that when there was the entrance of Araart, Araaraart, and Ra-Ta into Egypt, there was, even then, archaeological research. Artifacts, including textual material was discovered and translated by Ra-Ta. He shared it with those who would listen. These artifacts were evidence of the civilization that preceded them in the Nile Valley, which (the readings explain) had been submerged for nearly 250,000 years since civilization had been in this part of the country. Before this (the readings explain) there were a group of people or things that originally lived in Atlantis. They built a city and Araart, Araaraart, and Ra-Ta excavated the remains of this city when they entered into Egypt, circa the 11th millennium BC. Going back further in time, we find that Amilius was the creator of astronomical charts, which became a part of the civilization of Atlantis. With the upheavals in Atlantis, many left and took with them astronomical charts which were, in essence, calendars. These astronomical records were uncovered during the archeological efforts of Ra-Ta, and then translated. They were the sacred writings of the ancestors. These they recorded in the tombs of the kings of Egypt. So when we look at what is written in the tomb of Seti I, and Tuthmosis III, and Amenhotep II, and Ramesses VI, some of what we are looking at is from the Atlanteans themselves, even Amilius! Think about it when you read the translation from the tomb of Seti I.

Understanding the Text

In this section we will expand on what this text seems to mean, one piece at a time. The text being discussed will be presented in quotations using bold type.

> **"The utter darkness of the night is ended every day with the appearance of this god as he enters the horizon at the point of 120°, as if from an invisible gateway; moving through the sky like he is traveling above through an unseen canal. He travels in through the gateway of the horizon, his appearance is as the other world gods.** *Tuat of the Celestial Water of the Sun God* **is the name of this province of the beginning of the sky of the Tuat; to measure the land of his regions entrance. Those gods who are in follow him up to his domain."**

This text is referring to the serpent-constellation of Hydra and its appearance on the horizon. British Astronomer Norman Lockyer (1836-1920) stated that it would be possible to know the date a star rose in ancient times by its position on the horizon. The first star of Hydra appears on the horizon at 120°, on the Autumnal Equinox, September 21, 10390 BC at approximately 9:48 PM.

---

[33] For more information about The Edgar Cayce readings see page 204.

This is an illustration of the 4th Division of Am Tuat. If you look closely, you can see the canal.

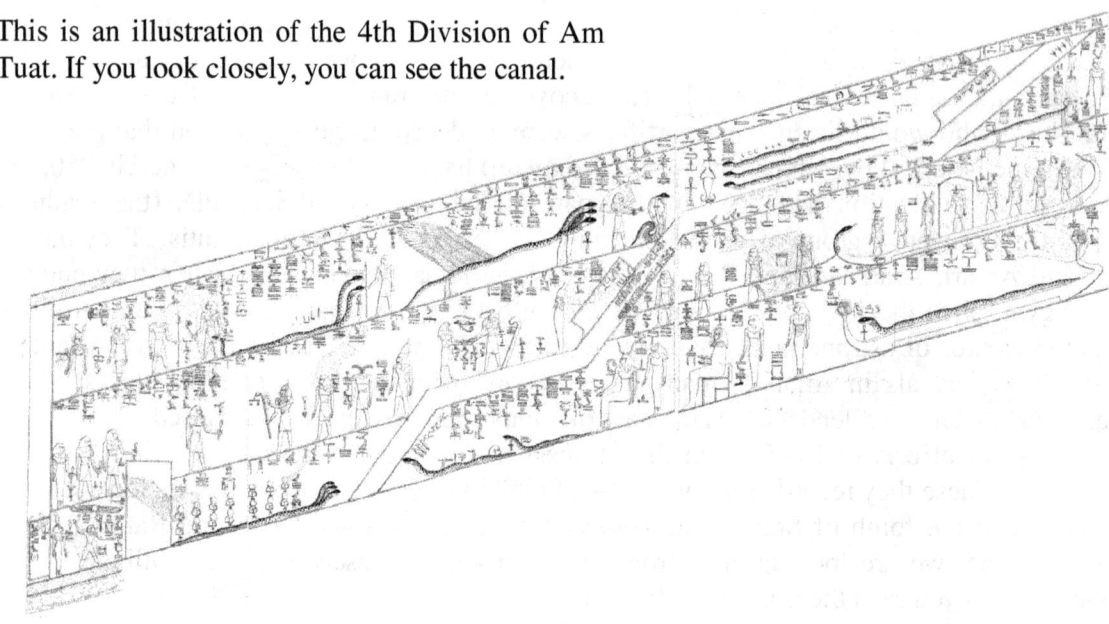

The ancient Egyptians illustrated the idea of the serpent following a canal at the beginning of the sky of the Tuat.

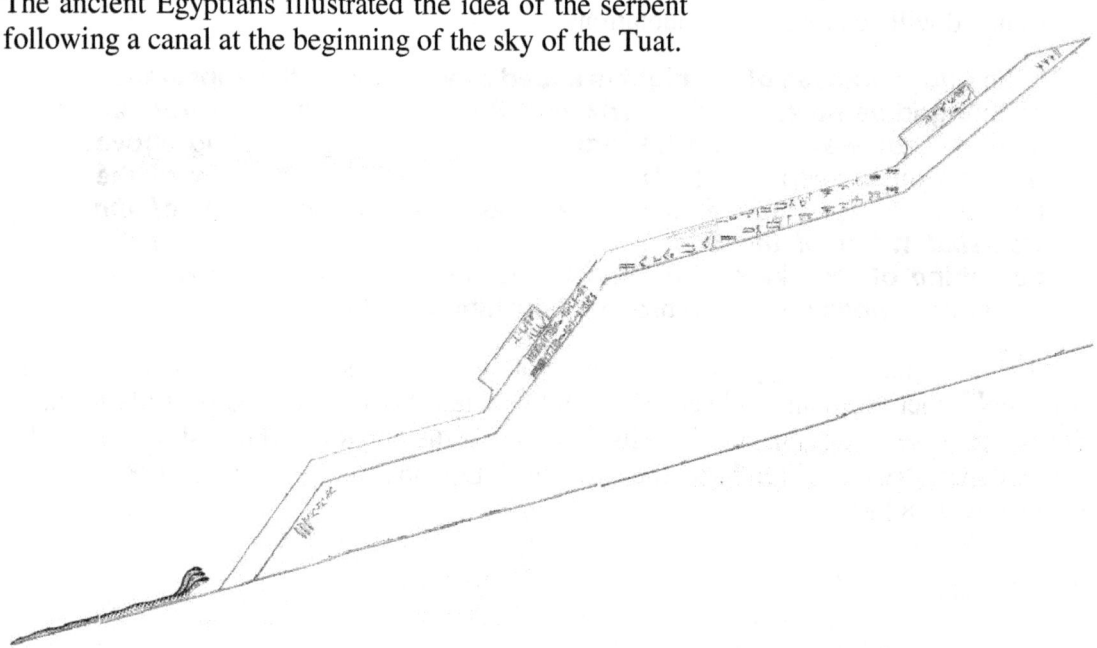

> "Come and see them together with this image of a god,[34] at the hidden house[35] in the morning. Know it by means of these guides together with the image of the great god himself! His spirit comes dweller on earth; in regular continuity forever. His spirit comes in the motionless Tuat."

The illustration below, from the fifth division of the book of Am Tuat in the tomb of Ramesses VI, is an illustration of the great god himself with other gods of the Tuat. The top or 'head' of the pyramid is the *hidden house*, the tomb of Osiris.

Egyptian Coffin Text, Spell 75: I have shown respect to the Lions, those who are about the shrine are afraid of me, those who encircle the tomb...the guardian of the limbs of Osiris...the earth gods. [36]

Marsham Adams in *The Book of the Master of the Hidden House*[37] reveals the fact that a tradition among the priests of Memphis was that the term "Secret house"[38] was used to refer to a pyramid. The necropolis of Memphis included Giza, where the two greatest pyramids are located.

---

[34] The constellations Hydra, Centaurus, and Leo taken together may represent Seker
[35] Pyramid
[36] See *Egyptian Coffin Texts*, R.O. Faulkner Translations, 3 Volumes, Volume I, p. 73 & 74, Spell 75: The lions may be the same as those in the 5th Division of Am-Tuat. If so, this reveals that what is in the center of the oval is the tomb. Additionally, "encircle" may also refer to the orbit of the constellations.
[37] Adams, W. Marsham, and E. J. Langford Garstin. 1933. *The Book of the Master of the Hidden Places*. London: Search Pub. Co.
[38] In the ancient Egyptian language, the word *sesheta* or *sheta* meant hidden or secret interchangeably.

> "The *Goddess of the First Hour of the Night*[39] is the name of the hour beginning this night sky, guiding this great god in the gateway. Therein he rests."

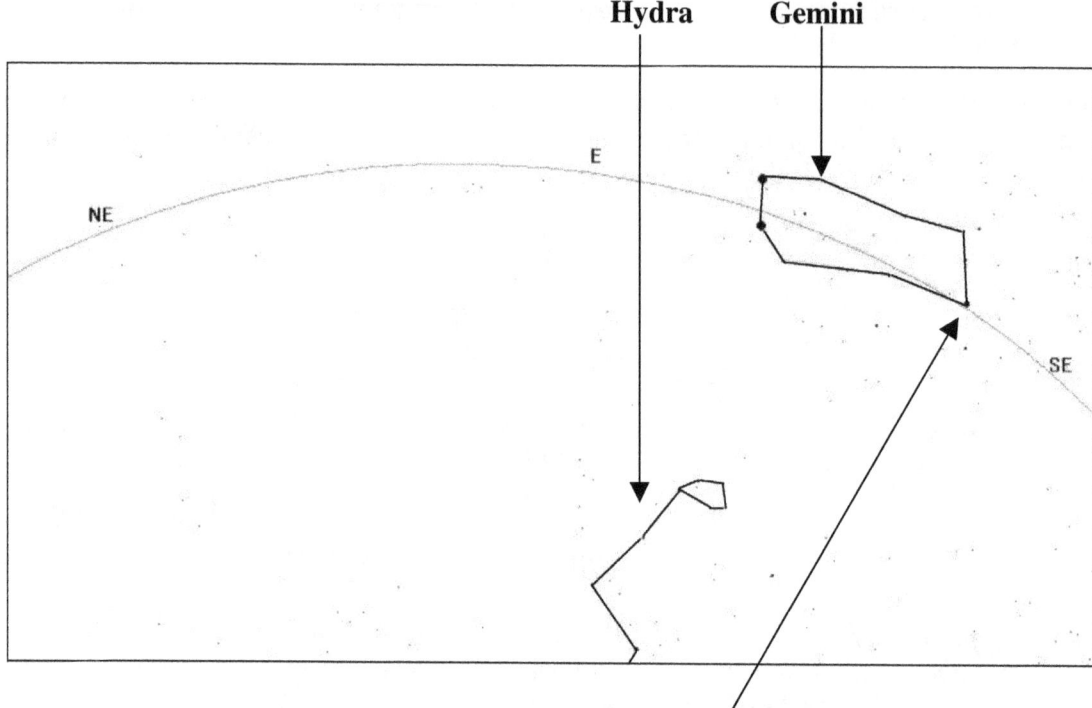

The star goddess of the first hour of night may refer to Alhena, just above the horizon. It is the third brightest star in Gemini, and the nearest star to the 120° point of entrance of the serpent-god constellation, guiding the way. The serpent-god can be seen at *"rest"* below the horizon.

---

[39] Dusk or civil dusk is the time at which the sun is 6° below the horizon in the evening. At this time objects are distinguishable but there is no longer enough light to perform any outdoor activities. The first star of the Gemini Twins is visible near the horizon, on September 21st, 10390 BC.

"**If you follow this great god in the great river that flows in the Tuat canal, in this length of 480 in this domain, the image at 120° is to be spread out. *Divine Souls, Gods, and Other Beings of the Tuat* are the names of the gods who are in this domain. Make known their names. He is with them to measure land for him, this great god regions entrance place in their domain, the great river that flows in the Tuat where the "Enemy God"[40] stands. He travels therein. Follow this great god.**"

This image of the canal that begins at 120° is to be spread out in length of 480. The diagrams of the fourth division and fifth division are located on opposite walls of a long corridor, and are each divided into three registers, *i.e. upper, middle, and lower.* If we begin counting these divisions from fourth division where the canal begins, we count 'one' in the lower register, 'two' in the middle register, 'three' in the upper register, and 'four' in the lower register of the fifth division, where the canal ends.

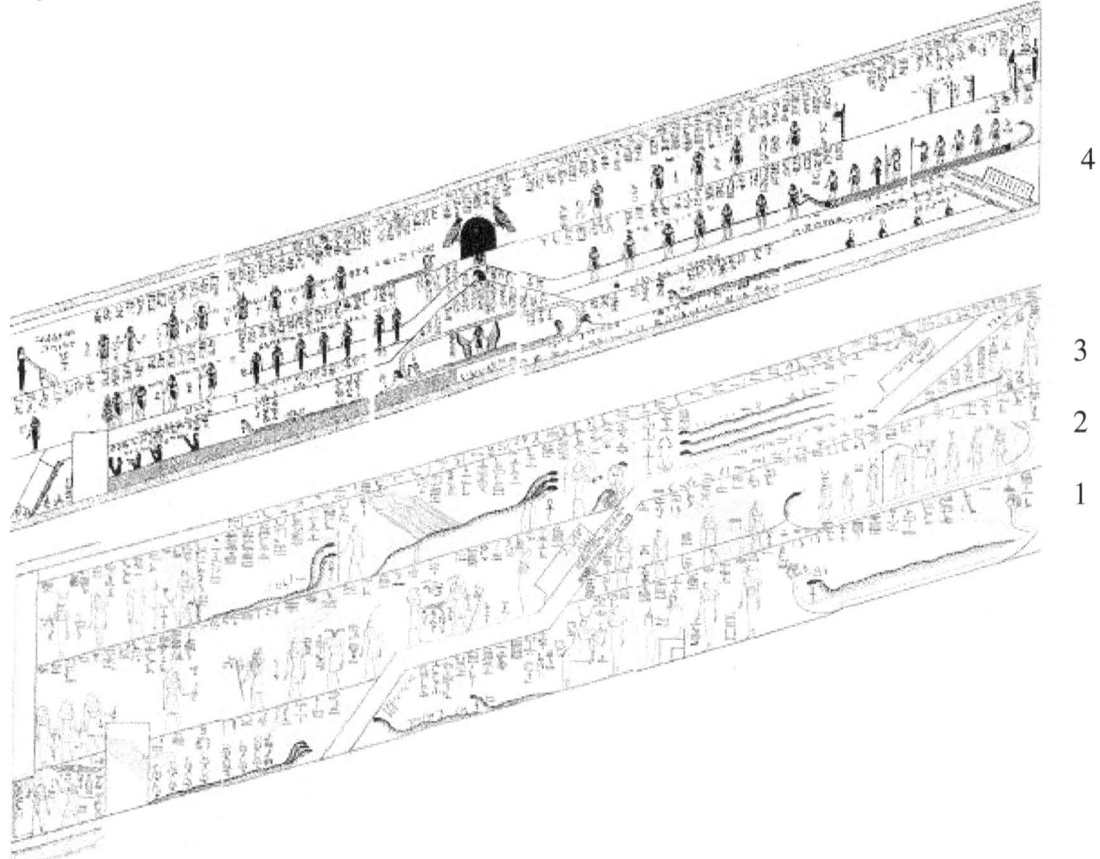

Each section is identified by its relationship to the *number* 120 (the number of degrees marking the location of the beginning of the canal). If we spread out all four sections, we have *four* number '120 sections'. In this way, there is an association of the 120 four times, and may explain its relationship to the number 480.

---

[40] Apep, the Egyptian serpent god was viewed as the greatest enemy of Ra, and thus was given the title "Enemy."

The serpent-god constellation moved within the invisible canal among other stars and constellations that were all known by names of their own. Distances could be measured for surveying or even travel upon the sea ascertained by the measure of the stars in the heavens.

The entrance place to the region of the sky, the territory of the serpent-god, located at 120° on the horizon, is where he **"stands."** He travels within the canal of the Tuat. Instructions are to **"follow this great god."**

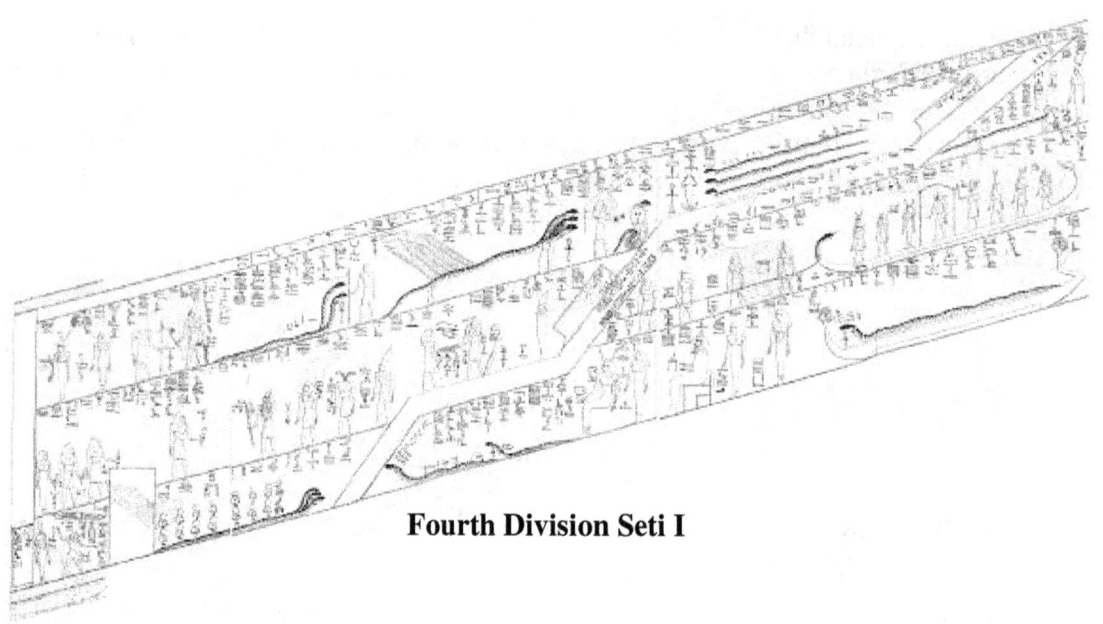

Fourth Division Seti I

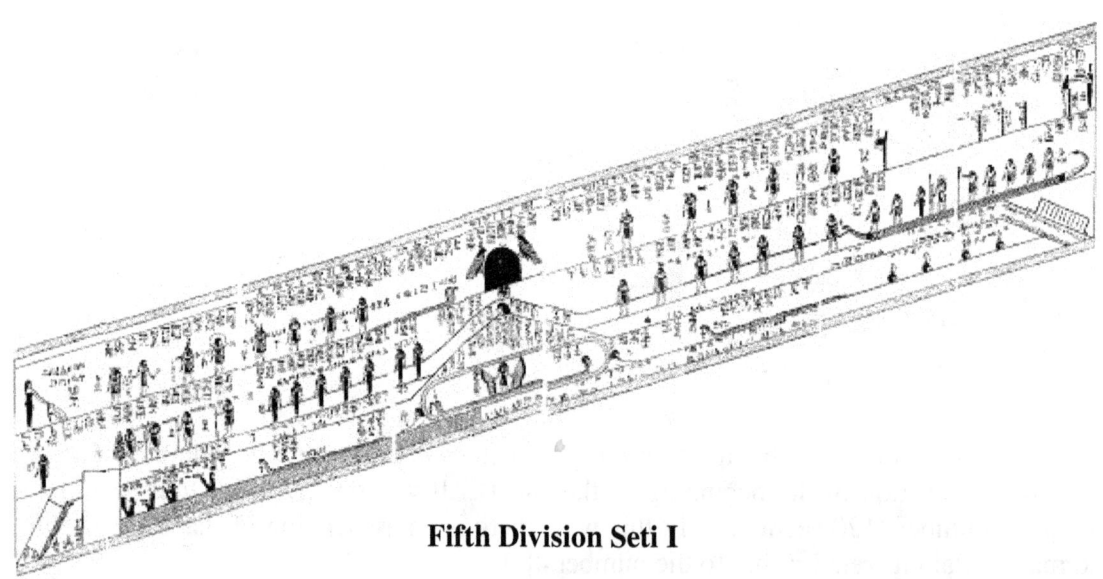

Fifth Division Seti I

Below, the fourth and fifth divisions as illustrated in the tomb of Tuthmosis III.

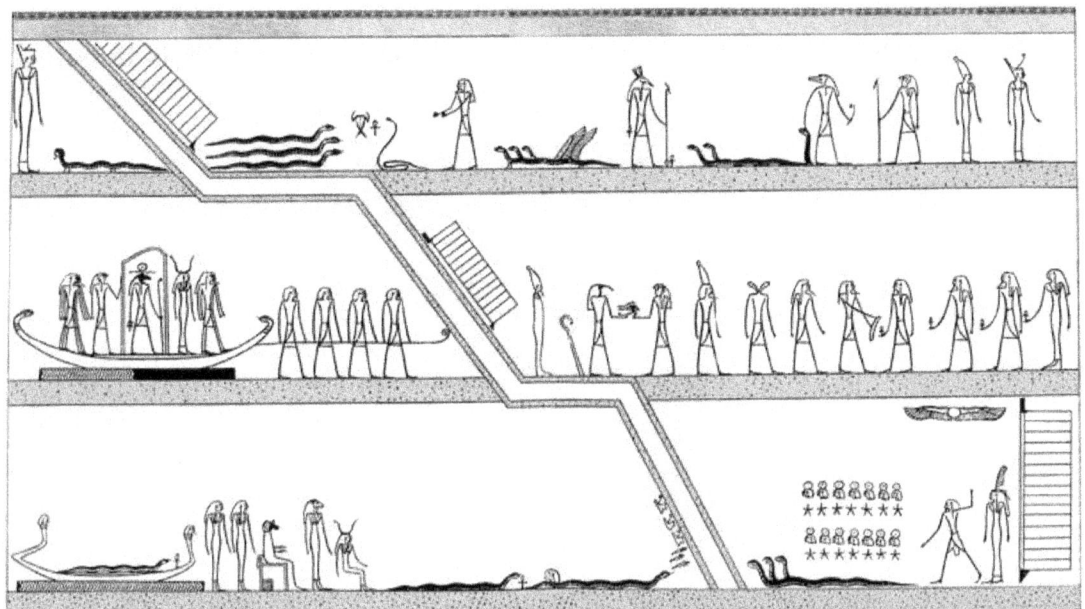

Fourth Division

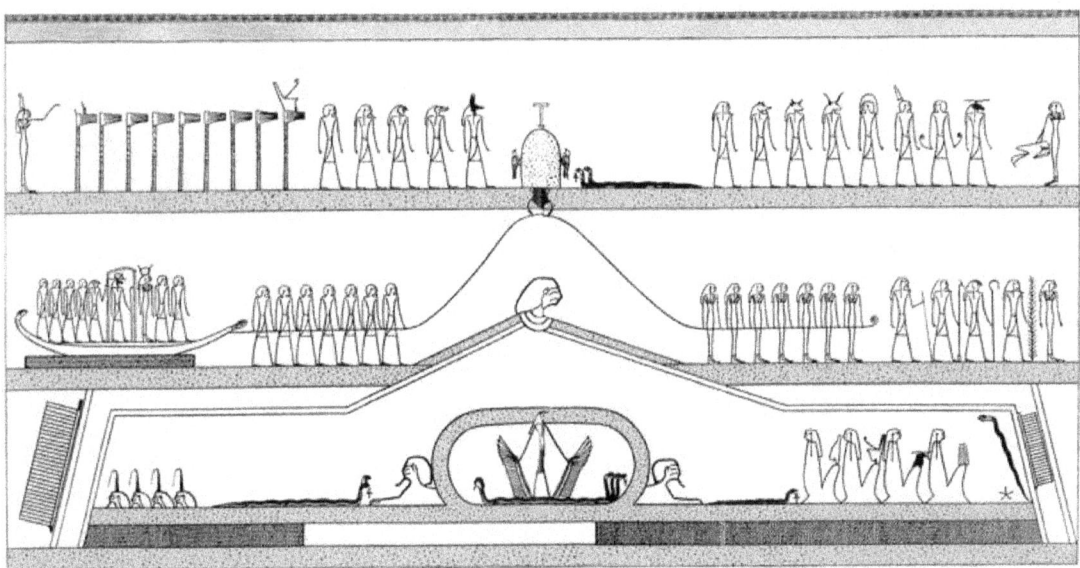

Fifth Division

"If you follow this great god in the great river that flows in the Tuat canal, in this length of 480 in this domain, the image at 120° is to be spread out."

Below the fourth and fifth divisions have been spread out.

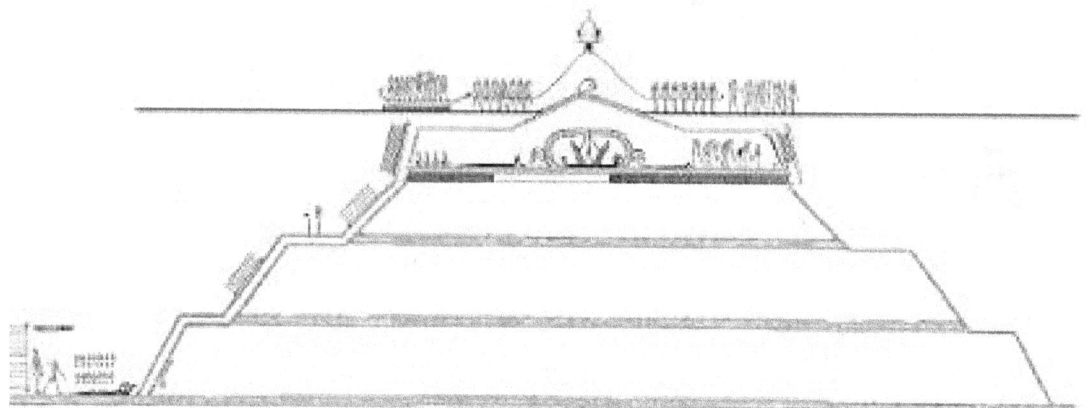

"He enters in the earth and his soul opens a way out to the Tuat to lead gods with side-locks.[41]"

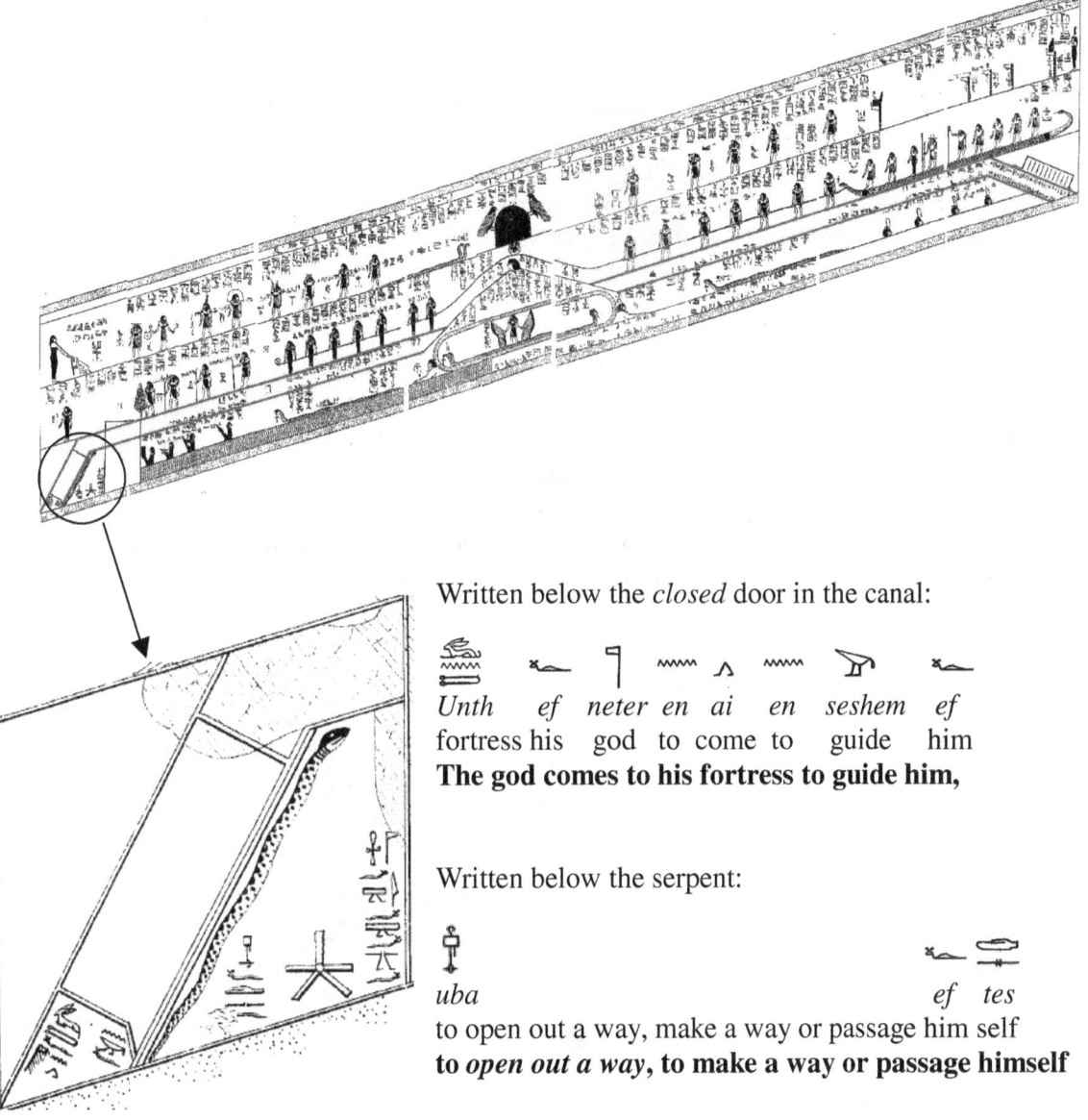

Written below the *closed* door in the canal:

Unth   ef   neter   en   ai   en   seshem   ef
fortress his god to come to guide him
The god comes to his fortress to guide him,

Written below the serpent:

uba   ef   tes
to open out a way, make a way or passage him self
to *open out a way*, to make a way or passage himself

Written near the star:

Neter   ankh   af   shem   ef   shem   sebi   ef
God living serpent[42] traveler he goes to lead him
The living serpent god, the traveler, he goes to lead him.

---

[41] The side lock was a hairstyle and was the side lock of youth.
[42] Budge, EHD, 43B, *Af*: Tuat III, a serpent hostile to Ra.

"He travels above to swallow the sun god."[43]

The great constellation of the serpent Hydra extended from the northeast to the southwest across the entire sky just before sunrise. This is why the legend grew that the great evil serpent god Apep waited to swallow Ra, the sun god, every day.

"Follow with the two Goddesses of Truth[44] to measure land.[45] He is bright and shining. He eats bread. To be removed, the earth gives him a towing rope for his boat. A form of the sun god comes; these images, the divine souls, gods, and other beings of the Tuat in writings, in their images. They are hidden in a hidden door."

The stars and constellations appear on the horizon as if they came through a hidden door.

"The first hidden writings place is the hill cemetery."

The hill cemetery may be the pyramid. The coffin texts explain in spell 1087 He possesses writing materials in djedu.[46] Djedu is the house of Osiris. Spell 399, vol. II, says: at the stairway…interred in it at the place where Osiris is. Spell 572, vol. II explains: The chamber of Osiris, and those who are on (the steps of) the throne in the secret chamber. The next few illustrations from various sources all depict this hill cemetery or house of Osiris.

---

[43] In the ancient Egyptian legend of the battle between the evil serpent god Apep and the sun god Ra, It was believed that Apep waited at Bakhu-the mountain of the horizon-to swallow the barque of Ra.
[44] Constellation Gemini
[45] The idea of measuring land has been discussed. The hieroglyph used here is *henbit*, Budge, EHD, 490A.
[46] *djedu* Web definitions; Abusir (Egyptian *pr wsjr*; Coptic: *busiri*, the House or Temple of Osiris; Greek: ; ابوصير) is the name given to an Egyptian archaeological locality – specifically, an extensive necropolis of the Old Kingdom period, together with later additions – in the vicinity of the modern capital Cairo. ... http://en.wikipedia.org/wiki/djedu
[47] Clark, Robert Thomas Rundle. *Myth and Symbol in Ancient Egypt*. (London: Thames and Hudson, 1978) 171.

Written on the second stone: "The Throne of Osiris"

From the Ancient Egyptian Coffin Texts:

Spell 584, vol. II:
A path was shown…Great One in hidden places…yonder…in darkness…on his side asleep … whose head is in the sky…whose face is to the east.

Spell 585, vol. II:
He sets on that seat which is north of the sky.

Cayce said, *"in the upper chamber of the northeast corner of the first pyramid builded."*

---

[48] Budge, *Osiris and the Egyptian Resurrection*, I, 43.

[49]

This image shows a star resting at the top of the pyramid

From the text of the Am Tuat:

> **"At the house the star comes to rest by this great god in the sky house of Osiris."**

[49] Perrot. *Essai Sur Les Momies.*

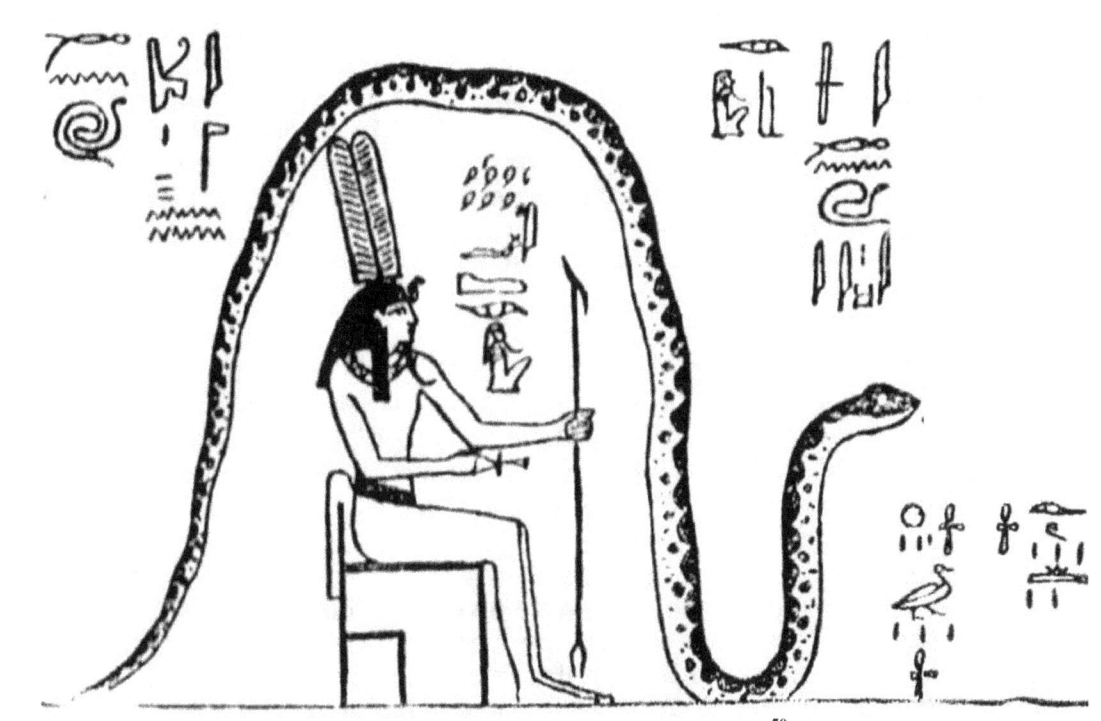

From the Seventh Division of Am Tuat[50]

Written behind the serpent:
hail god this in serpent's embrace

Written above the head of the serpent:
Osiris who is in embrace of Apepi[51]

Written in front of the serpent:
ankh-aru-tchefa
a serpent guardian of the body of Osiris.[52]

Written above the enthroned Osiris:
afi   Asar[53]
dead body of Osiris

---

[50] Budge, *Egyptian Heaven and Hell*, I, 149.
[51] **Apep** (also spelled **Apepi**, and **Aapep**, or **Apophis** in Greek)
[52] Budge, EHD, 125B, *ankh-aru-tchefa*: a serpent guardian of the body of Osiris.
[53] Budge, EHD, 43A, *Afi Asar*: Tuat VI, the flesh, i.e, dead body, of Osiris

> "Make an offering to them dweller on earth, they shine in their names, praise them dweller on earth. Their unit of measure is infinite time. Know these words spokesman, gods and other beings of the Tuat of this god, spokesman of words of this great god to ascend, with gods and other beings of the Tuat, to shine in him, dweller on earth, *"In Regular Continuity Forever"* is the name of the hour of night guiding this great god in this domain. Knowledge of the watercourse is protected by the star god. Follow in peace by majesty of this great god in this domain."

The stars and constellations shine and have names. They should be adored and held in high esteem by all who live upon earth, because they are the true measurers of time. The text admonishes the reader to know the words of the serpent-god that ascends the watercourse and protects the knowledge of it. The knowledge of the measure of the watercourse is the secret of the serpent-god. To know it, follow him in peace in his province.

> "The Harvest gods paddle by this god in the celestial water; the canal of Osiris is 480 in length in the domain, to be spread out 120°. This great god is bright and shining. Follow the words which are herein to the entrance. Make haste, he is in their regions, the entrance domain of these divine souls. *Secret Gods* is the name of the gods who are in this domain. Know them by their names dweller on earth."

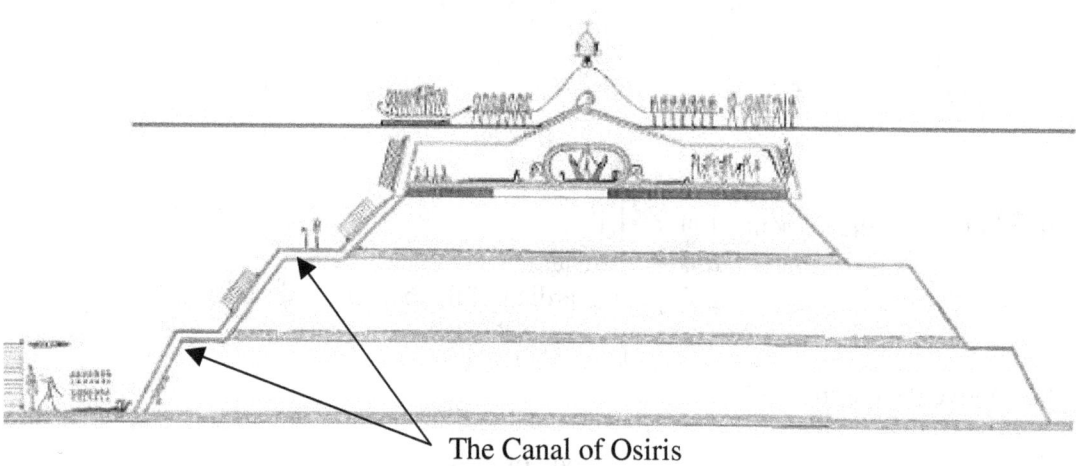

The Canal of Osiris

> "He comes to go up to his entrance place under Osiris within, give this in his domain of the celestial waters domain entrance, he this lord of celestial water. *One God Existent Largeness*[54] is the name of this domain. Come see the image; these images of the secret of the divine souls. Secrets of this image are not in writings, but are hidden in the Tuat first writings. Come know the entrance of the abode of the dead. They travel from above. They lead him in to roar. They do not travel in his entrance, their furnaces.[55] Come know them together with places this soul hides his entrance above with the Sun god."

The words in this document lead to the entrance of the place of Osiris. He is in their regions, high up in the sky. The names of the stars and constellations are secrets; those who dwell upon the earth should know them by their names.

> "Come know them with divine spirit power; his two legs are at the entrance. He does not enter in the place of destruction. He comes forth to shine in his images. Praise his winds; his great hour. The name of the hour guiding this god is *Earth Division*. Souls at peace follow in tow by the majesty of this great god in the secret circle of the abode of the dead. See the designs of the gods to come, conducted in with his voice. They do not see him. The name of this circle is *Living One*. *Images House* is the name of the door of this circle, this hidden corridor through which boats are towed."

'His two legs at the entrance' refer to the front legs of Centaurus. The place of destruction and the entrance refer to the horizon and the rising of the sun. The creator of heaven and earth comes forth to shine in His images, the images of the stars. In Egypt, the morning winds hailed the arrival of the sun each day. Sunrise was the "Great hour." The secret circle is an astronomical reference to the path of the ecliptic and the *'abode of the dead'* is the world of the stars in the heavens. The designs of the gods are star asterisms.

---

[54] This name could possibly be connected to the full expanse of the constellations Leo, Hydra, and Centaurus at the time when they fill the entire sky.
[55] Budge, EHD, 465, *Hatu* : ovens, furnaces

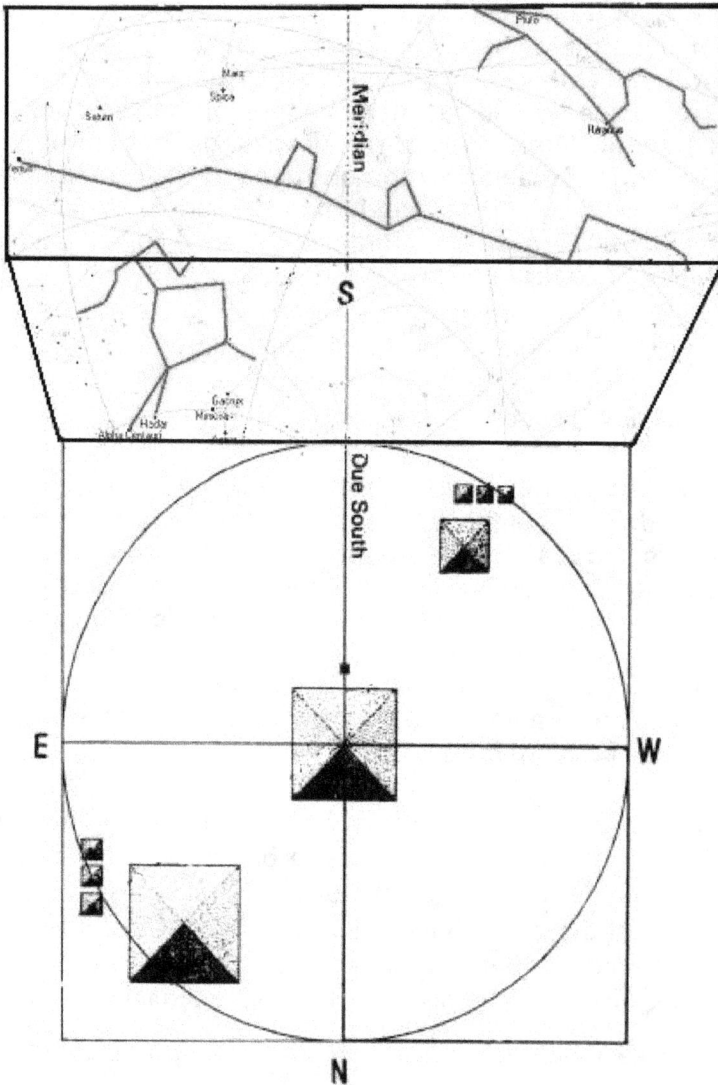

Giza Plateau 10390 BC, September 21, 4:50 AM

The ancient Egyptians illustrated the same idea of the central pyramid of the Giza necropolis, the horizon, the flying serpent-god and the double lion gods in this way:

> "Come know the images of the gods in these secret paths of the Memphite necropolis. Behold these paths. Among these large stones, the great house hidden doors which are in the earth. Seker over his sand to eat bread at the entrance of evil, the living gods in the great house of the creator of the heaven and the earth, come to know they give the paths of Amen of the other world.

The Giza plateau where the greatest pyramids are located is a part of the Memphite necropolis, the ancient Egyptian burial ground for the city of Memphis. The doors of the great hidden house among the megalithic stones at Giza are in the earth, and Seker is above the entrance in heaven, which is the house of the creator of heaven and earth. The astronomical paths of the stars are in heaven. Come to know them.

> ***"See the Images of the Gods in the Great House*** **is the name of the hour of night guiding this great god. Great powers star passages through which boats are towed for this great god in roads above. Houses of the Tuat with half of the sky circle hidden, of Sekri over his sand, not seen nor perceived, guiding this secret in the earth under."**

The Great House of Heaven

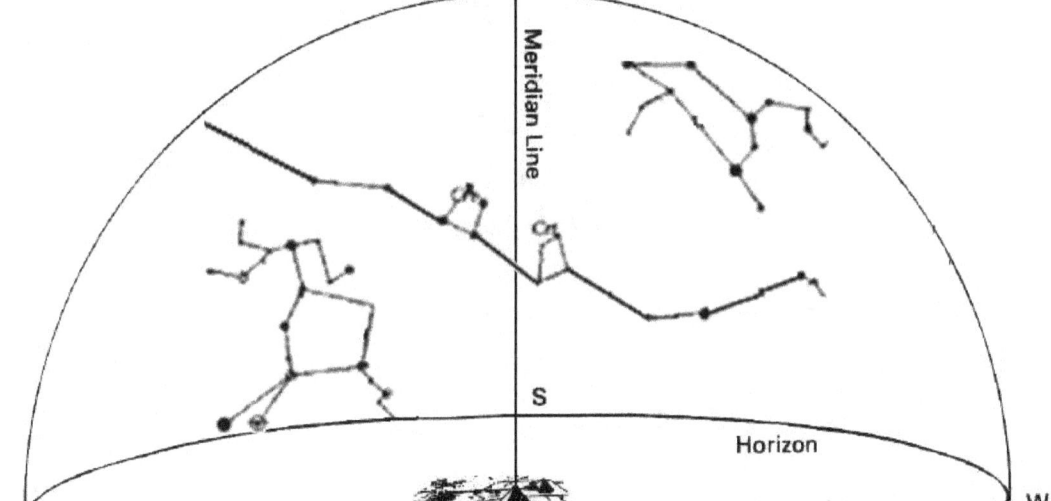

Half of the sky circle over Giza

"This god Af, the two man headed sphinxes, comes. The gods who are in this god hear their voice; the sun god calls out. *The Entrance Time of This God* is the name of the door to this place. *To Stand Mighty Gods* is the name of the circle of this god. The hidden hill cemetery roads, secrets of the abode of the dead, the doors of the hidden house, *The Holy Place of Sekri, the Two Man Headed Sphinxes, the Flesh of the Body in His Image Above* is the name of the gods who are in this circle."

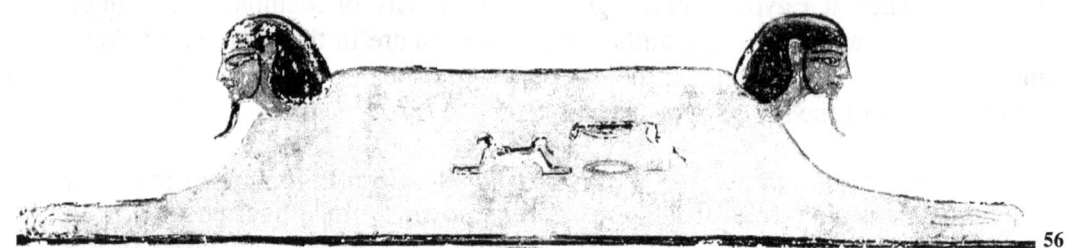

"The divine souls who are in door images, they who are in the hours, their images, their secrets, not known, not seen nor perceived; these images of the gods of Horus himself. Come see this image together with images of gods. This is not in writings; it is the secret of the Tuat over the South hidden house. Come to know them."

The star images of these gods are over the pyramid, the hidden house in the morning, just before sunrise. The megalithic stones of Giza are a part of the Memphite necropolis. The god Seker is in the sky with the double sphinx above the doors of the hidden house. They are in the southern sky over the hidden house.

---

[56] From the Book of Aker in the tomb of Ramesses VI. (Photograph by Francis Dzikowski, ©Theban Mapping Project, reprinted with permission.)
[57] Piankoff. *The tomb of Ramesses VI.*

"In peace his soul rests in his offerings. Khemit, the goddess of destruction, does not cut to pieces Sekri's dead bodies. He passes away over them in peace. Come to make an offering to these gods dweller on earth. The name of the hour of night guiding this great god in the circle is this guide *The Star of the Goddess of the Temple*. Rest by the majesty of this great god of deep celestial water. The gods and other beings of the Tuat become bright. His words to the gods therein become bright. His power is their divine offerings. This is their entrance place. He travels about equipped in a bright and shining boat in their regions in their entrance offerings they give him, in their celestial waters. Of their celestial waters entrance they travel in the Tuat daily."

"He travels about equipped in a bright and shining boat in their regions"

In 2084 BC, the Babylonians charted Hydra with two wings as can be seen in the illustration below.[59]

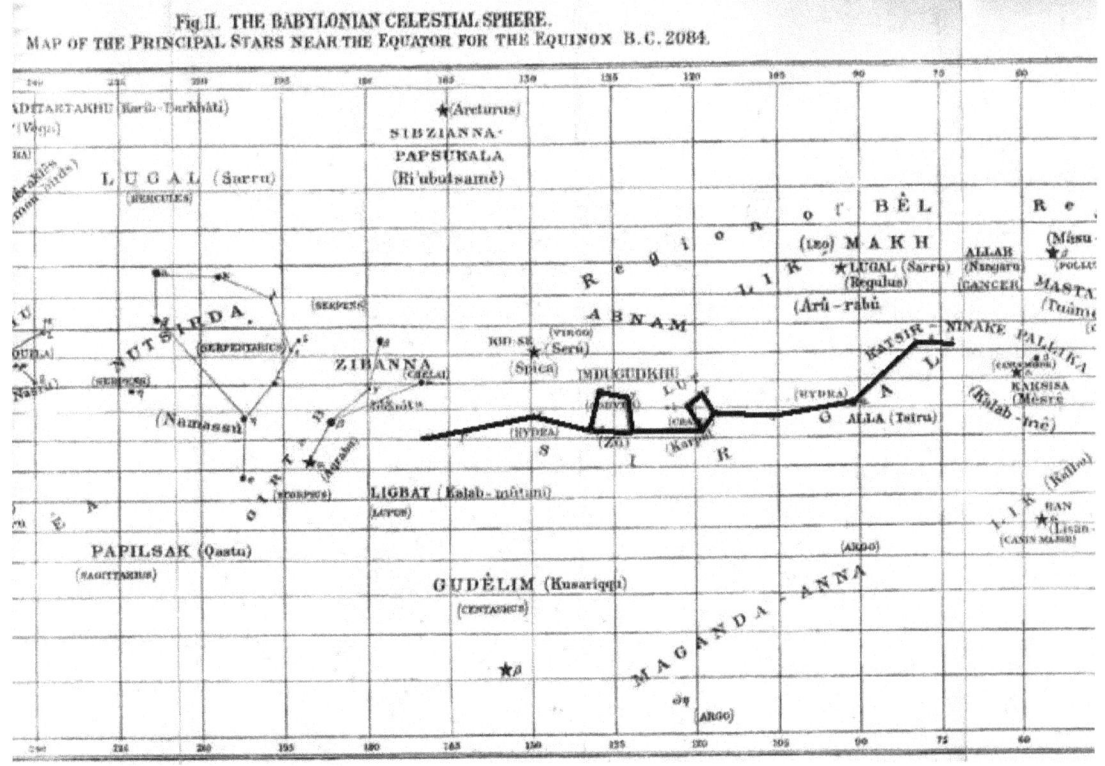

---

[58] Piankoff, *The Tomb of Ramesses VI*.
[59] Brown, *Primitive Constellations*, Vol. 2, Chart of the Northern Hemisphere between pages 148 & 149.

> **"The name of the door to this place is *Sothis Pierces the Hidden House Road of Ament*. This great god navigates the celestial water to conduct entrance in his boat. See the designs of the gods and other beings of the Tuat to unite within. Know their names together within images, their hours, their hidden course of events, and unknown images of gods. This is the secret in the Tuat. For mankind, the goddess comes. See these images of gods in these writings, altogether hidden in this house of the Tuat, come over the southern hidden house."**

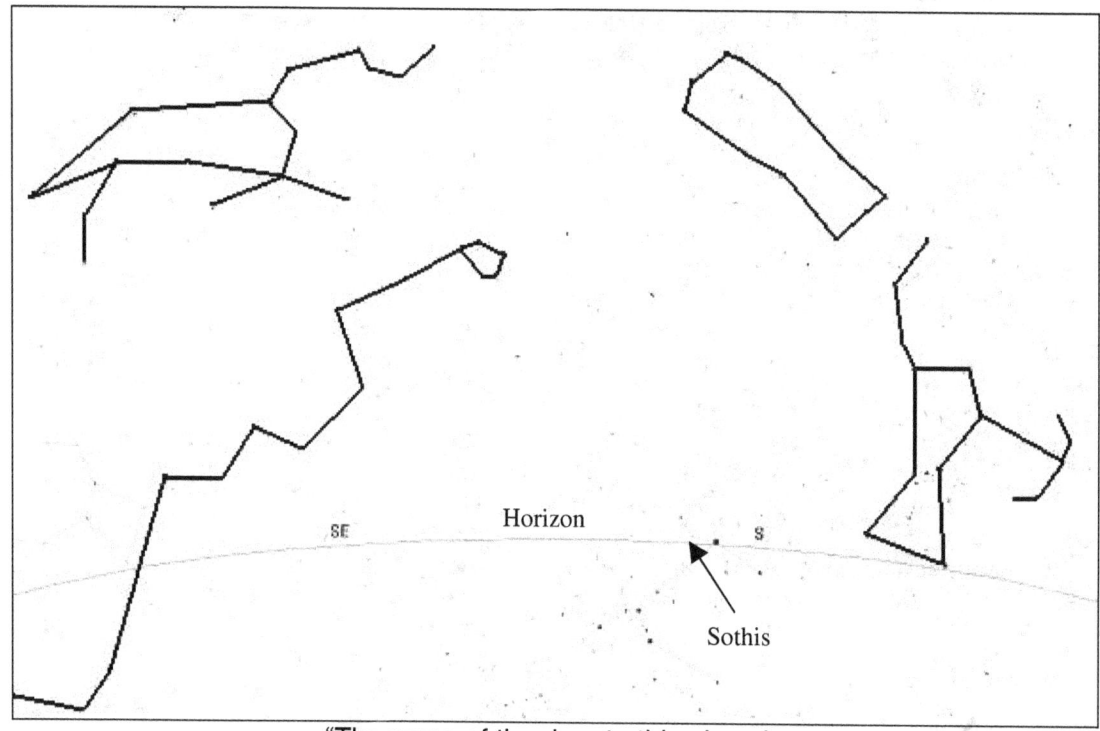

"The name of the door to this place is
Sothis Pierces the Hidden House Road of Ament."

The star Sothis pierces the Southern horizon on September 21, 10,390 BC for 1 hour, from 12:51 AM to 1:50 AM, before it quickly sets again.

An Overview of the Transliteration

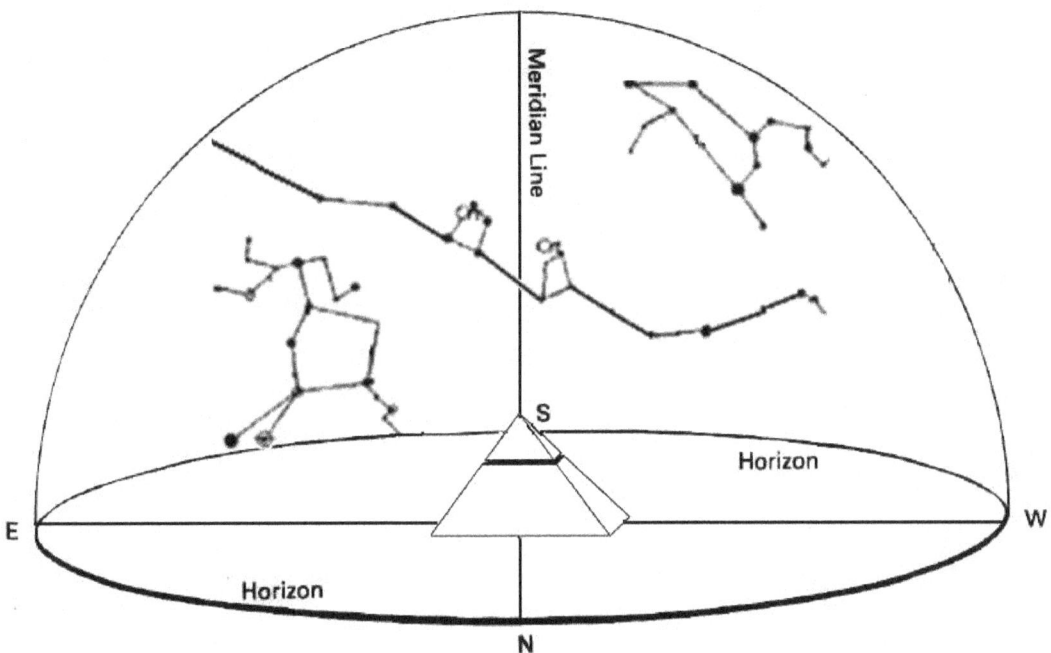

"See these images of gods in these writings, altogether hidden in this house of the Tuat, come over the southern hidden house."

The text continues:

> "To know, unite lengths in the Tuat. Satisfy him with offerings. Gods who are therein follow. Osiris come truth in his bright cycle of time. His people upon earth bright and shining recite the words of this god and give with divine offerings to the gods and other beings of the Tuat. He stands among them, see their powers, they in their domains the length of the horizons. They are Kheper in their shining brightness, this great god. *Metch-t-nebt-Tuat*[60] is the name of this domain. *Road of the Ship of the Sun-God* is the name of this hour of night guiding this great god in this domain, to lead to the land about the house. At the house the star comes to rest by this great god in the sky house of Osiris. Recite words by majesty of this great god, entrance this sky house, these great gods who are in."

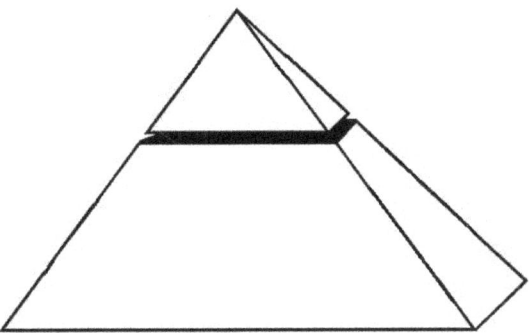

---

[60] Budge, EHD, 337A, *Metch-t-nebt-Tuat*: the name of the 6th division of the Tuat

ABRIDGEMENT OF THE AM TUAT TEXT, INTERLINEAR TRANSLATION, AND TRANSLITERSTION

The Text and Translation

The following pages include the text of the Am Tuat as copied by Eugène Lefébure from the tomb of Seti I, along with our original translation. In the last section of the book, we use Paul Bucher's extended transcription of the same text to complete the study.

We have used Bucher's method of underlining the text that originally appeared in red in the tomb throughout our translation. Footnotes provide explanatory references. The use of EHD in the footnotes refers to Budge's two-volume *Egyptian Hieroglyphic Dictionary*.

It can be challenging to read the transliteration, but this is due to the fact that the language, thought, and expression of the times were so far removed from that commonly used today. The sentence structure may appear archaic. But rather than lose or distort any of the original meaning, we chose to keep it as close to the original as possible.

There are however, some key points that become obvious. The main one is that we are being directed to observe the stars in the night sky. Understanding this puts everything else in proper context. The transliteration in bold type can be read to gain the essence of the message.

Summary of this Book

sehu[61]	en	sheftu	pen
Summary	of	book	this

Summary of this Book

hat	upt	net	Amentt[62]	pehui[63]
beginning	daily duty	of	abode of the dead	ends

The beginning of the daily duty, the abode of the dead ends

smau-keku[64]
utter darkness

the utter darkness.[65]

aq	neter	pen	em	ta	arit	net	aakhut	Amentt
enter	god	this	into	earth	gateway	of	the horizon[66]	the abode of the dead

This god enters into the earth gateway of the horizon,[67] **the abode of the dead**

atru	saa taut	pen	her	seqtut
canal[68]	120	this	over	a course on the river

canal 120 [degrees][69] **over this course on the river**[70]

---

[61] Budge, EHD, 683A, *sehu*

[62] Budge, EHD,163A, *Amentt*: , , the top part of *Amenti*, the brow of *Amenti*; , Ra in the zenith; , lord of the zenith

[63] Budge, EHD, 244A, *pehui*

[64] The hieroglyphs for this word are continued on the next page.

[65] Each day, at the beginning of the night, the stars appear in the sky ending complete darkness.

[66] The gateway of the horizon was the place on the horizon from which a star first appeared.

[67] The meaning is: This constellation appears on the horizon.

[68] The "abode of the dead canal" is an imaginary passageway in the sky that the constellation travels.

[69] 120° is a point on the horizon at the beginning of the course in the sky, which 'this god' follows. 'This god' is the Hydra star constellation; 'degrees' is implied. Sir Norman Lockyer (1836-1920) one of the major English astronomers of his time, became interested in a problem which had also attracted Newton, that of bringing in astronomy to assist the chronology of history. He derived his conclusions about the astronomical character of Egyptian religion on the solidest architectural measurements and astronomical calculations (Lockyer, p. IX-X). In 1894 he published his study of astronomy and mythology of the Ancient Egyptians, *The Dawn of Astronomy*. As he carried out his research, it soon became obvious to him that their mythology was intensely astronomical (Lockyer, p. XVI). The first star of Hydra appeared on the horizon at 120 degrees on September 21st, 10390 BC at 9:49 PM, the Autumnal Equinox.

[70] "River" refers to the river that flows in the sky, i.e. Urnes.

em	arit	ten	nt	sper[71]	ef	er
in	gateway	this	not	to arrive at a place	he	with

in this gateway, not to arrive at a place. He is with

Tuatiu
Gods and other beings of the Tuat
the gods and other beings of the Tuat.

net	mu	net	Ra	ren	en	sekhet
of	celestial water	of	sun god	name	of	field

Of the Celestial Water of the Sun God is the name of the field.

tepi[72]	net	Tuat
he who is leader	of	Tuat

He who is the leader of the Tuat.

henb	ef	aht	er	neteru	sen	amiu	khet	ef	shaa
to measure land	his	lands	with	gods		they who are in	follow	him	until

Measure his lands with the gods.[73] They who are in follow him until

ef	hetch	metu	ar-t[74]	skheru[75]
he	become bright	commands	seeing	designs

he becomes bright commands seeing designs[76]

Tuatiu		er	sekhet	ten
gods and other beings of the Tuat		near	field	this

the gods and other beings of the Tuat near this field.

---

[71] Budge, EHD, 661B, *sper*
[72] Budge, EHD, 828B, *tepi*
[73] This may be the idea of measuring land by using the stars for surveying.
[74] Budge, EHD, 68A, *ar-t*, the eye, a seeing, a looking, look, glance, the faculty or act of seeing, sight, vision.
[75] See Budge, EHD, 694A, *skher*:
[76] The designs may refer to star asterisms.

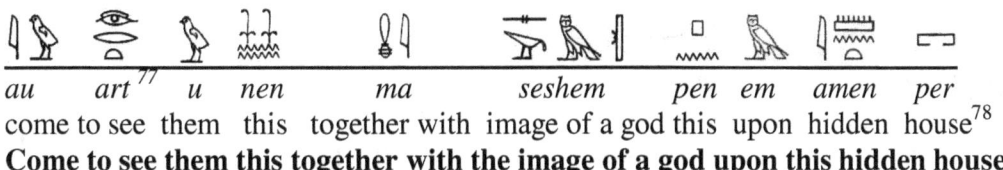

au	art[77]	u	nen	ma	seshem	pen	em	amen	per
come	to see	them	this	together with	image	of a god	this	upon	hidden house[78]

Come to see them this together with the image of a god upon this hidden house

en	tua
in	morning[79]

in the morning.[80]

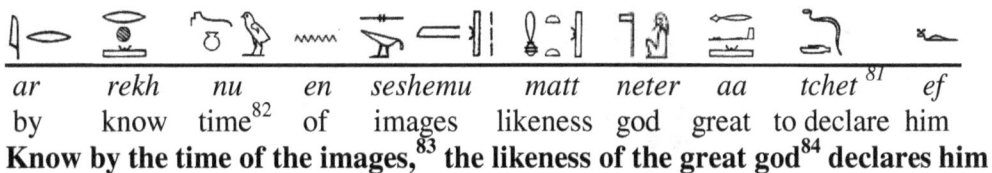

ar	rekh	nu	en	seshemu	matt	neter	aa	tchet[81]	ef
by	know	time[82]	of	images	likeness	god	great	to declare	him

Know by the time of the images,[83] the likeness of the great god[84] declares him

au	yah[85]	en	ef	tepi ta	maat-shes	maat	au
come	shine	for	him	dweller on earth	regularly	and always	come

and comes to shine for him, living man, regularly and always, come

khu	en	ef	em	Tuat	urt
spirit	of	him	in	Tuat	motionless

spirit of him in the motionless Tuat.

---

[77] Budge, EHD, 68A, *art*

[78] There was a tradition amongst the priests of Memphis that the "Hidden house" referred to one of the great pyramids. Basil Steward, *Witness of the Great Pyramid* 1927, Pages 219-221: reference to Marsham Adams from *The Book of the Master of the Hidden House.*

[79] The time of the images, early morning before dawn.

[80] The text is describing the configuration of multiple star constellations positioned above the pyramid of Khafra before sunrise. The upper portion of the pyramid is 'the hidden house.'

[81] Budge, EHD, 913A, *tchet*: to speak, to say, to tell, to declare, to narrate

[82] Budge, EHD, 351A, *nu*: time, hour

[83] The reference to the time of the images suggests the time of the night was known by the images of constellations.

[84] This likeness of the great god may be a reference to the combined images of Centaurus, Hydra, and Leo.

[85] Mercer, *Handbook of Egyptian Hieroglyphs*, page 156, Sign List, 57, 58 *yḫ* "to shine"

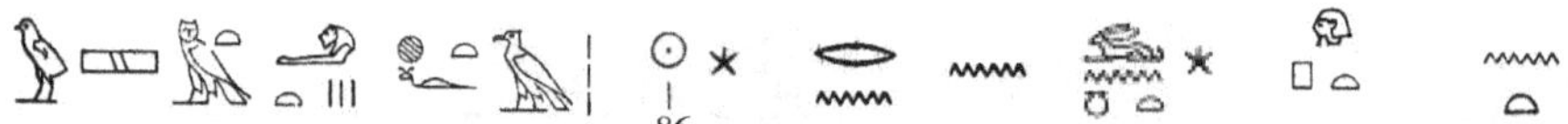

Ushem - hat - kheftiu-nu - Ra [86]   ren   en   unut   tep   net
goddess of the first hour of the night   name   of   hour   beginning   of
The Goddess of the First Hour of the Night,[87] the name of the hour beginning of

gerh   seshemt   neter pen   aa   em   arit
night   guidance   god this   great   in   gateway
the night guiding this great god in the gateway.[88]

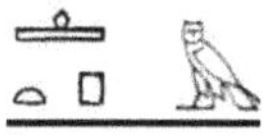

hotep   em
peace   in
[Follow] in peace

khet   ani   neter pen   aa   em   Urnes   atru
[follow]   bring   god this   great   in   river that flows in the Tuat   canal
bring this great god into the river that flows in the Tuat canal,

aftu saa   khemennui   pu   em   au[89]   *en   sekhet   ten   aru*
400   80   this   in   length   of   domain   this   image
480[90] in this length of this domain[91], the image

---

[86] Budge, EHD, 186B, *Ushem-hat-kheftiu-nu-Ra*:  goddess of the first hour of the night.

[87] As far as constellations, Gemini (the twin goddesses of truth) was the first constellation visible at the time referenced by these texts; the first twin star Castor of Gemini appears above the horizon at the beginning of the night on September 21, 10390 B.C. at 8:00 PM.

[88] The constellation of Hydra begins its appearance after the constellation of Gemini, as if the twins are its guide.

[89] Budge, EHD, 2A, *au*: length, largeness

[90] Tuthmosis III shows 309.

[91] The length of 480 is 4 times 120 (the position of the appearance of the first star of Hydra on the horizon). In the illustrations accompanying the fourth division in the full version of the Am Tuat, the journey of the serpent is shown to be through 4 levels of divisions, which begin with its initial appearance in the first level and lead through three more levels to its final position. See illustration on page 53.

saa taut em   usekh
100   20   of   to be spread out
of 120 to be spread out.[92]

baui   Tuati   ren   en   neteru   amiu
souls gods and other beings of the Tuat name of   gods   who are in
Souls, gods and other beings of the Tuat; the name of the gods which are in

sekhet   ten
field   this
this field.

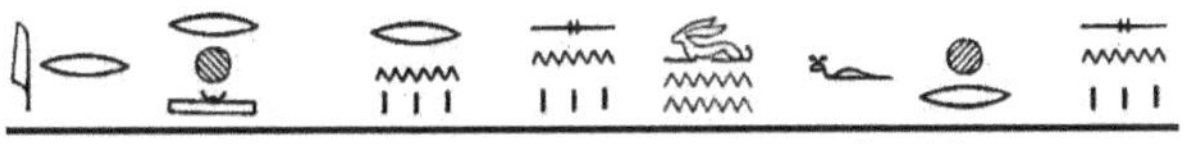

ar   rekh   ren   sen   unn   ef   kher   sen
by   to know names them to be   he   with   them
Know them by names. He is with them

---

[92] See image on next pages.

'120 to be spread out' is referring to the images of the 3 registers in the Fourth Division and the 1st register in the Fifth Division of the Book of Am Duat, which registers are to be spread out. In other words these registers, when combined and extended, represent a wide angle view of physical space. Here is the fourth and fifth divisions spread out.

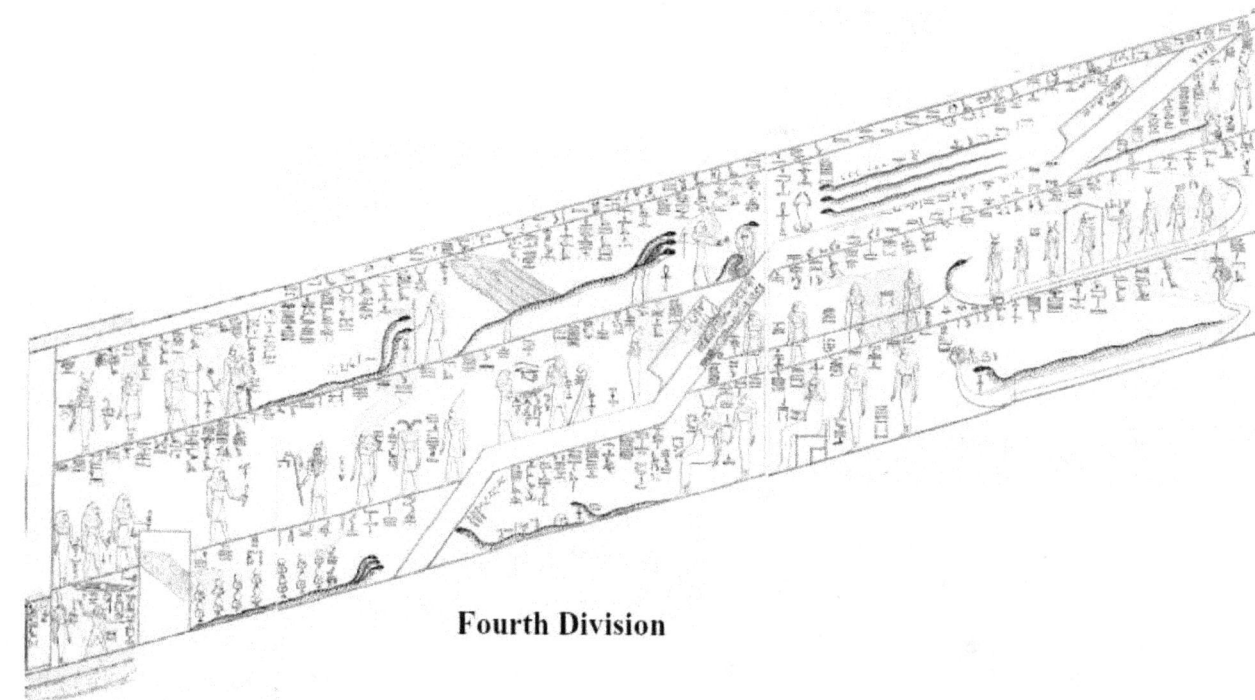

Fourth Division

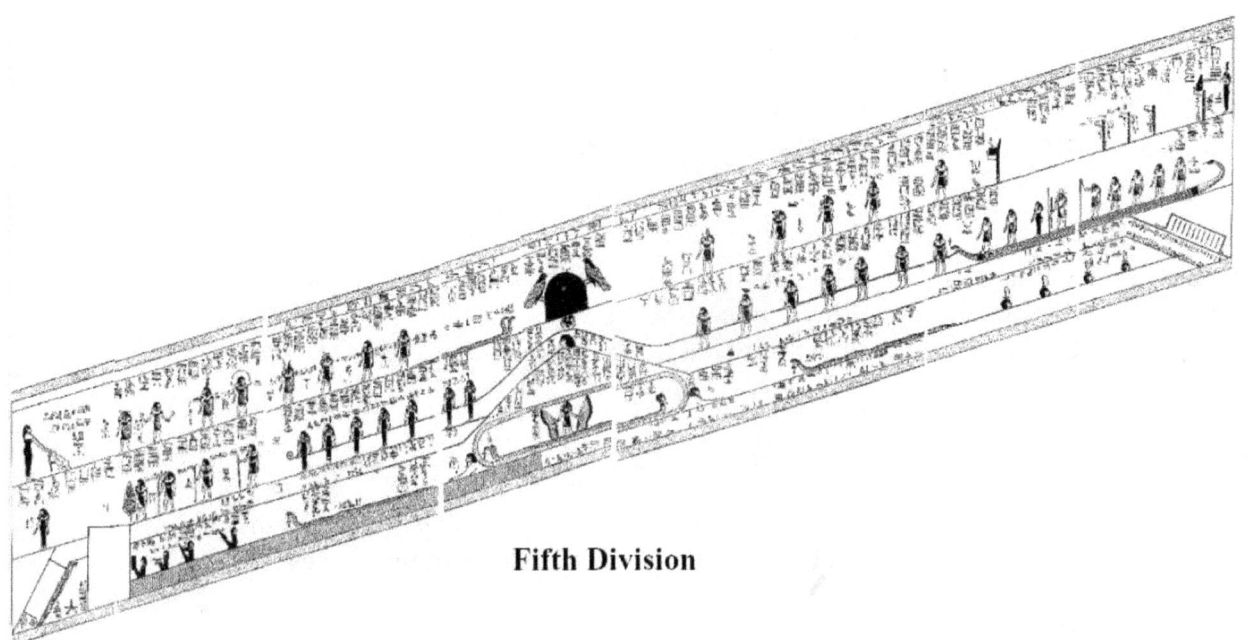

Fifth Division

henb	en	ef	neter	pen	aa	habt	er
to measure land for	him	god	this	great	lands	near

to measure land for him⁹³, this great god, the lands near

bu	sen	en	sekhet	Urnes	aha
place	their	in	domain	river that flows in the Tuat	stand

the place in their domain, stands the river that flows in the Tuat,

kheft	aha	neter	ap	ef	em	khet	neter	pen	aa	aq	ef	ta
enemy	stand	god	travel	he	in	follow	god	this	great	enter	in	he	earth

stands the enemy god.⁹⁴ He travels in. Follow this great god. He enters the earth

uba	ba	ef	em	Tuat	up	ef	sebt	em
open out a way	soul	his	in	Tuat	open up	his	lock of hair	with

to open out a way, his soul in the Tuat to open, his lock of hair with

hensekti
gods with side-locks

the gods with side-locks

ap	ef	her	am⁹⁵	aatui⁹⁶	em	khet	Maati
travel	he	above	to swallow	Sun god	to	follow	truth goddesses

he travels above to swallow the Sun God, following the truth goddesses⁹⁷

---

⁹³ In ancient Egypt, stars were used for surveying land. This is a reference to measuring land, which is elevated into their domain in the sky, in the Tuat.

⁹⁴ The enemy god was the great serpent Apep (Hydra), a star constellation in the sky just before dawn, the legendary archenemy of the Sun God, who waited each day to swallow him. The position of the appearance of this constellation is given as 120 on the horizon. The great serpent constellation Hydra entered the horizon at 120 degrees on September 21ˢᵗ, 10,390 BC.

⁹⁵ Bucher shows [hieroglyphs]..., page 84.

⁹⁶ Budge, EHD, 113A, *aatui*: One of the 75 forms of Ra.

⁹⁷ The twin truth goddesses (Gemini) precede the constellation Hydra in the sky.

henbit	hetcht	ef	qeq
domain	bright and shining[98]	he	to eat

bright and shining domain[99]. He eats

tau	er	uaa	ta	tu	en	ef	hat[100]
bread	upon	ship	earth	give	to	him	towing rope of a boat

bread upon the ship, the earth gives to him the towing rope,

ateb	tuba[101]
land	a form of the sun god

land of the Sun god.

au	ar	tu	nen	baui	Tuatiu	em
come	image	give	this	souls	gods and other beings of the Tuat	in

Come give image, these souls, gods and other beings of the Tuat in

sesh	em	qet	em	ament	ten	Tuat hat	sesh	er amentiu
writings	of	images	in	hidden	this	Tuat first	writings	concerning the dead

writings of images hidden in this Tuat. The first writings concerning the dead.

au	u	tent[102]	teben	en	sen	tepi ta	em	ren
come	they	plot of ground	go around	for	them	dweller on earth	in	names

They come go round the plot of ground for them, living man, in their names

sen	au	khu	en	sa	tepi ta	maa-shes-maat	en	sep
they	come	shine	for	man	dweller on earth	regularly and always	in	time

come shine for living man regularly and always in time.

---

[98] Budge, EHD, 522B, *hetcht*
[99] The domain of the night sky bright and shining with starlight.
[100] Budge, EHD, 461B, *hat*
[101] Budge, EHD, 824B, *Tuba*
[102] Budge, EHD, 881B, *tent*: plot of ground, field

au	rekh	nen	metu	techtu[103]	neteru
come to know	these words			spokesman	gods

Come to know these words spokesman of the gods

tuatui	en	neter	pen	metu	techtu[104]	en
gods and other beings of the Tuat	for	divine	this	words	spokesman	of

the gods and other beings of the Tuat for these divine words, spokesman of

neter	pen	aa	em	ar	kher	tuatui	au
god	this	great	to	ascend	with	gods and other beings of the Tuat	come

this great god to ascend with the gods and other beings of the Tuat come

khu	en	ef	tepi-ta	maat shes-maat	ren	en	unut
to shine	for	him	dweller on earth	regularly and always	name	of	hour

to shine for him, living man, regularly and always. Name of hour

net	gerh	seshem	neter	pen	aa	em	sekhet	ten
of	night	guidance	god	this	great	in	field	this

of night guiding this great god in this field,

Shesat-mak-t-neb-s [105]
knowledge protectress master star god

Shesat-mak-t-neb-s, the master star god knowledge protectress, an hour goddess in the Tuat.

hotep	em	khet
peace	in	follow

Follow in peace

---

[103] Budge, EHD, 913B, *tchetu*
[104] Budge, EHD, 913B, *tchetu*
[105] Budge, EHD, 288B, *m'kit*

an	het	en	neter	pen	aa	em	sekhet	nepertiu[106]	hept an
by	majesty of	god	this	great	in	field	harvest gods	paddle	by

by the majesty of this great god in [this] field. The harvest gods paddle by

neter pen	em	neth	mu	Asar
god this	in	which	celestial water	Osiris

this god which [is] in the celestial water, the Osiris

atru	aftu saa	khemennui[107]	em	aut[108]	en	sekhet ten
canal	400	80	in	length	of	field out

canal 480 in length of this field,

usekh	saa taut	hetch	neter pen	aa
this	to be spread 100 20	bright and shining	god this	great

this to be spread out 120,[109] bright and shining this great god

metu	amui	khet	en Asar	er
words	which are in	follow	to Osiris	at

follows the words which are herein to Osiris at

nuit[110]		ten	hent	ef en sen	ateb
sacred place created in the primeval age		this	journey	he in their	lands

this sacred place created in primeval time.[111] His journey in their lands

---

[106] Budge, EHD, 369A, *Nepertiu*, Tuat II, a group of grain gods or harvest-gods.

[107] Tuthmosis III shows 309.

[108] Budge, EHD, 2B, *aut*: length, largeness

[109] 'to be spread out 120' may be referring to the images of the 3 registers in the Fourth Division and the 1st register in the Fifth Division of the Book of Am Duat, which registers are to be spread out. See illustration on page 78.

[110] Reymond, *Mythical Origin of the Egyptian Temple*, page 14, ⊗ *niwt* the determinative of the name of any sacred place that was created in the primeval age.

[111] Osiris is at the sacred place created in primeval time. The stars lead the way to him. The text is telling the reader to follow the star constellations.

er   sekhet   ten   baui
near field   this divine souls
near this field. Divine souls,

shetau   neteru   ren   en   neteru   amu   sekhet   ten
secret   gods   names of   gods   who are in field   this
secret gods, names of gods who are in this field.[112]

ar   rekh   ren   sen   tepi-ta[113] *au   ef   ar   ef   er   bu*
by   know names their dweller on earth come he ascend he near place
Know by their names living man. He comes, he ascends near the place

kher   Asar[114] *am   tu   en   ef   mu   er   sekhet   ef   tu*
under Osiris   within give to him celestial waters near field his this
under Osiris within. Give to him celestial waters near his field, this

net   mu   neb   ua   neter   khepert   aut   ren   en   sekht   ten
of celestial water lord one god existent largeness name of field this
Lord of celestial water. One god existent largeness name of this field.

au   an   tut   nen   seshemu   sheta   en   baui   shetau   qett   pen
come see image these guides   secret of divine souls secrets image this
Come see the image, these secret guides of divine souls secrets. This image

nti   em   seshu   em   ament   net
not in   writings in   hidden   which
not in writings, which is hidden in

---

[112] The secret names of the gods refers to the names of the star constellations. Hydra ascends near the place where Osiris is under, within.

[113] Budge, EHD, 828B, *tepi ta*: Dweller on earth, i.e., a living man (as opposed to a dweller in the mountain, i.e., a dead man)

[114] Tuthmosis III shows , see: Bucher, page 86.

Tuat	hat	seshu	er	Amentiu	au	yah[115]	en	sa	tepi ta	em
Tuat	first	writings of		the dead	come	shine	for	man	dweller on earth	upon

the Tuat, the first writings of the dead, come shine for living man upon

khert neter	maat-shes maat	au	rekh	sen
necropolis	regularly and always	come	to know	them

the necropolis[116], regularly and always. Come to know them

em	ap	her	sen	sebi	en	ef	en	hemhemt	sen	n	ha
as	travel	over	they	lead	in	him	to	roar		they do not	descend

as travel over. They lead him in to roar.[117] They do not decsend

---

[115] Mercer, *Handbook of Egyptian Hieroglyphs*, page 156, Sign List, 57, 58 y3ḥ "to shine"

[116] cemetery, burial ground

[117] Reference to lion god Aker, the double lion constellations Leo and Centaurus. In the image of the 5th division of Am Tuat below, the oval is the horizon. The sphinx lion god on the right of the horizon is Leo, on the left is Centaurus, and in the center is Hydra, the flying serpent. The planet Venus is represented by the head at the end of the tail. This configuration is visible in the stars September 21st, 10390 BC, at 4:45 AM.

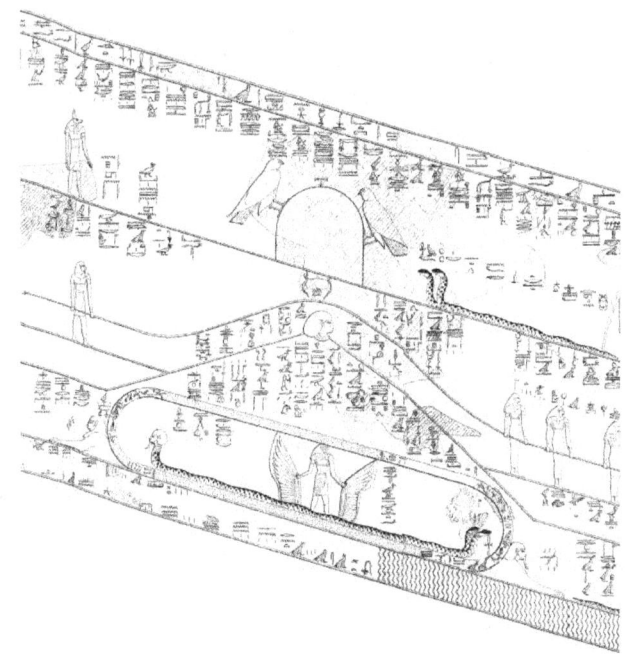

en	ef	er	hatu	sen	au
to	him	near	ovens	they	come

to him near their ovens. Come

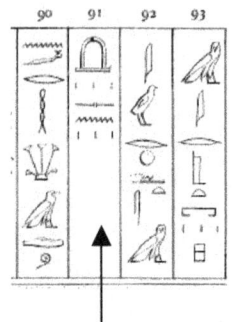

The same section from the tomb of Seti I, drawn by Lefébure in 1886, shows that Column 91 ends with *sen*. *Au* begins the next sentence, in the next column.

rekh	s	mm	ar	s-t	paut[118]	ef	er	her	hena
know	them	among	at	places	primeval	his	near	above	with

to know them among at the primeval places near his, above with

Ra	au	rekh	set	em	ba	khu	skhem
Sun God	come	to know	them	of	soul	spirit	divine power

the Sun God. Come to know them in soul spirit, the divine power

em	ret	efi	nti	aq	ef	hetemit	au	ef
of	two legs	his	not	enter in	he	place of destruction	come	he

of his two legs. He does not enter in the place of destruction.[119] He comes.

per	ef	em	aru	ef [120]
come forth	he	in	images	his

He comes forth in his images

---

[118] Budge, EHD, 230B, *pat*: , primaeval time, remote ages. *Paut*, , is consistently associated with the idea of "primeval." and both represent the letter 't', and were sometimes used interchangeably.

[119] The place of destruction may refer to the tomb and/or may refer to the sunrise.

[120] Bucher omits , page 86

em	thepa	ef	nef	unut	ef
in	to breathe	his	wind	hour	his

to breathe in his winds, his hour.[121]

ren	en	unut	seshemt	neter pen	ta ten	tent	seshem	ba sba [122]
name	of	hour	guidance	god this	earth this	belonging to	guide	souls star

Name of hour guiding this god, this earth's guide star souls.

hotep	em	khet	em	stau	an	het	neter pen	em
peace	in	follow	as	tow	by	majesty	god this	in

In peace follow as tow by the majesty of this god in the

qerut	shetaut	en	Ament
circle	hidden	of	the dead

hidden circle of the dead.

art	skher	neta [123]	neteru	ames	em	kheru	ef
see	designs	advance	gods	conduct	with	voice	his

See the designs. The gods advance. Conducted with his voice.

n-t	maa	ef	sen	ren	en	qerrt	net	ankh [124]
without	see	him	they	name	of	circle	of	living person or thing

They do not see him. The name of the circle of living things

kheperu	per	ren	en	sba	en	qerrt	net	ament
images	house	name	of	door	of	circle	of	hidden

images house is the name of the door of the circle of hidden

---

[121] The dawn in Egypt was accompanied by wind.

[122] Bucher includes ✶ , page 86.

[123] Budge, EHD, 1B, *neta*

[124] Budge, EHD, 124B, *ankh*

sethau
corridors or passages through which boats are towed[125]
corridors or passages through which boaus are towed.

au	*rekh*	*seshem*	*pen*	*en*	*uat*
Come	to know	guides	this	in	paths

Come to know the guides in these paths

shetat	*net*	*er*	*restau*	*ma*	*net*	*Nu*
hidden	of	entrance	the abode of the dead of Memphis[126]	behold	of	sky-god

of hidden entrance of the abode of the dead of Memphis. Behold the sky-god of

uat	*teseru*[127]	*na*	*mm*	*het*[128]	*sbau*	*amenu*
paths	large stones	a kind of stone	among	great house	doors	hidden

paths. Large stones among the great house hidden doors[129]

amiu	*ta*	*sekri*	*heri*	*sha*	*ef*
which are in	earth	Seker[130]	over	sand	his

which are in the earth, Seker[131] **over his sand**

Em	*kek*	*ef*	*ta*	*er*	*er*	*khent*[132]	*Ankhu*	*neteru*	*em*	*het*
as	eat	his	bread	near	entrance	before	living	gods	in	great house

as he eats his bread near the entrance before the living gods in the great house

---

[125] Budge, EHD, 629B, *setha*

[126] The Giza necropolis forms part of the huge necropolis of Memphis, the capital of Egypt during the Old Kingdom.

[127] Budge, EHD, 888B, *teseru*:

[128] Budge, EHD, 453A, *het*: , great house, temple

[129] This sentence may be a reference to the large stones of a pyramid in the necropolis of Memphis and a secret door to the hidden house (of Osiris).

[130] Compare with Bucher, page 87 (first line): .

[131] *Seker* or *Sekri* may be a term that refers to the configuration of three constellations: Leo, Hydra, and Centaurus

[132] Budge, EHD, 554A, *khent*: in the front, in the forepart, before, aforetime, formerly, previously, in advance, the beginning, the land south of Egypt.

Temu
creator of heaven and earth
of the creator of heaven and earth.

au	*Rekh*	*set*	*em*	*maa*	*ten*	*uat*	*shemt*[133]	*em*
come to know	them	as	to give	this	roads	journey	of

Come know them as give these roads, the journey of

Athen		*uat*	*en*	*er*
Amen god of solar disk		roads of entrance	of	entrance

Amen the god of the solar disk, roads of entrance

sethau[134]	*semit*	*maa*
passages through which boats are towed	desert	see

desert passages through which boats are towed[135]**, see**

seshem	*mm*	*het*	*ren*	*en*	*Unut*	*net*	*gerh*
images of gods	among	great house	name	of	hour	of	night

the images of the gods among the great house.[136] **The name of the hour of night**

seshemt	*neter*	*pen*	*aa*	*urt*	*neter*	*aa*	*her*	*sen*
guidance	god	this	great	motionless	god	great	over	them

guiding this great god, the motionless great god above them

em	*skhemu*[137]	*s*	*sba*
with	powers	her[138]	star

with the star of her powers.

---

[133] Budge, EHD, 739A, *shemt*, ; [Bucher omits the ⌒, page 87]

[134] Budge, EHD, 629B, *sethau*

[135] These roads that Amen travels in the desert are the corridors in the sky through which boats are towed. In other words, the paths followed by star constellations as the slowly move across the heavens.

[136] Here the great house is the universe and the images of the gods are star constellations. The name of the hour of night, is the name of the star goddess of this hour. It is she who guides the great motionless star constellation above.

[137] Budge, EHD, 690B, *skhemu*

[138] This may refer to the hour goddess of this particular hour.

Sethau — *neter* *pen* *aa* *her*
corridors or passages through which boats are towed — god this great over
corridors or passages through which boats are towed this great god over

uat
paths
paths

Maati — *net* *Tuat* *er ges* [139] *Herit* [140]
Twin Goddesses of Truth — of Tuat near Goddess of heaven a form of Nut
Twin Goddesses of Truth of Tuat near Nut, the Goddess of Heaven, [141]

qerrt *shetat* *net* *Sekri* — *ᶜ* *nt* *maa* *nt* *petr*
circle secret of Sekri — s not perceive not seen
the secret circle of Sekri over his _____, ___ _____, not seen

shemit
guides (plural fem.)
guides;

From tomb of Seti I, Lefébure, 1886:

Pen *sheta* *en* *ta* *kher* *auf* [142] *neter* *pen* *au* *neteru*
this secret in earth under bodies divine this come gods
this secret in the earth under these divine bodies. [143] **The gods come**

---

[139] Budge, EHD, 813A, *er ges*; Bucher, page 87 (in Tuthmosis III), and page 205 (in Amenhotep II) is written

[140] *Herit;* Bucher, page 87 (in Tuthmosis III), and page 205 (in Amenhotep II) is written .

[141] The Twin Goddesses of Truth are the constellation Gemini which is seen at the beginning of night on September 21st, 10390, after sun has set and darkness has begun.

[142] Budge, EHD, A34, *auf*

[143] The secret is in the earth under Sekri (Seker)

amiu	neter	pen	setchem	sen	kheru	Ra
who are in	god	this	hear	they	voices	Sun God

who are in this god. They hear the voice of the Sun God.

tua	ef	er	ha [145]	neter	pen
to call out	he	near	in place near at hand	god	this

He calls out nearby this god.

Ren	en	sba	en	nuit [146]		aha [147]
name of		door	of	sacred place which was created in the primeval age		stand

The name of the door of the sacred place created in primeval time stand

neteru	per [148]	ren	en	qerrt	neter	pen
gods	house	name	of	circle	god	this

gods house. The name of the circle this god

ament	semit
hidden	hill cemetery

hidden hill cemetery.

uat	shetat	net	Ament	sba	en	at	amen
roads	secrets	of	the west bank of the Nile	doors	of	house	hidden

Secret roads of the west bank of the Nile. The doors of the hidden house,

---

[144] *ef* was missing in Seti I

[145] Budge, EHD, 438A, *ha*

[146] Reymond, *Mythical Origin of the Egyptian Temple*, page 14, ⊗ niwt the determinative of the name of any sacred place which was created in the primeval age.

[147] Incorrectly written; compare Tuthmosis III (Bucher, page 87), and Amenophis II, (Bucher, page 205).

[148] Missing from Seti I, but included in both Tuthmosis III (Bucher, page 87) and Amenophis II (Bucher, page 205).

bu	teser	en	Sekri
place	holy	of	Sekri

the holy place of Sekri.[149]

Afu		ha	ef	tchet	em
two man headed sphinxes		the flesh of the body	his	body	in

the two man headed sphinxes[150]**; the flesh of his body in**

kheperu	tepi
images	first

the first images.

ren	en	neteru	amiu	qerrt	ten	baui	amiu
name	of	gods	who are in	circle	this	divine souls	who are in

The name of the gods who are in this circle; the divine souls who are in

Tuat	aru	sen	ami	unut	kheperu	sen	shetau
Tuat	images	they	who are in	hours	images	their	secrets

the Tuat images, they who are in the hour images, their secrets

n-t	rekh
without	know

unknown,

n	maa	n	petr	seshemu	pen	en	Heru[151]	tches
not	perceive	not	see	images	this	of	an ancient sky god	himself

not perceived, not seen, images of this ancient sky god himself.[152]

---

[149] *Seker* or *Sekri* may be a term that refers to the configuration of three constellations: Leo, Hydra, and Centaurus.

[150] The two man-headed sphinxes may refer to the constellations of Leo and Centaurus.

[151] Both Tuthmosis III and d'Amenophis II show 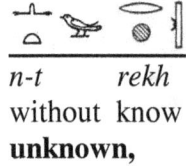 (Bucher)

[152] This is most likely a reference to the god Seker (see footnote 149)

au	maa	tut	nen	ma	seshem	pen	nti	em
come	see	image	this	together with	images	this	not	in

Come see this image together with these images,[153] not in

seshu	em	amen	net	sba	her	Res	en	at	amen
writings	in	hidden	of	Tuat	above	South	of	house	hidden

writings; of the hidden Tuat above, South of the hidden house.

au	rekh	set	em	hotep	ba	ef	hotep	ef	em
come	to know	them	in	peace	soul	his	rest	his	with

Come to know them. His soul rests in peace with his

hotept[155]	Sekri	n	ten	Khemit[156]
offerings made to the dead	sekeri	not cut to pieces		goddess of destruction

sepulchral meals. Sekri is not cut to pieces by the goddess of destruction,

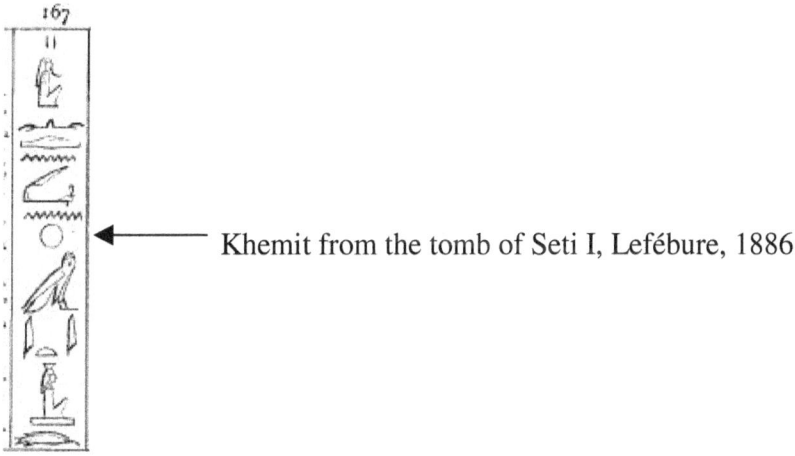

Khemit from the tomb of Seti I, Lefébure, 1886

---

[153] This is a reference to star asterisms.

[154] Bucher, pages 87 and 206, both tombs show *Sekri* as [glyph].
[155] Budge, EHD, 518A, *hotep*
[156] Budge, EHD, 547B, *Khemit*

khat	ef	sua[157]	ef	heri	sem[158]	hotep	au
bodies without life	his	to pass on	his	above	image	rest	come

his bodies without life pass away above, his image rests. Come

uten[159]	en	nen	neteru	tepi-ta	ren	en	unut	en
to make an offering	to	these	gods	dweller on earth	name	of	hour	of

make an offering to these gods living man. The name of the hour of

gerh	seshemit	neter	pen	aa	em	qerret	ten
night	guidance	god	this	great	in	circle	this

night guiding this great god in this circle,

Ten	seshit	heri ab[160]		uaa	sba
this	guide	the goddess dwelling in the temple		ship	star

this guide the goddess dwelling in the temple star ship.

Hotep	an	het	en	neter	pen
rest	by	majesty	of	god	this

Rest by the majesty of this great god

aa	em	Metch[161]	Mu	nebt[162]
great	in	a gulf in the other world	celestial water	goddess

in a gulf in the other world, the celestial water goddesss,

---

[157] Budge, EHD, 592A, *sua*: to pass, to pass on, to pass away

[158] Budge, EHD, 666B, *sem*, form, image, kind, manner, practice

[159] Budge, EHD, 189A, *uten*: to make an offering

[160] Budge, EHD, 494B, *heriabt*

[161] Budge, EHD, 337A, *Metch*, Tuat VI

[162] Budge, EHD, 337A, *Metch-t-Nebt-Tuat*, , the name of the sixth division of the Tuat.

Tuatui	*hetcht*	*ef*	*metu*	*en neteru*
gods and other beings of the Tuat	bright and shining	his	words	to gods

gods, and other beings of the Tuat bright and shining. His words to the gods

amiu
who are in
who are in

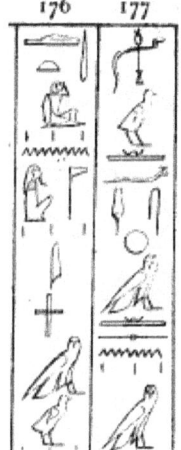

from the tomb of Seti I, Lefébure, 1886; there is no ⎯ before .

ef	*sekhem*	*sen*	*em*	*Neter*	*hotept*[163]	*sen er*
his	divine power	they	in	divine	offerings made to the dead	they near

his divine power, in their divine power. Their sepulchral meals near

nuit[164]		*ten*	*seqtt*	*ef em ten*
sacred place created in primeval time		this	travel about in a boat	he in this

this sacred place created in primeval time, he travels about in a boat in this,

aper	*em*	*uaa*
equipped	as	ship

equipped as in a ship,

---

[163] Budge, EHD, 518A, *hotept*: sepulchral meals, the offerings made to the dead.

[164] Reymond, *Mythical Origin of the Egyptian Temple*, page 14, ⊗ *niwt* the determinative of the name of any sacred place which was created in the primeval age.

hetch	ef	en	sen	aht	en [165]	sen	er
bright and shining	he	in	their	regions	to	their	near

bright and shining he in their regions, near to their

hotept		sen	ta	ef en sen	Mu
offerings made to the dead		they	give	him in their	celestial waters

sepulchral meals they give to him in their celestial waters,

sen	ra [166]	pu	ai	Tuat	em	ra [167]
their	place	this	journeys	Tuat	in	daily

their place, this journeys in the Tuat daily.[168]

ren	en	sba	en nuit [169]	ten	Septit	temetu [170]	per
name	of	door	of place	this	Sothis	to pierce	house

The name of the door of this place: Sothis Pierces the House,

uat	shetat	net	Amentt	khenn
way	secret	of	the abode of the dead	navigate

the secret way of the abode of the dead,

neter	pen	Aa	mu	ames	em	uaa	ef	er	art
god	this	great	celestial water	to conduct	in	ship	his	with	see

this great god [navigates] the celestial water to conduct in with his ship. See

---

[165] Bucher, page 88, uses [hieroglyphs].

[166] Budge, EHD, 419A, *ra*

[167] Budge, EHD, 417B, *ra*

[168] The stars journey in their place every day

[169] Reymond, page 14, ⊗ *niwt* the determinative of the name of any sacred place which was created in the primeval age.

[170] Bucher, page 88: [hieroglyphs].

skheru	*tuatui*	*Temt*	*em*
designs	gods and other beings of the Tuat	to unite with	with

the designs of the gods and other beings of the Tuat united with

renu	*sen*	*rekh*	*ma*	*then*	*em*	*aru*	*sen*	*unut* *sen*
names	their	to know	together with	this	in	images	their	hours their

their names. Know together with this in their images, their hours

shetat	*khert*
secret	natures

and secret natures.[171]

nt	*rekh*	*seshemu*	*pen*	*sheta*	*en*	*Tuat*	*an*	*reth* *nebt*
not	to know	images of gods	this	secret	of	Tuat		for mankind goddess

Unknown images of gods, this secret of the Tuat, the goddess for mankind.[172]

au	*art*	*seshemu*	*pen em*	*seshu*
come	see	guides	this in	writings

Come see the guides in this book

ma qet[173]	*pen em*	*amen*	*per net*	*Tuat*	*her*	*resi*	*at*
altogether	this in	hidden	house of	Tuat	over	southern	house

altogether in this hidden house of the Tuat, over the southern house

amentt[174]
abode of the dead
abode of the dead.

---

[171] Natures may refer to astrological influences.
[172] The goddess for mankind may be referring to the sky (*Nut*).
[173] Budge, EHD, 779B, *ma qet*: altogether, in a body, collectively, in entirety, whole, totality.
[174] Bucher, page 88,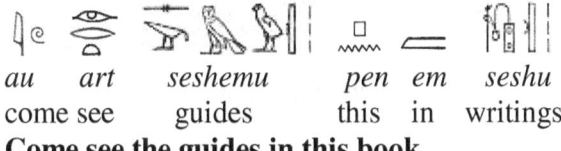

au	Rekh	set	m	ar [175]		au	
come to know	them	in proportion to	largeness				

Come to know them in proportion to the largeness[176]

em	Tuat	hotep ef	em	hotept	neteru	ami khet	Asar
in	Tuat	rest he	in	offerings to the dead	gods	who are in follow	Osiris

in the Tuat. He rests in sepulchral meals. The gods who are in follow Osiris

au	maat	en	ef	aabti	neteru
come	truth	to	his	eastern	gods

come to his truth, eastern gods,

ef	em	ta
his	to	earth

to his earth.

utcht metu	an	neter	pen	er	ta	neter	hotept	en
utter words	by	god	this	to	give divine offerings made to the dead			to

Words uttered by this god to give divine sepulchral meals to

neteru	Tuatiu	aha	ef	er	sen
gods	gods and other beings of the Tuat	stand	he	near	them

the gods and other beings of the Tuat. He stands near them

maa	sen	su	sekhem	Sen	en	sekhet	sen	uat
see	they	his	divine powers	they	in	domains	their	wide

they see his divine powers in their domains, their wide domains,

akhut	sen	kheper	sen	em	hetch	en	sen	neter	pen
horizons	they	Kheper	them	in	to become bright	in	them	god	this

their horizons. Kheper in them becomes bright, this [great] god in them.

---

[175] Budge, EHD, 277A, *ar*

[176] This page really makes a strong emphasis to recognizing the stars in their vast domain.

aa
great

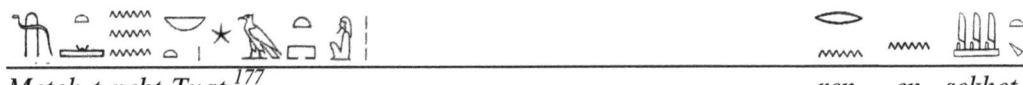

Metch-t-nebt-Tuat [177]						*ren*	*en*	*sekhet*
gulf in the other world-goddess-gods and other beings of the Tuat						name	of	domain

The gulf of the goddess, gods, and other beings of the Tuat is the name of

ten	*uat*	*pu*	*net*	*uaa*	*ra*	*ren*	*en*	*unut*
this	path	this	of	ship	Sun god	name	of	hour

this domain. This Path of the ship of the Sun God is the name of the hour

neth	*gerh*	*seshemt*	*neter*	*pen*	*aa* [178]	*em*	*sekhet*	*ten*
of	night	guidance	god	this	great	in	field	this

of the night guiding this great god in this field,

em	*sper*	*it*	*ar*	*atma*	*au*	*sba*
as	to come forth	food	to	offering	comes	star

as comes forth to food offering. The star comes

hotep	*an*	*neter*	*pen*	*aa*	*em*	*Thepht*	*n-t*	*Asar*	*utch metu* [179]	*an*
rest	by	god	this	great	upon	storehouse[180]	of	Osiris	to give orders	by

to rest by this great god upon the storehouse[181] of Osiris. Commands by

het	*en*	*neter*	*pen*	*aa*	*er*	*thepht* [182]	*ten*	*en*	*nen*	*neteru*
majesty	of	god	this	great	near	storehouse	this	of	these	gods

the majesty of this great god near this storehouse of these gods

---

[177] Budge, EHD, 337A, *Metch-t-nebt-Tuat*: the name of the 6th Division in the Tuat
[178] Bucher, p 89, line 33, omits "Great"
[179] Budge, EHD, 192A, *utch metu*
[180] Budge, *A Hieroglyphic Vocabulary*, page 451, *thephet*: storehouse, cave, cavern, hole.
[181] In the Cayce readings, storehouse is a synonym for pyramid. Reading 1925-1, text, paragraph 10: *those storehouses in those pyramids*; reading 275-33, text, paragraph 22: *...among those things preserved in the pyramid of unknown origin, as yet, but in the storehouse of records.*
[182] Budge, EHD, 854B, *thepht*: hole in the ground, cavern, cave.

ami
who are in
who are in ...

The text of Seti I, as recorded in Lefébure's book ends here. But the continuation of the text can be found in Paul Bucher's work, which is presented in the next section.

THE CONTINUATION OF THE ABRIDGEMENT OF THE AM TUAT

Paul Bucher

Father Paul Bucher
(1887 –1966)

Paul Bucher was also interested in a comparative study of the Am Tuat, and the early 1930's saw the publication of his work in this area, including a portion of the text that was not in Eugène Lefébure's rendition. In this section, we complete our translation using the hieroglyphs as recorded by Bucher.

The Obituary of Father Paul Bucher

The life and work of Father Paul Bucher, French priest and Egyptologist, is summed up well in his obituary, written by colleague, Jean Leclant, and here translated from the original French.

> On May 22, 1966 Father Paul Bucher died, a man whose life and work were very closely linked to the University of Strasbourg. On May 15, 1887, in Guebwiller, in the heart of the lovely landscape of a vineyard, this native of Haut-Rhin came to study at the seminary of Strasbourg. Under the influence of distinguished masters, the Old Testament sciences were in full bloom there at that time. The young student completed his training with the courses of the faculty, where he enrolled in particular for Arabic and Semitic studies with Noeldeke and Enno Littmann; for Assyrian, he was a pupil of the late Canon Dennefeld. But it was in Wilhelm Spiegelberg he was to meet the Master par excellence. Exceptionally early (born in 1870, he was Dozent in 1894), the latter gave the Institute of Egyptology extraordinary brilliance. He set up a remarkable collection there. His teaching of the hieratic and the demotic were then

probably without equal in Europe. The Master's charm and kindness, how many times, over decades, has it been the object of admiration by Father Bucher! Eschau priest, he loved to recall the release of ancient remains, ambulance driving during a conflict where there was no doubt about his deep sympathies for the Alsatian patriot, Father Bucher continued to attend his beloved Institute of Egyptology. In June, 1917 he defended his doctorate. His thesis was dedicated to Papyrus 2 and 7 of the collection of the National University Library of Strasbourg. These, which are hymns to Sobek-Re, the crocodile god, master of Semnou, will be published later in the journal founded by P. Montet, *Kémi* (I, 1928, p. 41-52, 147-166, III, 1930, p. 1-19.).

In November 1918, Alsace had again become French. In 1919, P. Montet was named Master of Conferences in the chair made vacant by the departure of Spiegelberg for Heidelberg. A long collaboration would be established between Father Pierre Montet and Bucher which his superiors deliberately maintained close to the university, in the parish of La Madeleine at first, then from 1923 in the village of Avenheim, huddled in the picturesque landscape of hills covered with vineyards and hops, not far from Truchtersheim.

The first missions in Egypt of Father Bucher in Deir-el-Medina were in the framework of the work of the French Institute of Oriental Archeology. Later after 1930, he regularly participated in excavations at Tanis, linking his name solidly to the resounding findings made in the Delta by Professor P. Montet. Thus, in February 1940, he removed, in the presence of Father Droiton, the magnificent silver casket contained in the anthropoid sarcophagus of black granite of Pharaoh Psusennes. There is a large volume of hieroglyphic texts copied by him in the Theban necropolis, Volume 60 of the memoirs of the I.F.A.O., entitled The Texts of the tombs of Thutmosis III and Amenophis II; often the friends of the Father have pressed to have published the translation and the commentary he had prepared - but to no avail. Previously, Father Bucher had already edited "The Texts at the end of the First, Second and Third Hours of The Book of What is in the Duat". Texts compared the tombs of Thutmosis III and of Amenophis II and Seti I, in the Bulletin *I.F.A.O.*, 30, 1930, p. 229-247.

To articles already cited by Kêmi, Father Bucher added Volume IV, 1931, p. 157-160, the publication of the Inscription of Kasr es Saijad, giving the beginnings of the Psalms LI to XCIII; then in volume V, 1935, p. 64-70 publishing several individual steles of Tanis. Finally, he contributed an article with Pierre Montet on "A Canaanite God at Tanis: Houroun of Ramesses", in *Revue Biblique*, 44, 1935, p. 153-165.

In 1948, it was only natural that Father Bucher, Doctor of Letters from the University of Strasbourg and assistant for many years to Professor P. Montet, was responsible for Egyptology when the latter was elected to the College of France. In 1954 I was to join him at the Institute of Egyptology in Strasbourg for a long and amicable collaboration which would last ten years. Father Bucher then absorbed himself in a grammar course intended for students as well as the teaching of Demotic and Coptic, of which he was one of the few specialists. Students from the Faculties of Catholic and Protestant theology were his frequent listeners. Our first work together was the rehabilitation of the collection which had suffered the many tribulations of war, occupation and the post-war period, and its increase due to a very large donation given from the collection of Barr. Those long hours spent in the company of Father Muller, of Miss Ortscheit and dedicated students! The joy of the Father was great when the objects were stored in the display cases, inventories put in order, the collection could be presented to the Dean Marcel Simon and Y. Béquignon his Assessor, and then to the Rector himself and many visitors.

At the invitation of our colleagues Dr. Dollinger and G. Livet, we could soon publish (1956) a note on the collection of the Institute of Strasbourg, in the Bulletin of the Academic Society of Bas-Rhin, 1953-1956, v. LXXV-LXXVIII, p. 100-109. Among the three illustrations published, was the head of the god Amon bearing the name of Ramses III, in fact one of the few known effigies of this ruler.

The promotion of Father Bucher to Officer of the Order of Academic Palms was during a small intimate ceremony, which the participants fondly remember. Very regularly, he continued coming to Avenheim, where his colleagues and pupils often came to visit him, always sure of a warm-hearted reception. Then, after forty years of devotion to the parish of Avenheim, it was from the nursing home San José in Strasbourg that he came almost daily to his dear Institute. A few days before his death, he returned to the Haut-Rhin he loved so much. Dean G. Livet, Professor Dr. Derchain, his most faithful followers, A. Gutbub, A. Heyler then gave a moving account of the last visit with one who has done so much for the reputation of the Institute of Egyptology at the University of Strasbourg.

Jean Leclant

The Text and Translation

The first line below is the last line of hieroglyphic text recorded in a book published in French in 1886: Memoirs published by Members of the French Archaeological Mission in Cairo 1882-1884, Second Volume, The Royal Tombs of Thebes, The Tomb of Seti I, by Eugène Lefébure. The remainder is from the work of Paul Bucher.

het en neter pen aa er thept
majesty of god this great near storehouse
the majesty of this great god near this storehouse

ten en nen neteru amiu s au [183]
this of these gods who are in they come
of these gods who are in they come.

neter pen maa ef ki aru er thepht
god this see his other forms near storehouse
See this god, his other forms near storehouse

then stem [184] ef uat er Apep [185] em heka [186]
this to turn back his way against Apep with beneficent spells
this to turn back his way against Apep with beneficent spells,

As-t heka semsu
Isis divine incantation
Isis divine incantation.

---

[183] This text begins in line 45 of Bucher's *Les Textes Des Tombes De Thoutmosis III et D'Amenophis II*, hieroglyphs from the tomb of Amenhotep II continue with , *s au*, which means *they come*.

[184] Budge, EHD, 711A, *stem*

[185] Budge, EHD, 111A, *Aapep*: , , , , , , , a monster mythological serpent which produced thunder, lightning, storm, hurricanes, mist, cloud, fog, and darkness, and was the personification of evil. He was called by 77 "accursed names."

[186] Amenhotep II reads ...

ren	en	sba	en		nuit[187]		ten	app
name of		door	to		sacred place created in primeval time		this	travel

The name of the door to this sacred place created in the primeval age, travel

neter	pen	her	ef	ruti		Asar	per
god	this	over	him	entrance to any large building		Osiris	house

this god over his entrance to the house of Osiris[188]

ren	ef
name	his

his name.

ren	en		nuit		then	thepht
name of			sacred place that was created in primeval time		this	storehouse

The name of the sacred place created in the primeval age, this storehouse,

shetat	per	uat
secret house		way

hidden house. The [secret] way

shetat	net	Ament	ap	neter	aa	her	sen	em	uaa
secret	of	abode of the dead	travel	god	great	over	them	in	ship

of the Abode of the dead. This great god travels over them in [his holy] ship.

---

[187] Reymond, page 14, ⊗ *niwt* the determinative of the name of any sacred place which was created in the primeval age.

[188] This text refers to a large building, created in the primeval age that was called the House of Osiris, a storehouse, a hidden or secret house. In the ancient Egyptian language, *seshat* meant hidden and secret. There was a tradition amongst the priests of Memphis that the "Hidden house" referred to one of the great pyramids. Basil Steward, *Witness of the Great Pyramid* 1927, Pages 219-221: reference to Marsham Adams from *The Book of the Master of the Hidden House*. Giza was a part of Memphis which was the capital of Egypt during the Old Kingdom.

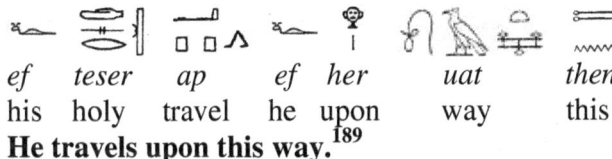

ef	teser	ap	ef	her	uat	then
his	holy	travel	he	upon	way	this

He travels upon this way.[189]

nti	nu	sen
without	water	they

Without water, they,

Nti	sethau	seqtt
without	corridors or passages through which boats are towed	travel about in a boat

without passages through which boats are towed,[190] **travel about in a boat,**

---

[189] This 'way' is the orbit or trajectory of its course.

[190] In Egypt, boats moved through waterways, canals, corridors, or passages. However, the boats of the star constellations sailed on boats in the sky without water.

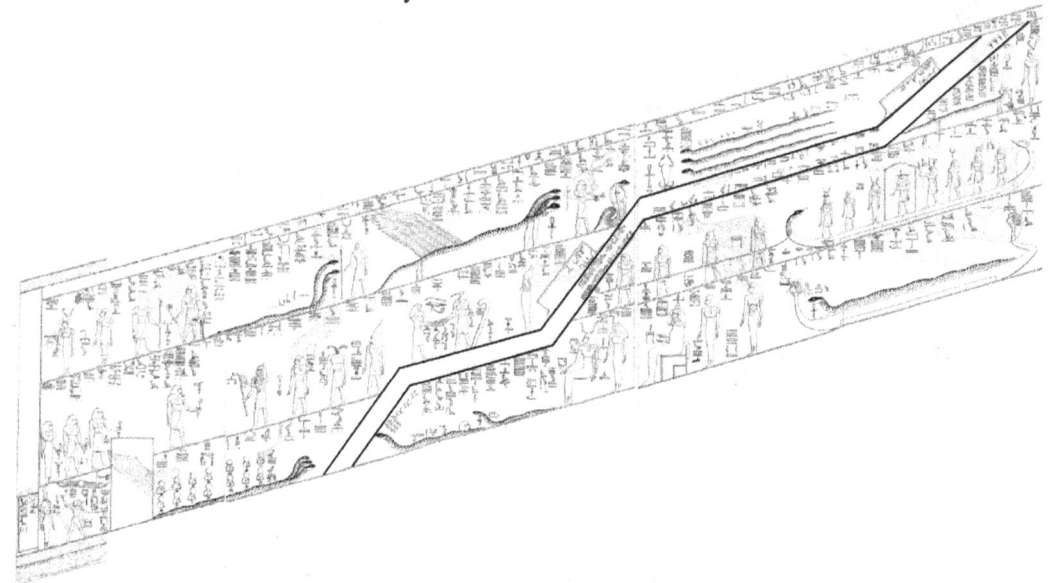

Above is an illustration from the tomb of Seti I, that shows the 4th Division of the Am Tuat filled with divine gods and other beings of the Tuat, and a corridor through which the three-headed serpent god must pass. Apep is the serpent in the horizon. The oval is the Ancient Egyptian hieroglyph for horizon. Below, Apep is illustrated as a three headed serpent in the 5th Division of the book of Am Tuat (this illustration from Ramesses VI tomb).

ef	*em*	*hekau*	*hetem*	*neter*		*semsu*[191]		*em*
he	according to	beneficent spells	throne	god		eldest		of

according to his benevolent spells, the throne of the eldest god.

khut	*tepi*	*er*	*en*	*neter*	*pen*	*tches*	*art*	*shat*	*apep*
spirits	above	entrance	of	god	this	himself	look	wounds	Apep

Spirits above the entrance of this god himself seeing the wounds of Apep

Em	*Tuat*	*qerrt*	*hau*[192]	*ef*
in	Tuat	circle	things in a state of ruin	his

in the circle in the Tuat, his things in a state of ruin,[193]

pu	*em*	*pet*
this	in	sky

this in the sky.

au	*maa*	*tu*	*nen*	*ma-qet*[194]	*pen*	*em*	*sesh*	*her*	*mehti*	*at*	*ament*
come	see	this	these	altogether	this	like	writing	over	north	house	hidden

Come see this, these altogether in this, like writing over the north hidden house

em	*Tuat*	*au*
of	Tuat	[come]

of the Tuat.

Upon reading this section of text, it became strikingly obvious that they were telling us to look at the sky. We were able to access an astronomical software program that allowed us to view the sky from 10,390 BC, the year we believe the Hall of Records was sealed. Looking directly overhead just before sunrise, we could see the constellations of Leo and Centaurus (the double-lion god Aker) and Hydra (the serpent).

---

[191] Budge, EHD, 602B, *semsu*

[192] Budge, EHD, 439B, *hau*

[193] We can begin to understand that this text is conveying information in terms of astronomy. When the sun begins to bring dawn, the constellation of Hydra (Apep) is wounded (by the rays of the sun) and ruined.

[194] Budge, EHD, 779B, *ma qet*: altogether, in a body, collectively, in entirety, whole, totality.

The next image is from Skyglobe planetary software. It shows an image of the sky over Giza on September 21st, 10390 BC, at 4:45 AM. with relevant constellations darkened.

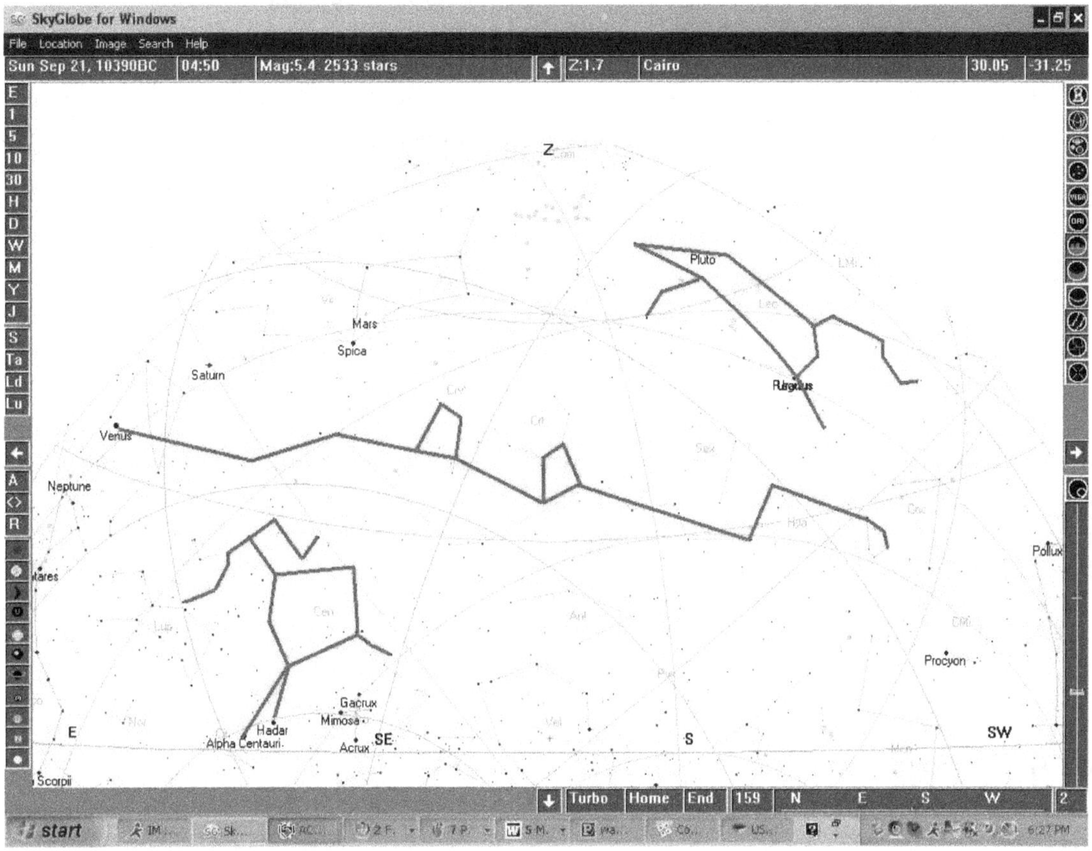

The text's instructions are:

> See this God, His other forms near the storehouse...spirits of images of His, they come in the sky of the earth. Come see these beneficent spells ... benign enchantments in their images of the greatest age. (*See translation pages 114 to 114*)

Next, we considered the readings from Edgar Cayce[195] that indicate that 'storehouse' was used as a synonym for 'pyramid.'

> 5748-7, #7: With the storehouse, or record house (where the records are still to be uncovered) there is a chamber or passage from the right forepaw to this entrance of the record chamber, or record tomb.[196]

> 4748-5, #-3: Yes. In the information as respecting the pyramids, their purpose in the experience of the peoples, in the period when there was the

---
[195] For more information about Edgar Cayce see page 204.
[196] For an explanation regarding the right forepaw, see p. 221.

> rebuilding…10,500 years before the coming of the Christ into the land, there was first that attempt to restore and to add to that which had been begun on what is called the Sphinx, and the treasure or <u>storehouse</u> facing same, between this and the Nile, in which those records were kept by Araart and Araaraart in the period ... there began the building of that now called Gizeh
>
> 1925-1,#10: there may be found still those of the storehouse of El-Dhli, those <u>storehouses</u> in those <u>pyramids</u> or mounds not yet uncovered;
>
> 249-151, 7-9: Hence there began the first preparation for what has later become that called The Great Pyramid, ... Then began the laying out of the pyramid and the building of same, ... This building, as we find, lasted for a period of what is termed now as one hundred years. <u>It was formed according to that which had been worked out by Ra-Ta in the mount as related to the position of the various stars ...</u>

With this insight, we can suggest that the Egyptian text may be telling us that the forms are near the pyramid, which rises into the sky among the stars.

The text continues:

khu	en	aru	en	ef	set	em	pet	em	ta
spirits	of	images	of	his	they	in	sky	of	earth

Come spirits of images of his. They in the sky of the earth.[197]

au	rekh	set	em	ba baui	kher	Ra	au	maa	tu
come to	know	them	of	soul of souls	with	sun god	come	see	this

Come to know them of the soul of souls with the Sun God. Come see this

nen	hekau[198]	ast	heka
these	beneficent spells	Isis	beneficent spells

these beneficent spells, Isis benign enchantments

semsu	aru	sen	em
eldest	images	their	in

in their images of the greatest age,

---

[197] The text says that his images are in the sky of the Earth. There can be no doubt that this is a reference to patterns of the stars recognized in the Earth's night sky.
[198] Budge, EHD, 515A, *heka* (plural *hekau*)

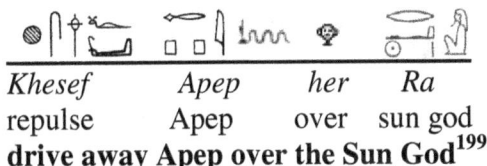

Khesef	*Apep*	*her*	*Ra*
repulse	Apep	over	sun god

drive away Apep over the Sun God[199]

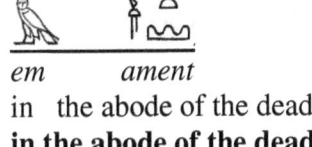

em	*ament*
in	the abode of the dead

in the abode of the dead.

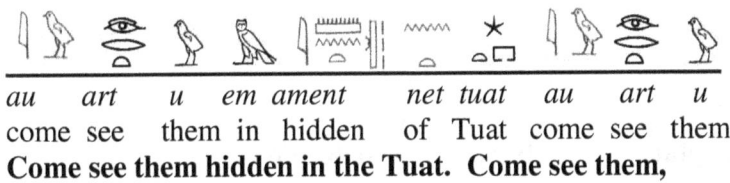

au	*art*	*u*	*em ament*	*net*	*tuat*	*au*	*art*	*u*
come	see	them	in hidden	of	Tuat	come	see	them

Come see them hidden in the Tuat. Come see them,

tepi-ta	*em matt*	*au*	*rekh*	*set*	*em*
dweller on earth	in likeness	come	to know	them	in

living man, as images. Come to know them among

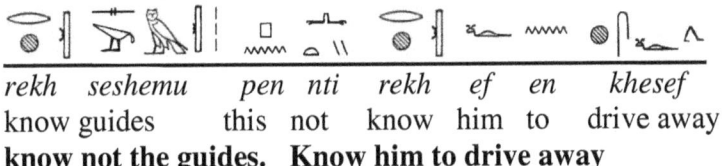

amiu	*u*	*uaa*	*en*	*Ra*	*em*	*pet*	*em*	*ta*	*an*	*ant*
who are in	they	ship		of sungod	in	sky	of	earth	for	destitute

who are in their ship of the Sun God in the sky of the earth, for the destitute

rekh	*seshemu*	*pen*	*nti*	*rekh*	*ef*	*en*	*khesef*
know	guides	this	not	know	him	to	drive away

know not the guides. Know him to drive away

En	*ha*	*her*	*Apep*
the	evil	above	Apep

the evil Apep above.

---

[199] Just before dawn, over Giza, on September 21st, 10390 BC, the constellation of Hydra (Apep) is in the sky, and the sun is just below the horizon. One could imagine that the array of gods visualized in the patterns of the stars had been responsible for repelling the Hydra constellation.

ar	thes	ta	nen	ha	her	Apep	pen	em
image	tie	earth	this	evil	above	Apep	this	in

The evil image of Apep above is bound to the earth in the

Tuat	meh [200]		pu	em	au [201]	ef	au
Tuat	cubit	400 50	this	in	length	his	come

Tuat,[202] in his length of 450 cubits.   He comes

ef	meh [203]	ef	su [204]	em	Aq [205]	bu	teben	ef	art	utcha [206]
he	to be full	he	this	to	diminish	place	revolves	he	seeing	to judge

to his fullness this to diminish the place he revolves, seeing to decide

qentiu [207]	ef	er	ef
boundaries	his	near	him

his boundaries near him.

ap	neter	pen	her	ef	s-thenem [208]	ef
Travel	god	this	above	him	to turn back	him

This god travels over him to turn him back[209]

uat	er	ef	thept	Asar
road	near	him	storehouse	Osiris

the way near him, the storehouse of Osiris.

---

[200] Budge, EHD, 316A, *meh*: cubit, i.e., seven handbreadths or 28 fingerbreadths, or 0.525 meter, or about 20 inches.
[201] Budge, EHD, 2A, *au*: length, largeness
[202] The Tuat was in the sky. (*see* Hancock & Bauval, *The Message of the Sphinx*, page 134-135, quoting Salim Hassan, "Excavations at Giza," Cairo, 1946, p. 277: *"If we consider the evidence afforded by the meaning of its name during the Old Kingdom, [The Pyramid Age], we shall see that the Tuat, the future underworld, was located in the sky."*)
[203] Budge, EHD, 316B, *meh*: to fill, to fill full, to be full, filled, to be occupied with
[204] Budge, EHD, 648A, *su*: personal pronoun 3rd singular masculine; also used as a particle.
[205] Budge, EHD, 10B, *aq, aqa*: to fail, to be weak, to be weary, to be tired, diminish, come to an end, be exhausted perish, die
[206] Budge, EHD, 194B, *utcha*
[207] Budge, EHD, 773A, *qentiu*
[208] Budge, EHD, 630A, *s-thenem*: to turn back, to turn aside or away, to lead astray
[209] The text seems to convey the idea that at the culmination of the constellation of Hydra (Apep) over the house of Osiris, the brightness of the rising sun causes it to diminish and disappear.

sqett	*neter*	*pen*	*em*		*nuit* ²¹⁰		*then*
travel	god	this	to		sacred place that was created in primeval time		this

This god travels to this sacred place that was created in the primeval age,

seshemu	*en*		*Mehen*
guides	of		serpent god who protected Afu-Ra in the Tuat

the guides of the serpent god who protected Afu-Ra in the Tuat.²¹¹

au	*rekh*
come	know

Come, know

set	*tepi ta*	*em*	*nti*	*sura*	*en*	*Ha-her*
them	dweller on earth	of	not	to drink	of	a form of Apep

them living man. Drink not of Apep

nu	*ef*
celestial water	his

his celestial water

nn	*sebi*	*en*	*ba*	*en*	*rekh*	*set*	*en*	*qent* ²¹²	*net*	*neteru*	*ami*
not	to lead	in	soul	in	to know	them	in	rage	of	gods	who are in

not lead in the soul of. Know them in the rage of the gods who are in

qerrt	*then*
circle	this

this circle.

---

²¹⁰ Reymond, *Mythical Origin of the Egyptian Temple*, page 14, ⊗ *niwt* the determinative of the name of any sacred place which was created in the primeval age.

²¹¹ See page 61 for an illustration of the protective serpent in Egyptian art.

²¹² Budge, EHD, 774B, *qent*: to be wroth, to rage, to be furious

au	*rekh*	*set*	*em*	*Temu*		*ab*	*am*[213]
come to know	them	with	the creator of heaven and earth		enemy	to devour

Come to know them with the creator of heaven and earth. The enemy to devour

ef	*ren*	*en*	*unut*	*neth*	*gerh*
him	name	of	hour	of	night

him the name of the hour of night

seshemt	*neter*	*pen*	*aa*	*em*	*arit*	*ten*	*kheft*
guidance	god	this	great	in	gateway	this	to drive away

guiding this great god in this gateway to drive away

hau[214]		*hesqt*	*en*	*ha*	*her*	*Apep*	*sba*
a serpent fiend in the Tuat	mutilation	of	evil	above	Apep	a star god

the serpent fiend in the Tuat, the mutilation of evil above,[215] Apep the star god.

hotep	*em*	*khet*	*an*	*het*	*en*	*neter*	*pen*	*aa*	*er*
peace	in	follow	by	majesty	of	god	this	great	among

Follow in peace by the majesty of this great god among

qerrt	*shetau*	*her*	*u*
circles in the Tuat	secret	over	their

the secret circles in the Tuat over their

sha	*sen*	*hetch*	*ef*	*en*	*sen*
sand	they	to become bright	he	to	them

sand. They become bright, his [words] to them

---

[213] Budge, EHD, 120B, *am*: to eat, to swallow, to devour
[214] Budge, EHD, 443B, *hau*
[215] The legend of the Sun God and Ra was that the great serpent Apep (Hydra) waited to devour the Sun God as he was about to rise each day. Ra always won, because his shafts of light pierced and destroyed the constellation of the serpent in the sky.

metu	em	uaa	ef	neteru	ef
words	from	ship	his	gods	his

from his ship. His gods

sethau	au	em
passages or corridors through which boats are towed	come	with

passages or corridors through which boats are towed come with

skhenu [216]	tesert [217]	en	Mehen
embraces	holy	of	a serpent god who protected Afu-Ra in the Tuat

the holy embraces of the serpent god who protects Afu-Ra in the Tuat[218]

Ren	en	sba	en	nuit	aha	en
name	of	door	of	a sacred place created in primeval time	stand	by

the name of the door of the sacred place created in the primeval age stands by

Urt [219]	ur	ef	aa	ren	en	nuit	ten
a motionless god	great	his	door	name	of	sacred place created in primeval time	this

a great motionless god his door name of this sacred place created in primeval age

tebat [220]	neteru	s	per
tomb	gods	their	house

the tomb, the house of the gods.

qert	shetat	net	Ament	ap	neter	aa	her	sen	em	uaa	ef
circles	secret	of	the west	travel	god	great	over	them	in	ship	his

The great god travels over them in the secret circles of Ament in his ship

---

[216] Budge, EHD, 616B, *skhenu*: embraces

[217] Budge, EHD, 888B, *tesert*: , something splendid or holy, see ; , splendid or beautiful things

[218] See page 61 for an illustration of the protective serpent in Egyptian art.

[219] Budge, EHD, 175B: *Urt*, Tuat VI, a motionless god = *Urt-ab* (or ha)

[220] Budge, EHD, 874B, *tebat*: funerary chest or coffer, coffin, sarcophagus, tomb

em   sethau
in   corridors or passages through which boats are towed
in passages or corridors through which boats are towed[221]

neteru   em   amiu   neter   Tuatiu
gods   his   who are in divine   gods and other beings of the Tuat
his gods who are in the divine gods and other beings of the Tuat.

au   art[222] *nen   together with   seshem*
come to see these together with the images of gods
Come to see these together with these the images of gods,

pen   nti   em   seshu   her   mehti   at
this   not   in   writings   over   North land   house
not in writings; Above the North the abode of

Amentt   em   Tuat
The abode of the dead   in   the Other World
Ament in the Tuat.

au   rekh   set   em   ren   sen   em   menkh-t[223] *em   ta   nt*
come to know them by names they in change of raiment near earth without
Come to know them by their names in change of array near the earth. Without

shetau   terpt[224] *ef   er   ahat*[225] *aa   shes*[226] *ma*
secret   supply   he   near   tomb   great   rope   to give
his secret supply near the tomb give great rope.

---

[221] See footnote 190 on page 111.
[222] Budge, EHD, 68A, *art*
[223] Budge, EHD, 304B, *menkh-t*: a piece of cloth or stuff of any kind, bandlet, veil, ceremonial girdle or fillet, a change of raiment
[224] Budge, EHD, 884B, *terpt*: a gift, an offering, supply, provision
[225] Budge, EHD, 134A, *ahat*: tomb, grave,
[226] Budge, EHD, 751A, *shes*: cord, string, rope

ren	*en*	*Unut*	*net*	*gerh*	*seshemt*	*neter*	*pen*	*aa*	
name	of	hour	of	night	guidance	god	this	great	

The name of the hour of night guiding this great god

nebu	*aakhut*	*gerh*	*u*	*sba*
lords	horizon	night	their	star[227]

Night Horizon Lords, their star.

hotep	*an*	*het*	*en*	*neter*	*pen*	*aa*	*em*	*qerrt*	*ten*	*hetch*	*ef*
reposed	by	majesty	of	god	this	great	in	circle	this	to become bright	he

Rest by the majesty of this great god in this circle. He becomes bright.

metu	*em*	*uaa*	*ef*	*en*	*neteru*
words	from	ship	his	to	gods

Speech from his ship to the gods

amiu
those who are in

who are in

hotep[228]	*neter*	*uaa*	*neter*	*pen*	*aa*	*er*
sepulchral meal	divine	ship	god	this	god	near

sepulchral meal the divine ship of this great god near

nuit[229]		*pen*	*ren*	*en*	*sba*	*en*
sacred place created in primeval time	this	name	of	door	of

this sacred place created in the primeval age, the name of

---

[227] Bucher, page 209,

[228] Bucher, page 209; *hotep* written , Budge, EHD, 518A, *hotep*: .

[229] Reymond, *Mythical Origin of the Egyptian Temple*, page 14, *niwt* the determinative of the name of any sacred place which was created in the primeval age.

	nuit		ten	ap
	sacred place created in primeval time		this	travels

this sacred place created in primeval time, travels

neter	pen	aa	her	er	ef	hotep	ef	net	nu [230]	amit
god	this	great	over	near	he	rest	he	of	celestial water	which is in

this great god above near his rest he of celestial water which is in the

nuit [231]		pen	Sa em Geb [232]
sacred place created in primeval time		this	the gate of the 9th division of the Tuat

sacred place created in the primeval age the gate of the 9th division of the Tuat

nuit		ten	bes-aru [233]
sacred place created in primeval time		this	a title of Ra

this sacred place created in primeval time Bes-aru.

ren	en	qerrt	shetat	net	amentt	hotep	neter	aa	qet [234] [235]
name	of	circle	hidden	of	the abode of the dead	rest	god	great	design

The name of the hidden circle of the abode of the dead rest the great god design,

neteru	ef	res	em	Tuat
gods	his	belonging to	in	Tuat

gods belonging to him in the Tuat.

---

[230] Budge, EHD, 349B, *nu*: The mass of water which existed in primeval times, Celestial waters

[231] Reymond, *Mythical Origin of the Egyptian Temple*, page 14, ⊗ *niwt* the determinative of the name of any sacred place which was created in the primeval age.

[232] Budge, EHD, 587A, *Sa em Geb* :

[233] Budge, EHD, 222B, *bes*: form, figure, body, statue, visible image of a god, a re-incarnation (?)

[234] Bucher, line 54, page 209,

[235] Budge, EHD, 779B, *qet*: design, drawing, plan, the draughtsman's craft

au	art	u	nen	em	ren	sen
come	see	them	these	by	names	they

Come see them, these by their names

ma	seshem	pen	nti	em	seshu	her	aabti	at
together with	images	this	not	in	writings	above	eastern	house

together with images. This not in writings. Above eastern house,

ament	net	Tuat
the abode of the dead	of	Tuat

the abode of the dead of the Tuat

au	rekh	ren	sen	tepi-ta
come	to know	names	their	dweller on earth

come to know their names living man

rekh	nest	sen	em	Ament	em	hotep	nest	ef	em	Tuat
to know	thrones	their	in	Ament	in	rest	throne	he	in	Tuat

know their thrones in the West rest in throne he in Tuat

aha	em	maki[236]	khert[237]	neteru	em	maa-
to stand still[238]	in	to protect	things which concern	gods	in	true-

stands still in to protect things which concern the gods in true-

---

[236] Budge, EHD, 288B, *m'ki*
[237] Budge, EHD, 561A, *khert*
[238] This may indicate the equinox or solstice.

kheru   em   tchattchat²³⁹   heru   hesbt²⁴⁰   aa²⁴¹   au   khu   en²⁴²
voice   of   judges   day   a reckoning doors come spirit in

voice of the judges, the day reckoning the doors spirit comes in.

rekh   set   tepi-ta
know   them   dweller on earth

know them living man.

ren   en   unut   then   gerh
name   of   hour   this   night

The name of this hour of night

seshem   neter   pen   aa   em   qerrt   ten   Tua-ti
guidance   god   this   great   in   circle   this   the god of the Tuat

guiding this great god in this circle, the god of the Tuat

Maket²⁴³   neb   sba
protection   lord   star god

protection lord star god.

hotep   em   khet   an   het   en   neter   pen   aa   em   qerrt   ten
peace   in   follow   by   majesty   of   god   this   great   in   circle   this

Follow in peace by the majesty of this great god in this circle

---

²³⁹ Budge, EHD, 901A, *tchatchat*: One of the later forms [hieroglyphs], judges, council of statesman, board of guardians, college, board of overseers, the task masters of the Other World [Tuat], chiefs, foremen

²⁴⁰ Budge, EHD, 510B, *hebst*: an account, a reckoning, a calculation, an estimate, the total, scheme, plan, design, a measuring stick, a result arrived at by thinking, the right, or true, or correct measure.

²⁴¹ Budge, EHD, 107A-B, *aa*; also see Bucher, line 52, page 92, from tomb of Thuthmosis III, [hieroglyphs]

²⁴² Bucher, line 56, page 210, from tomb of Amenhotep II [hieroglyphs]

²⁴³ Budge, EHD, 288B, *m'kit*

hetch   *ef*   *metu*
to become bright   he   words
becomes bright. His words

aa   *her*   *ef*   *aa*   *kheperu*   *mesi* [244]   *aru*   *aa*
great   over   him   great   manifestations   fashion   images   door
great, over him great manifestations fashion images door

ren   *en*   *nuit*   *then*
name of   sacred place created in primeval time   this
the name of this sacred place created in primeval time,

metch-t-qua-utchebu [245]   *nuit*
name of the 10th division of Tuat   sacred place created in primeval time
the name of the 10th division of the Tuat sacred place created in the primeval age,

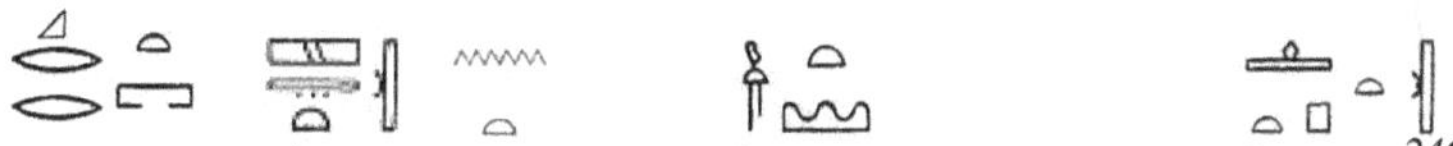

qerrt   *shetat*   *net*   *Ament*   *hotept* [246]
circle   hidden   of   the West   sepulchral meals
hidden circle of the West offerings made to the dead.

Khepra   *er*   *sen*   *kher*   *Ra*
Khepera who makes every form of his being   near   them   with   sun god
Khepera who makes every form of his being near them with the Sun God,

---

[244] Budge, EHD, 321A, *mesi*: to bear, to produce, to give birth to, to fashion, to form, to make a likeness of

[245]

[246] Budge, EHD, 518A, *hotept*

kenat[247] *neteru ikm khu muti*[248] *er sen her*
angry gods spirits the dead near them above
angry gods, spirits, and the dead near them, above

seshemu seshat en akert[249] *au art u nen ma*
images of gods secret of abode of the dead come see them these together with
images of gods, secret of the abode of the dead. Come see them, these together with

seshem pen nti em seshu her abti at ament net Tuat
images this not in writings above eastern house hidden of Tuat
images. This not in writings. Above eastern hidden house of the Tuat

au rekh set em ren sen em khens[250] *Tuat er sen tcha*[251]
come to know them by names they as to sail over Tuat near they travel
Come to know them by names as they sail over the Tuat. They travel near

ef er sen hetch pet kher Ra
he near them become bright sky with Sun God
him. Near them the sky becomes bright with the Sun God.

ren en
name of
The name

---

[247] Budge, EHD, 794 B, *kenat*: [glyph], wrath, anger, reviling, anger, curse, abuse; see also Budge, EHD, 794B, *ken*: [glyph], to be angry, to feel indignation, to revile, to curse. See also Bucher, line 57, page 210, [glyph]

[248] Budge, EHD, 295B, *muti*: the dead, the damned

[249] Budge, EHD, 96B, *Agertt*: [glyph] the abode of the dead in the Tuat of the souls of An; also see Budge, EHD, page lix: "The following is the transliteration of the letters of the Egyptian Alphabet which Brugsch printed in the first volume of his *Worterbuch* (1867): [glyph] =k"

[250] Budge, EHD, 552B, *khens*: to traverse, to travel over, to stride over, to fly over, to sail over

[251] Budge, EHD, 894B, *tcha*: to set out on a journey, to make a passage, to travel

unut	net	gerh	seshemt	neter	pen	aa	er	uat
hour	of	night	guidance	god	this	great	ner	roads

of the hour of night guiding this great god near the [secret] roads

shetat	net		nuit [252]		ten	
secret	of	sacred place created in primeval time			this	

of this sacred place created in the primeval age

Tentenit-uhesq-t- khak-ab [253]

the hour goddess of the 10th division of the Tuat.

hotep	An	het	en	neter	pen	aa	em	qerrt	ten	hetch
rest	by	majesty	of	god	this	great	in	circle	this	become bright

Rest by the majesty of this great god in this circle become bright

metu	neteru	ami	sen
words	gods	who are in	them

words gods who are in them.

ren	en	sba	en	nuit	then	ap	neter	pen
name	of	door	of	place this		travel	god	this

The name of the door of this place created in primeval time this god travels

her	ef		*Skhen-tuatiu* [254]
over	his		Tuat XI, the gate of the 11th Division of the Tuat

over his gate of the 11th division of the Tuat.

---

[252] Reymond, *Mythical Origin of the Egyptian Temple*, page 14, ⊗ *niwt* the determinative of the name of any sacred place which was created in the primeval age.

[253] Budge, EHD, 881B, *Tentenit-uhesq-t- khak-ab*:

[254] Budge, EHD, 617A, *Skhen-tuatiu*

ren	en		nuit [255]	er	en
name	of	sacred place which was created in primeval time		entrance	to

The name of the entrance to the sacred place which was created in primeval time.

qerrt	aptf [256]	khat	nuit [257]
circle	these	bodies without life	sacred place created in primeval time

These bodies without life circle the sacred place created in the primeval age.

qerrt	shetat	ten	Tuat	ten	ap	neter	pen	aa	her	sen
circle	secret	this	Tuat	this	travel	god	this	great	over	them

This secret circle, this Tuat. This great god travels above them,

pert [258]	em	tu	aabti [259]	pet	am [260]
what comes forth	from	mountain	eastern	sky	to devour

comes forth from the eastern mountain sky to devour

tche-t	ta	seshemu	s	m-bah [261]	petra
bodily form	earth	images	they	before	the name of a fiend in the Tuat

the bodily form earth images, they in the presence of the fiend in the Tuat

---

[255] Reymond, *Mythical Origin of the Egyptian Temple*, page 14, ⊗ *niwt* the determinative of the name of any sacred place which was created in the primeval age.

[256] Budge, EHD, A43, *aptf*: , demonstrative pronoun plural of

[257] Reymond, *Mythical Origin of the Egyptian Temple*, page 14, ⊗ *niwt* the determinative of the name of any sacred place which was created in the primeval age.

[258] Budge, EHD, 240B: *pert*: , exit, issue, what comes forth, manifestation, outbreak of fire, offspring

[259] Budge, EHD, 18B, *aabti*: , left, eastern

[260] Budge, EHD, 120A, *am*: , to eat, to swallow, to devour

[261] Budge, EHD, 205A, *bah- m bah*: before, in the presence of

129

ami   *nuit* [262]   *ten*   *as* [263]   *sen*
which is in   sacred place which was created in the primeval age   this   behold   they

which is in this sacred place created in the primeval age. See them as

em   *khet*   *er*   *mesut*   *khepera*   *em*
in   follow   near   births   the self produced Beetle God   in

follow near the births of Khepera in

ta
earth

the earth.

au   *art*   *nen*   *em*   *qet*   *ma*   *seshemu*   *nti*   *em*   *shemu*
come   see   these   in   designs   together with   images of gods   not   in   writings

Come see these in designs together with images of gods, not in writings,

em   *ament* [264]   *net*   *Tuat*   *her*   *aabti*   *at*
in   secret   of   Tuat   over   eastern   house

in secret of Tuat over eastern house

Ament
the abode of the dead

the abode of the dead.

---

[262] Reymond, *Mythical Origin of the Egyptian Temple*, page 14, ⊗ *niwt* the determinative of the name of any sacred place which was created in the primeval age.

[263] Budge, EHD, 79A, *as*: an enclitic conjunction, often used as a mark of emphasis, or to draw special attention to the phrase to which it is attached; it also serves to mark an explanation, and may be translated "namely," "to wit," "that is," "behold"

[264] Budge, EHD, 53A, *ament*

au   rekh   set   em   pesesh [265]   *hotept* [266]   *ef   em   khu   neter*
come to know them   in   to share   sepulchral meals his   with spirit divine

Come to know them to share in his sepulchral meals in divine spirit

aper   em   pet   em   ta   shes maa [267]
equipped in   sky   in   earth in regular continuity forever

equipped in the sky in the earth in regular continuity forever.

ament
name of

The name of

unut   net   gerh   seshemt   neter   pen   aa   em   qerrt   ten
hour   of   night   guidance   god   this   great   in   circle   this

the hour of night guiding this great god in this circle

sbait [268]   *sba   ra* [269]   *uaa*   *khesft* [270]
teaching   star   daily   ship   repulse

teaching that the daily star ship repulses

---

[265] Budge, EHD, 248B, *pesesh*: to cleave, to split, to slit, to divide with, to share or participate with someone, to open the legs or arms, to distribute

[266] Budge, EHD, 518A, *hetep-t*: ⟨hieroglyph⟩, sepulchral meals, the offerings made to the dead.

[267] Budge, EHD, 751A, *shes maa*

[268] Budge, EHD, 655A, *sbait*: teaching, instruction, training, education, learning, wisdom, lore of books, doctrine, punishment, correction, tax, impost

[269] Budge, EHD, 41B, *ra* ⟨hieroglyph⟩ every day, daily

[270] Budge, EHD, 564AB, *khesft*

seba[271]	*em*	*pert*[272]	*unut*[273]	*netrit*
enemy	by	appearance	hour	goddess

the enemy by the hour goddess appearance.

hotep	*an*	*het*	*en*	*neter*	*pen*	*aa*	*em*	*qerrt*	*ten*
rest	by	majesty	of	god	this	great	in	circle	this

Rest by the majesty of this great god in this circle

pehui	*smau-keku*	*mess-t*	*neter pen*
end	utter darkness	something which is born	god this

the birth of this [great] god ends utter darkness

aa	*em*	*kheperu*	*em*	*en*	*Kheper*	*er*	*qerrt*	*ten*
great	by	images	his	of	Kheper	near	circle	this

by his images of Kheper near this circle.

Text from Thuthmosis II (missing from Amenhotep II):

Kheper	*Nu*	*nen*	*hehu*
Kheper	Tuat XII, the Sky-god	this	eternity

Kheper this eternal sky god.

hehnu	*er*	*qerrt*	*net*
eternity	near	circle	of

Eternity near the circle of

---

[271] Budge, EHD, 657A, *seba*: [hieroglyphs], to be inimical, hostile, unfriendly, to act as an enemy; also see Budge, EHD, 657A, *seba*: [hieroglyph], enemy, foe, demon, devil wicked man

[272] Budge, EHD, 242A, *per-t*: the appearance of a heavenly body, or of a figure of a god or goddess, which was usually celebrated by a festival

[273] Budge, EHD, 167A, *unut* [hieroglyph], hour, time, regular duty, service

Here we resume with text from Amenhotep II:

mesut	neter	pen	aa	per	ef	em	Tuat	hotep	ef	mm
birth	god	this	great	come forth	he	in	Tuat	rest	he	among

the birth of this great god, he comes forth in the Tuat, he rests among

antit				kha	ef	em
boat in which Ra sailed from dawn to midday				to rise like the sun	he	in

the boat in which the Sun God sails from dawn to midday to rise like the sun.

ahti [274]	thebit [275]	Nu
neck	dual sandals	Sky god

The neck and dual sandals of the Sky God.

ren	en	sba	en	nuit	ten
name	of	door	of	sacred place created in primeval age	this

The name of the door of this sacred place created in the primeval age:

thennt [276]	neteru	aa
sanctuary of Seker	gods	door

the sanctuary of Seker gods door.

ren	en	sba	en	nuit	ten
name	of	door	of	sacred place created in primeval age	this

The name of the door of this sacred place created in the primeval age:

khepert	keku	kha
exists	darkness	rise like the sun

darkness exists. Rise like the sun

---

[274] Budge, EHD, 77A, *ahti*: see *ahtit*: neck, throat, windpipe, lung

[275] Budge, EHD, 853B, *then-t, thenn-t,* [hieroglyphs], place, abode, sanctuary of Seker

[276] Budge, EHD, 856A, *thennt*

mesut	*nuit* [277]	
birth	sacred place created in primeval time	

the birth the sacred place created in the primeval age

qerrt	*seshat*	*net*	*Tuat*	*messut*	*neter*	*pen*	*aa*
circle	hidden	of	Tuat	something which is born	god	this	great

the hidden circle of the Tuat, something which is born, this great god

per	*Nu*	*hotep*	*ef*	*em*	*khat*	*Nu*
come forth	Sky-god	rest	he	from	womb	Sky-god

comes forth, the Sky-god rests, he from the womb of the Sky-God.

au	*art*	*u*	*nen*	*ma*	*seshemu*	*pen*	*nti*	*em*	*sesh*	*her*
come	see	them	these	together with	images	this	not	in	writings	over

Come see them, these together with these images, not in writings; over

abti	*at*	*ament*	*net*	*Tuat*
left, eastern	house	hidden	of	Tuat

the eastern hidden house of the Tuat.

au	*kha*	*en*	*rekh*
come	spirit	of	to know

Come the spirit of to know

set	*tepi-ta*	*em*	*pet*	*em*	*ta*
them	dweller on earth	in	sky	in	earth

them living man, in the sky in the earth.

---

[277] Reymond, *Mythical Origin of the Egyptian Temple*, page 14, ⊗ *niwt* the determinative of the name of any sacred place which was created in the primeval age.

hat	hetchut	pehui	keku
beginning	light	end	darkness

The first light ends the [utter] darkness

smau [278]	seshemt	Ra
utter	guidance	Sun God

guiding the Sun God

em	Ament	skher	sheta	aru	neter	pen	ames
in	the abode of the dead	designs	secret	images	god	this	to conduct

in the abode of the dead designs, the secret images, conduct this divine

aftit [279]		ant-t	seshu	sheta Tuat
sarchophagus		the minority as opposed to the majority	writings	secret Tuat

sarchophagus, a small number of Tuat secret writings

nti	rekh	an	reth
not	to know	by	everybody

not known by everyone

up	her	ant
to open	over	the destitute man

open over the destitute man.

au	an	tu	seshemu	pen	ma qet	pen	em amen	net	Tuat
come	see	this	guides	this	altogether	this	in hidden	of	Tuat

Come see these guides, this altogether hidden in the Tuat.

---

[278] Bucher, page 212, line 65, ;

also see Budge, EHD, 600B, *sma[i]u keku*

[279] Budge, EHD, 120A, *aftit*

nt   maa   nt   petr
not perceive not see
Not perceived and not seen.

au   rekh
come to know
Come to know

nen   seshemu   sheta   khu   aper   ef   per   ef   ha[280] *ef*
these images of gods secret spirit equipped he come forth he enter   he
these secret images of gods, his equipped spirit, he comes forth, he enters

em   Tuat   au   ef   metu   ef   en   ankhu
in   Tuat come he   word   his   to   the living
in the Tuat, he comes, his word to the living,

shes maa[281]   *en   sep*
in regular continuity forever   in   time
in regular continuity forever in time.

This last line is from Thuthmosis III

aper   ef   per   ef   ha[282] *ef   em   Tuat   au   ef   metu*
equipped he come forth he enter   he   in   Tuat come he   word
Equipped he comes forth. He enters in. In his Tuat he comes. [His] word

ef   en   ankhu   heh   hena   tchet
his   to   the living eternity with everlastingness
to the living: eternity with everlastingness.

---

[280] Budge, EHD, 439A, *ha*: to descend, to go down into a boat, to embark, to travel by sea, to fall down, to enter
[281] Budge, EHD, 751A, *shes maa*
[282] Budge, EHD, 439A, *ha*: to descend, to go down into a boat, to embark, to travel by sea, to fall down, to enter

neter	pen	aa	her	er	ef	*hotep*	*ef*	*net*	*nu* [283]
god	this	great	above	near	he	*rest*	*he*	*with*	*celestial water*

This great god above, near him he rests with celestial water.

---

[283] Budge, EHD, 349B, *ha*: The mass of water which existed in primeval times, Celestial waters

FURTHER EXPLANATORY MATERIALS

DISCUSSION OF THE FOURTH DIVISION OF AM TUAT

When studying the translation of the Fourth Division, it is important to understand the context of this information. It is possible that the original date of the information in the ancient Egyptian book of Am Tuat, predates any known document. By using Skyglobe shareware computer planetary software[284], we can view the positions of stars in the ancient past, and thereby know the dates that the stars were in a particular position and/or configuration. For example, the beginning of the book of Am Tuat starts out with the appearance of the constellation of Gemini, recorded as the Two Goddesses of Truth. Further on into the First Division, the ancient texts give the position of the rising of Hydra, referred to as The God of Evil, at 120 degrees ESE. The only time Hydra ever rose over Giza at 120 degrees ESE was September 21st, 10,390 BC.

Cayce tells us that when there was the entrance of Araart and Araaraart into Egypt, they began to build upon a mound that was discovered through archaeological research.[285] A storehouse or record house, which they constructed upon one of the mounds, could be located by following a way (or a path or passage) to the entrance, from the right forepaw of the Sphinx. Until recently, it was not known that the ancient Egyptians depicted the constellation of Centaurus as a sphinx. This means that Cayce may have been talking about a star constellation.

The Sphinx constellation as illustrated in the zodiac of Esne, the ancient Egyptian city of Latopolis, [286] where the Temple of Hathor contains two representations of the heavens, a round zodiac ceiling (Denderah Zodiac) and a square zodiac (Grand Temple) in the outer hypostyle hall. In the zodiac of the Grand Temple of Hathor, the sphinx is portrayed in the position of the constellation Centaurus.[287] The star in the right or foremost paw is Alpha Centauri.

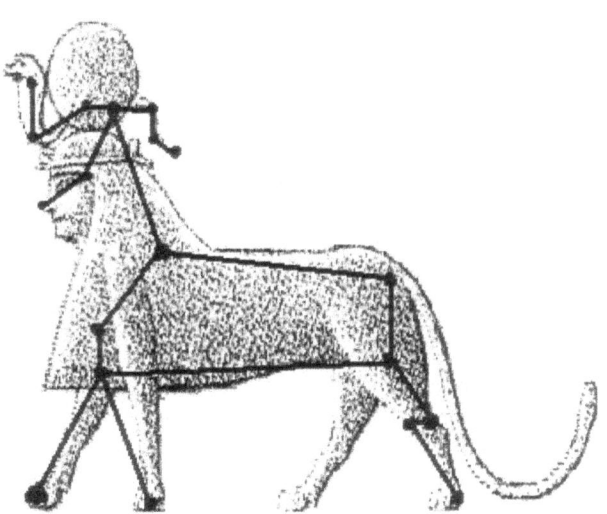

Sphinx overlaying Centaurus constellation

---

[284] Haney, Mark A. *Sky Globe*. Twinsburg, OH: International Computer Concepts, 1992. Computer software.
[285] ECRS, 5748-6, paragraph 17
[286] Aufrère, Sydney. *Description de l'Egypte: ou, Recueil des observations et des recherches qui ont été faites en Egypte pendant l'expédition de l'armée française.* ([Paris]: Inter-Livres, 1995.) Plate 79, Esne (Latopolis) - A vol. 1.
[287] Aufrère, *Description de l'Egypte,* Plate 79, Esne (Latopolis) - A vol. 1.

Alpha Centauri

Sir Norman Lockyer (1836-1920), one of the major English astronomers of his time, became interested in a problem which had also attracted Newton, that of bringing in astronomy to assist the chronology of history. In 1894 he published his study of temple worship and mythology of the ancient Egyptians, *The Dawn of Astronomy*, and explained the significance of Alpha Centauri:

> "Alpha's splendor naturally made it an object of worship upon the Nile, and it's first visible emergence from the sun's rays, in the morning at the autumnal equinox, has been connected by Lockyer with the orientation of at least nine temples in northern Egypt dating from 3800 BC"[288]

Lockyer proved that certain temples were oriented to the stars on the autumnal equinox.[289] These stellar temples were constructed so that their axis (the alignment of the main corridor) captured the beam of starlight and focalized it into the central passageway.

---

[288] Allen, Richard Hinckley. *Star Names: Their Lore and Meaning*. (New York: Dover Publications, 1963) 153; also Lockyer. *The Dawn of Astronomy*, 308-309.
[289] Lockyer, *The Dawn of Astronomy*, 167.

Stars Mark the Location of the Hall of Records

The ancient Egyptians may have used stars in the sky to mark the path to the entrance of the Hall of Records. The following quotations from ancient Egyptian texts show that the double lion god was in the sky and it was he that could open the path.

- From *The Book of the Dead*:
    Hail, god in the form of two lions, who comest forth from heaven.[290]

- From the Declaration of Innocence of the Dead Before the Gods of the Tribunal:
    O Double Lion who came forth from the sky[291]

- From the papyrus of Mut-hetep:[292]
    Thou Openest the path of the double Lion God.

- From the *Ancient Egyptian Coffin Texts* (Spell 649, vol. II):[293]
    Lion-man of his, open a path ...
    Lion-man of his, open a path ...
    Lion-man of his, open a path ...
    Lion-man of his, open a path ...
    Lion-man of his, open a path ...
    Lion-man of his, open a path ...

It is interesting to see the term "Lion-man," which is a description of a Sphinx. If we consider that the image from the Fifth Division of Am Tuat, below, is a Double Sphinx, **and** it is directly connected with a flying serpent in the horizon, the Fifth Division of Am Tuat takes on a whole new appearance!

[294]

---

[290] Budge, *Egyptian Book of the Dead* (New York: Barnes & Noble, 2005) 347.
[291] Andrews, Carol, and Raymond O. Faulkner. *The Ancient Egyptian Book of the Dead*. (Austin: University of Texas Press, 1990) 31.
[292] *Egyptian Literature; Comprising Egyptian Tales, Hymns, Litanies, Invocations, The Book of the Dead, and Cuneiform Writings*. (New York: Collier, 1901) 11.
[293] Faulkner, Raymond Oliver, *The Ancient Egyptian Coffin Texts*, II, Spells 355 - 787. (Warminster: Aris & Phillips, 1977) 224.
[294] Piankoff, *The Tomb of Ramesses VI*.

THE FOURTH DIVISION SETI I TOMB

The Upper Register

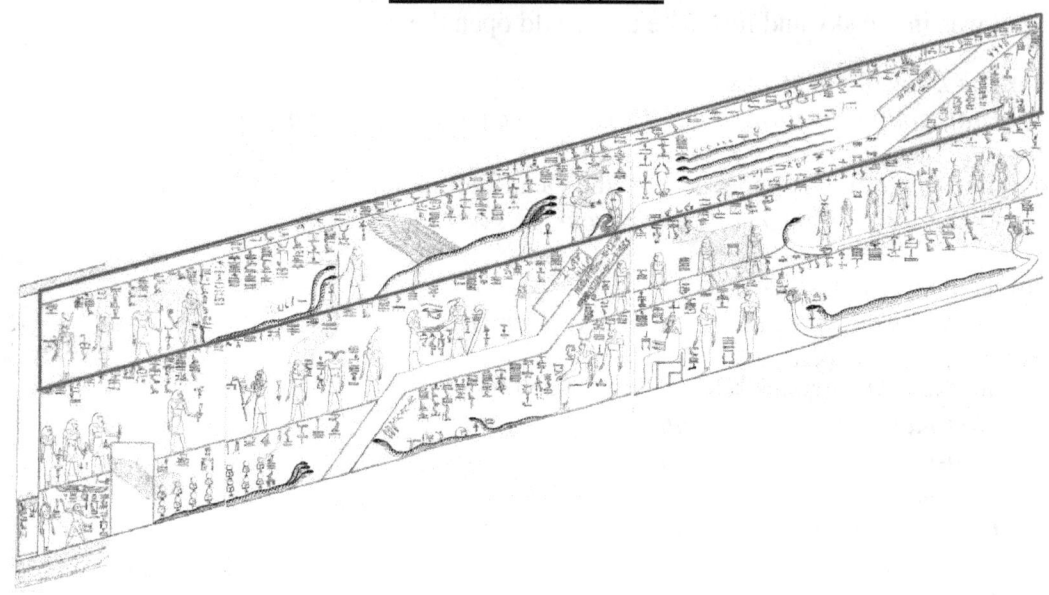

The Narrow Line Across the Very Top

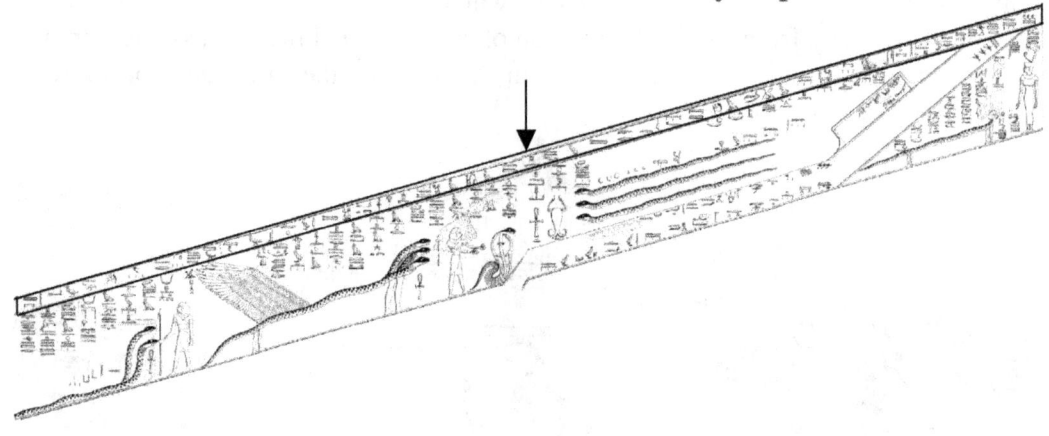

We will look at this line of text more closely in 2 sections on the next pages, dividing at the location of the arrow above, and beginning with the upper right end and then working down.

FOURTH DIVISION – UPPER REGISTER

Narrow Line – Right Side

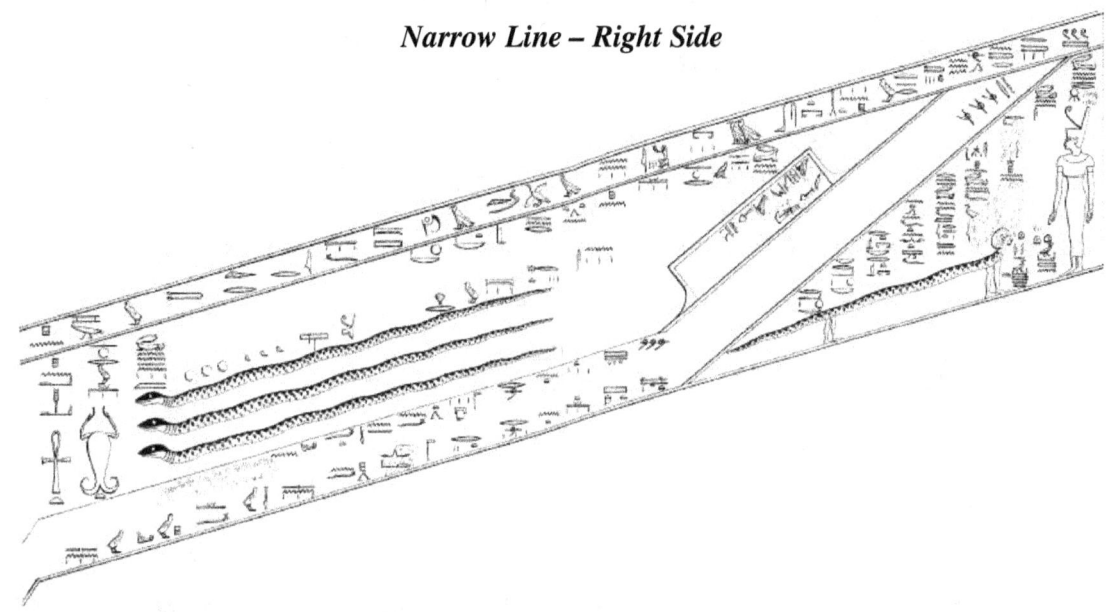

Beginning at the right side:

ah	sheta	neter	sta	nut [295]	teseru	en	thept [296]	sba
ropes	hidden	divine	tow	canal	large stones	to	shrine	doors

Divine hidden ropes tow[297] the canal to large stones of the shrine doors,

a	nen	em	pa	maa	seker	pet	sheta	ef	ar	ar
praise	these	as		fly	see	Seker	over	secrets	his	to make	image

praise these. See fly with Seker over his secrets to make image

thu	m [298]	seshem	pen
thou	canal	guide	this

thou this canal guide

---

[295] Budge, EHD, 349B, *nut*: a mass of water, lake, pool, stream, canal. Bunker/Pressler note: "passage" is a synonym of "canal."
[296] Budge, EHD, 854B, *thept*
[297] Star appears to move from east to west, as if being towed, because the Earth rotates from west to east.
[298] Budge, EHD, Vol I, A List of Hieroglyphic Characters, cxxvi, , *m*: canal, any collection of water

Similar Text from the Tomb of Amenhotep II[299]

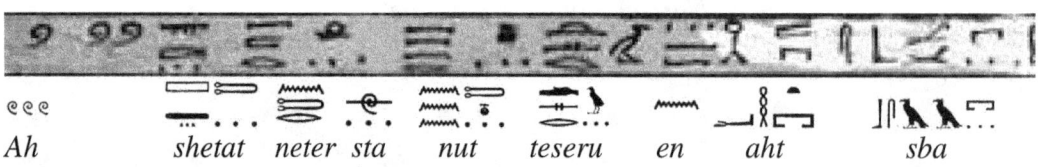

Ah	shetat	neter	sta	nut	teseru	en	aht	sba
Ropes	hidden	god	tow	canal	large stones	of	chamber	doors

Hidden ropes tow the god through the canal, large stones of chamber doors.

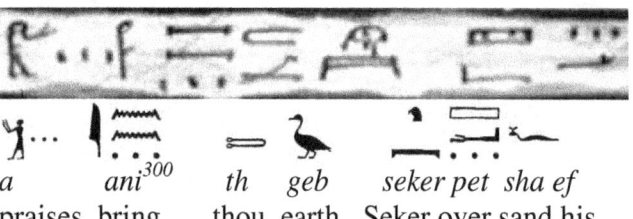

a	ani[300]	th	geb	seker	pet	sha	ef
praises	bring	thou	earth	Seker	over	sand	his

Bring praises thou on earth, Seker is over his sand.

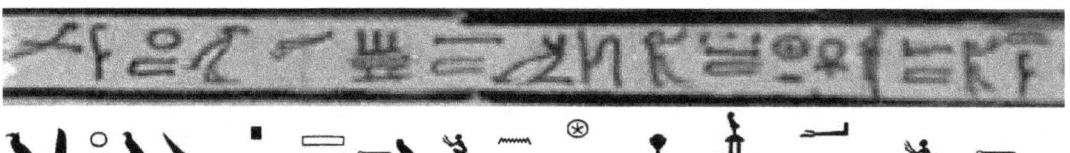

aakhut	seshem	pen	shen	them	a	neth	Tuat	her	ament	at	a	thou
horizon	guide	this	hover	over	praises	of[301]	Tuat	above	hidden house[302]		praise	thou

This horizon guide hovers over this, praises of Tuat above the hidden house praise thou.

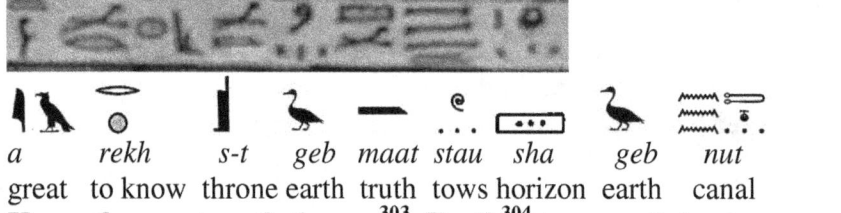

a	rekh	s-t	geb	maat	stau	sha	geb	nut
great	to know	throne	earth	truth	tows	horizon	earth	canal

Know the great earth throne.[303] Truth[304] tows earth horizon canal

---

[299] These hieroglyphic images are from photographs by Francis Dzikowski, c Theban Mapping Project, reprinted with permission.

[300] Budge, EHD, 56A, *ann*: [glyphs] ; ani: [glyphs]

[301] Corrected Text from Amenhotep II, Bucher, page 23.

[302] Hidden house = pyramid, Davidson & Aldersmith, The *Great Pyramid: Its Divine Message*; Adams, The *Book of the Master of the Hidden Places*.

[303] Inside the door to the Fifth Division

[304] "Truth Tows" may be a reference to the first division of Am Tuat where the two truth goddesses (Gemini) go in front of the boat of the sun god (Leo). Gemini rises before Leo and apparently tows Leo behind.

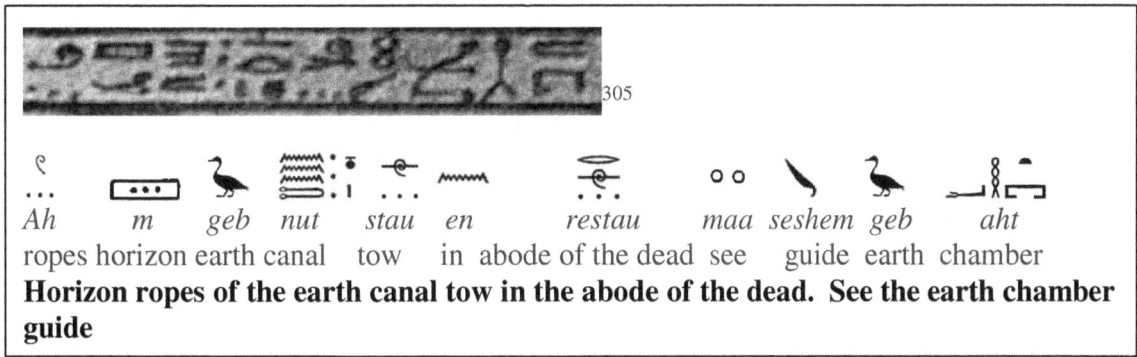

Ah	m	geb	nut	stau	en	restau	maa	seshem	geb	aht
ropes	horizon	earth	canal	tow	in	abode of the dead	see	guide	earth	chamber

Horizon ropes of the earth canal tow in the abode of the dead. See the earth chamber guide

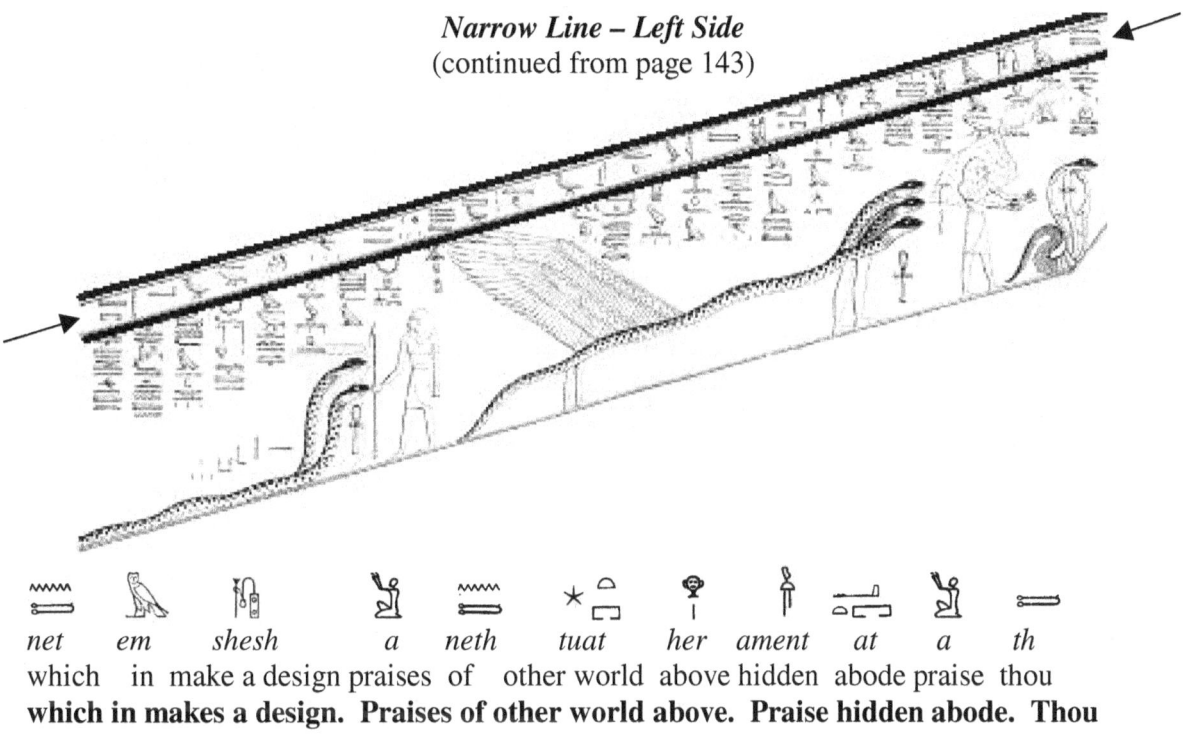

net	em	shesh	a	neth	tuat	her	ament	at	a	th
which	in	make a design	praises	of	other world	above	hidden	abode	praise	thou

which in makes a design. Praises of other world above. Praise hidden abode. Thou

au	rekh	hetem	geb	maat	stau	m	geb	nut	en
to be	to know	throne	earth	truth	tows	canal	earth	canal	in

art to know the earth throne. Truth tows[306] to pass over the earth canal in

restau	seker	seshem	geb	aht
abode of the dead	Seker	guide	earth	chamber

the abode of the dead, Seker, the guide of the earth chamber

This is the illustration referred to in footnote 306 (previous page) from the unabridged version of Am Tuat

---

[305] Comparison of text from Tuthmosis III and Amenhotep II
[306] This refers to the two goddesses of truth (Gemini constellation) who tow the boat of the sun god, illustrated in the unabridged version of the Am Tuat, as shown in illustration on facing page.

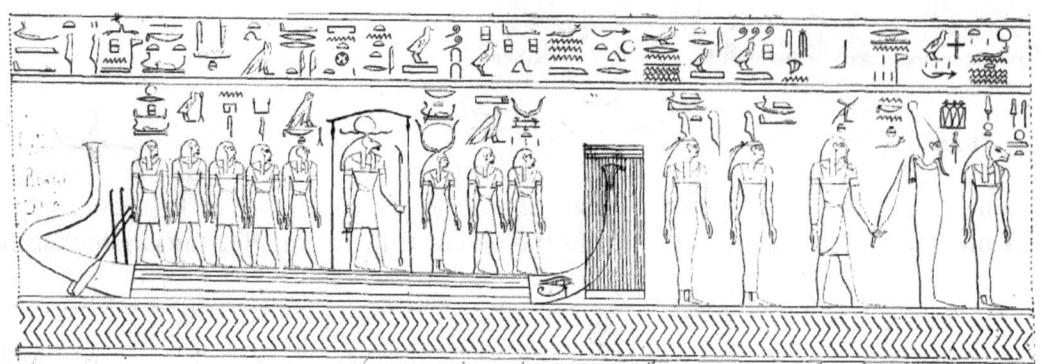

The hieroglyphic text across the top is written from left to right:
The twin goddesses of truth are not in the boat of the setting sun.
The journey to the gateway of this place belongs to 220 degrees.
He travels behind in the celestial water in this birthplace of the entrance of the gods who are following him, who are in follow the celestial water.

The mat or door at the prow of the boat may represent the gate of the entrance to the horizon.

Above the gods in the ship is written from left to right: *In front place the look out, the double truth goddess and the path. Praise the name of the Sun god of night. The goddess of the ship and the knowledge of the opener of the ways.*

Above the two goddesses standing in front of the ship is written: *The two goddesses of truth.*

Above the three remaining standing figures is written:
The murder of Osiris, the Age (period of time) of the Goddess Sekhmet

This may be referring to a date. i.e., The Legend of the Goddess Sekhmet and the destruction of mankind.

FOURTH DIVISION – UPPER REGISTER

Upper Register Continued

We will examine this section in 5 parts as shown here.

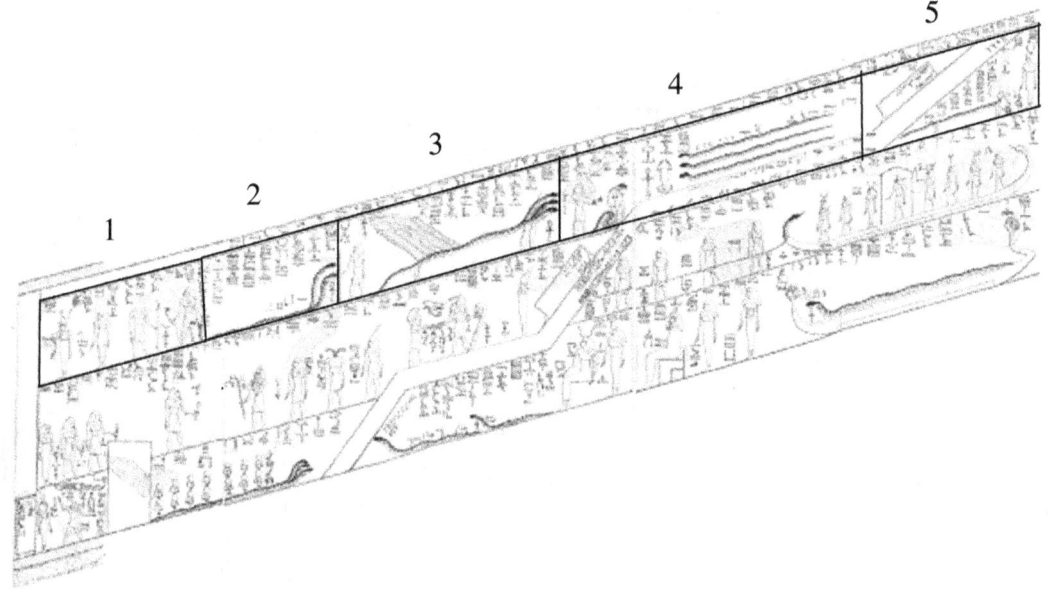

Upper Register – Part 1 - Text

Above the people, read from the right side toward the left side:

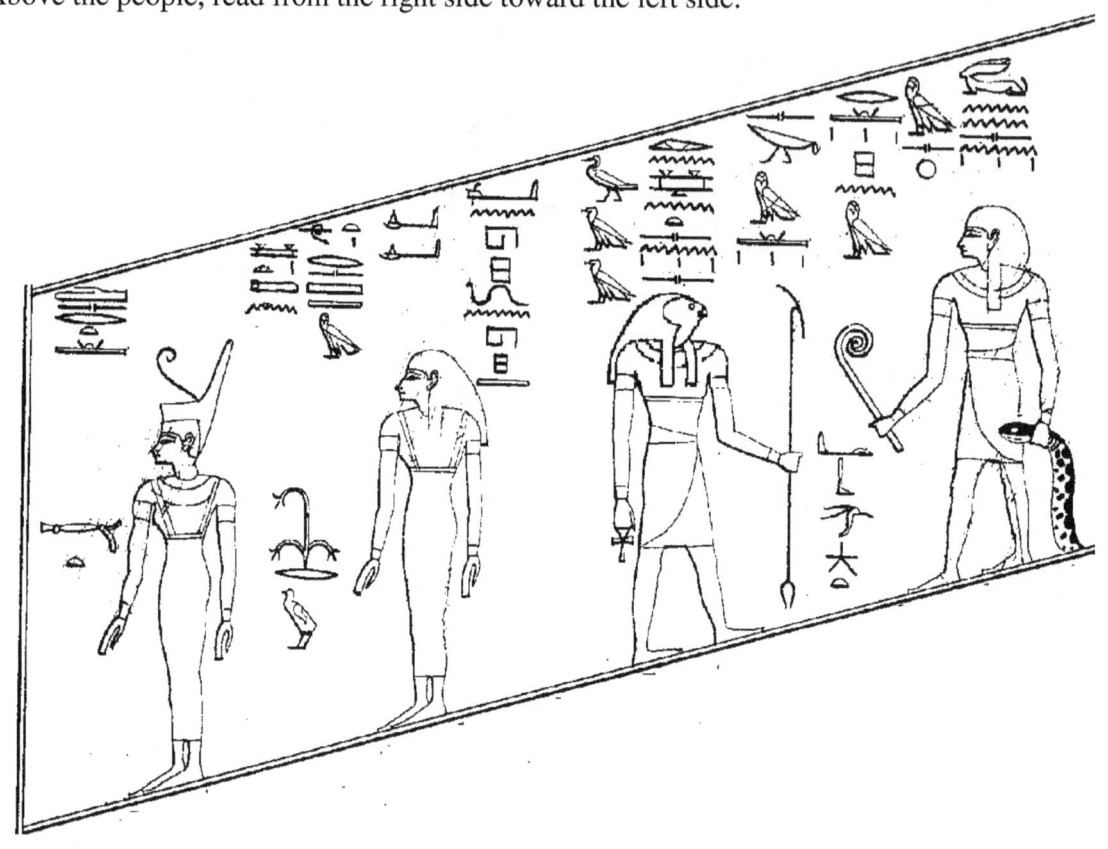

unn	sen	em	skher	pen	em	seshemu	an	ua	net	sen	saa
are	they	in	designs	this	as	guides	see	path	of	their	guardian

They are in this design as guides. See the path of their guardian.

Nehp	nehp	ta	tata	stat
serpent god	guard	earth	to give	arura[307]

The serpent god guards, and the earth gives an area of 100x100 cubits.

---

[307] Budge, EHD, 707A, *stat*: a measure of land, the arura (area of ground 100 x 100 cubits - see explanation next page)

Arura

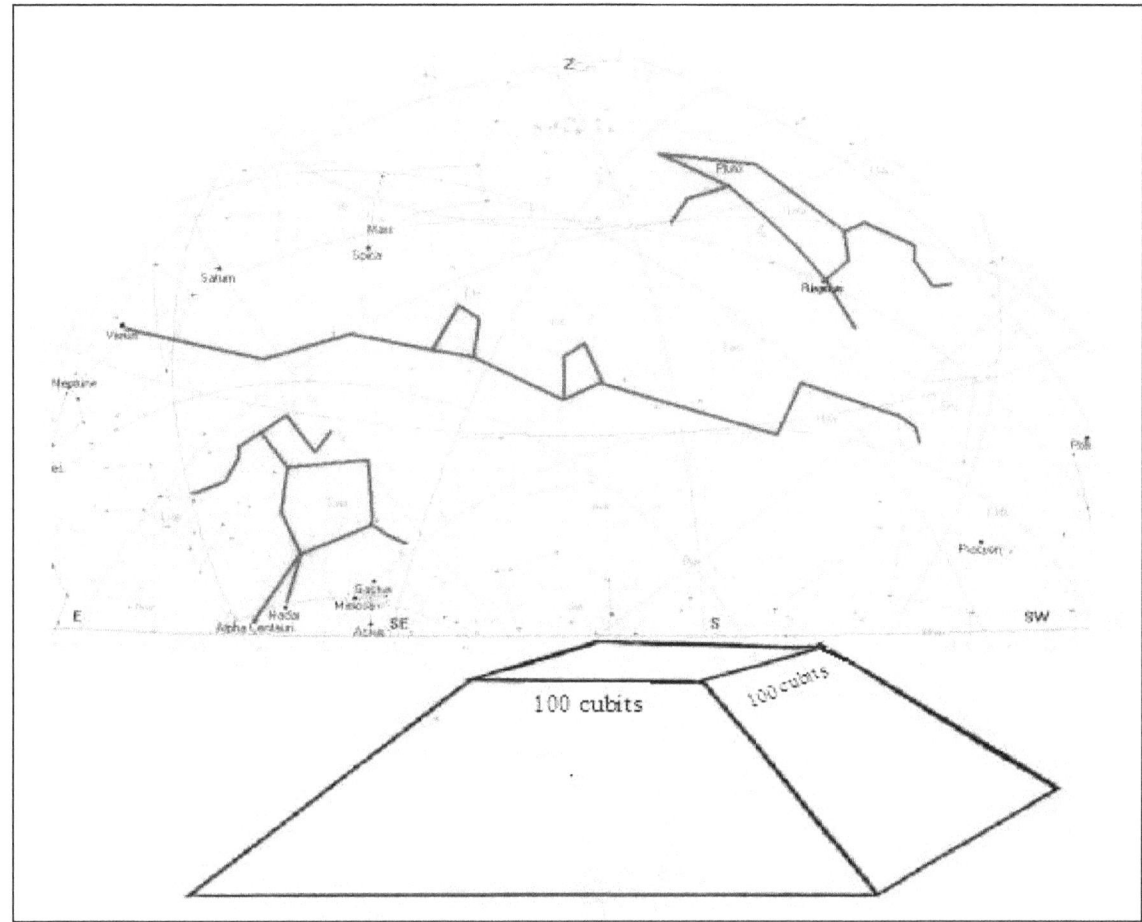

The sky as it appeared over the flat top of the pyramidal mound

The arura, 100x100 square cubits guarded by the serpent, may be the pyramid of Khafrae (above).

The hieroglyphic inscription on this stone block (right) reads: "The Throne of Osiris."

150   FURTHER EXPLANATORY MATERIALS

Upon the door of the Fifth Division is written:

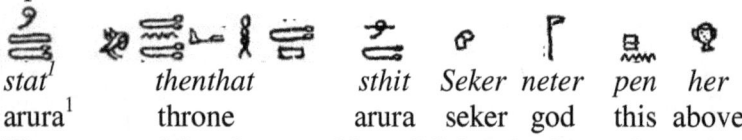

| stat[1] | thenthat | sthit | Seker | neter | pen | her |
| arura[1] | throne | arura | seker | god | this | above |

The arura of the throne; this god Seker is above the arura.

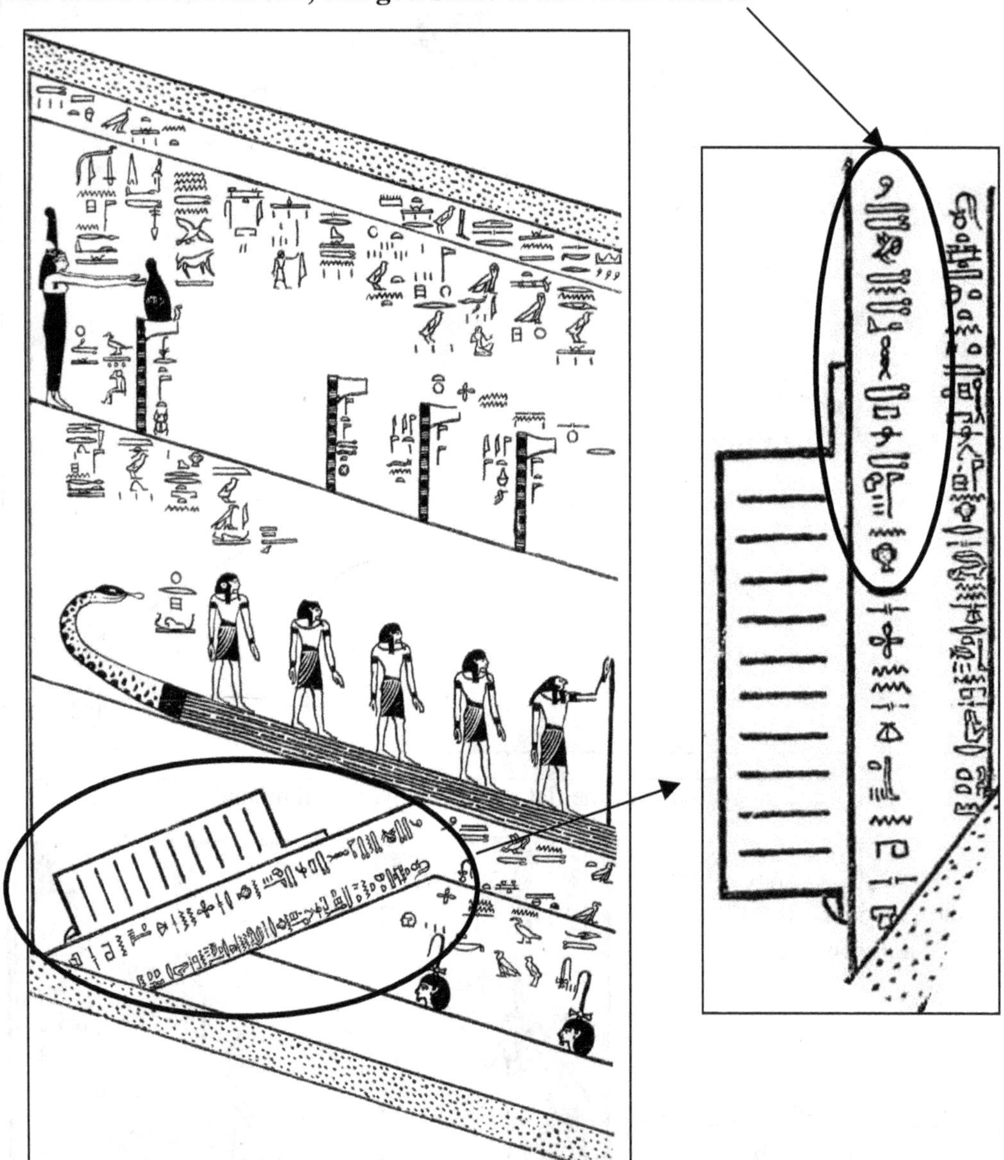

The Kingdom of Seker.

Fourth Division – Upper Register

The Serpent Aligned with the Flat Top of the Pyramidal Mound

The hieroglyphic determinatives of the serpent and the star indicate the ancient Egyptian word *tchuat*: the period of culmination of a star. This may imply that the constellation of Hydra culminates above the pyramid tomb of Osiris.

Illustration found on a 21st dynasty coffin discovered in Thebes

The Serpent Guardian of Osiris

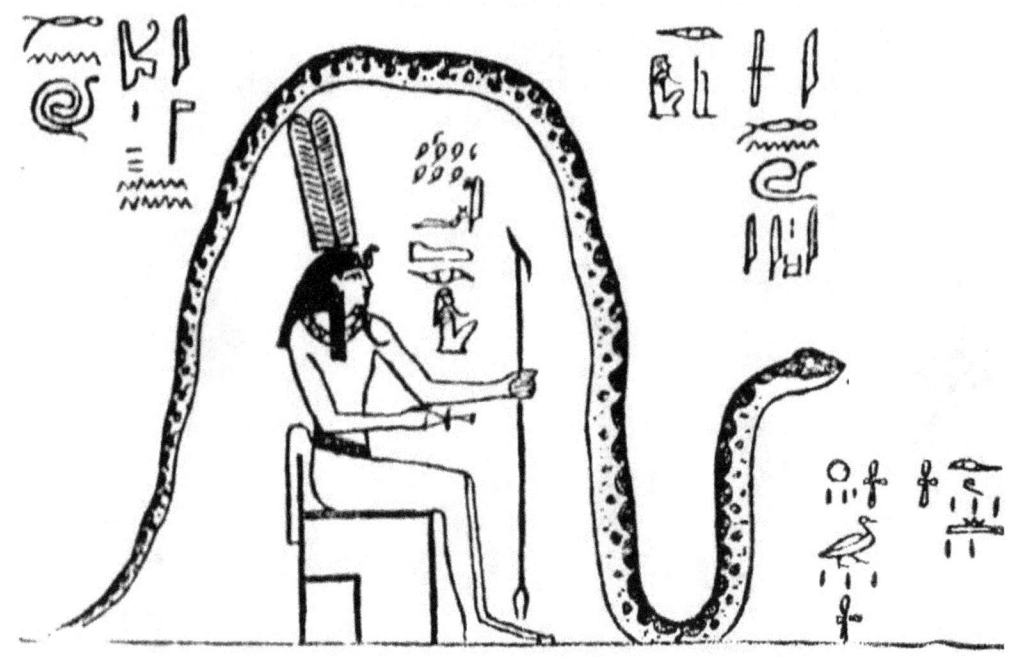

From the Seventh Division of Am Tuat [308]

Written behind the serpent:

An neter pen en mehen
hail god this in serpent's embrace

Written above the head of the serpent:

Asar ami mehen Apepi
Osiris who is in embrace of Apepi [309]

Written in front of the serpent:

ankh-aru-tchefa [310]
a serpent guardian of the body of Osiris

Written above the enthroned Osiris:

afi Asar [311]
dead body of Osiris

---

[308] Budge, *Egyptian Heaven and Hell*, I, 149.
[309] Apep (also spelled Apepi, and Aapep, or Apophis in Greek)
[310] Budge, *EHD,* 125B, *ankh-aru-tchefa*
[311] Budge, EHD, 43A, *Afi Asar*: Tuat VI, the flesh, i.e, dead body, of Osiris

Upper Register – Part 2 - Text

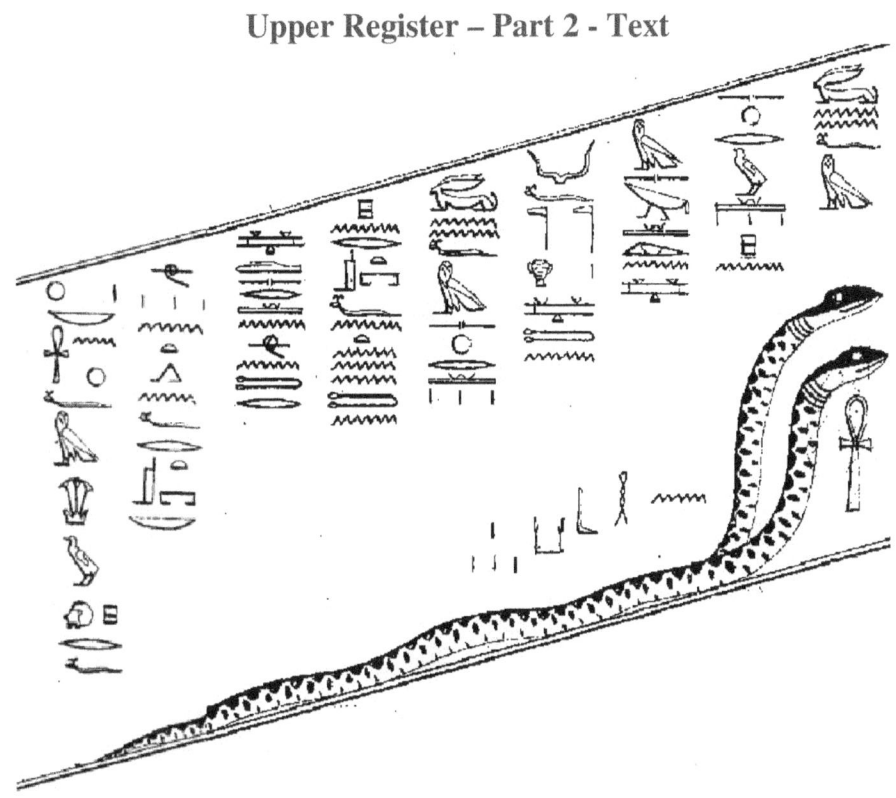

Above the serpent, read from the right side toward the left side:

unn	ef	em	skher	pen	em	seshem	an	uat	up	ef	neterui	her	uat	then
is	he	in	designs	this	as	guide	see	path	open	his	double god	upon	path	this

He is in this design as the guide. See the open path. He is the double-god upon this path.

Unn	ef	em	skher	pen	er	s-t	ef	net	nu	then	uat	teser	en	stau
is	he	in	designs	this	entrance	place	his	of	celestial water	this	path	holy	to	tow

He is in this design, his entrance place of celestial water, this holy path to tow the

neter	stau	net	ai	en	ef	er	s-t	ra	ankh	ef	em	hau
god	tows	which	to go	to	him	entrance	place	daily	live	he	in	addition to

god, which tows him to go to the entrance place every day. He lives in addition

tep	er	ef
he who is over	entrance	his

[to] he who is over his entrance.

Upper Register – Part 1 & 2 – The Figures

In front of the goddesses:

meht — res — pen ta
North — South — this earth

North and South of this earth.

In front of the hawk headed god:

ab[312] — benu — tuat[313]
to unite with — Venus — the planet Venus as the early morning star

To unite with Venus, the early morning star,

Above the 2 headed serpent: In front of the 2 headed serpent:

neheb — ka — ankh
to conquer[314] — images — to live

to be entrusted with living images

---

[312] Budge, EHD, 116B, *ab*: to face someone or something, to meet, to join, to unite with
[313] Budge, EHD, 870B: *tuat*: the planet Venus as the early morning star
[314] Budge, EHD, 384A *neheb*: to yoke cattle or horses, to put under the yoke, i.e., conquer, to be entrusted with something.

Fourth Division – Upper Register

Star Chart Illustration of the Serpent united with Venus

"The North and South of this Earth"

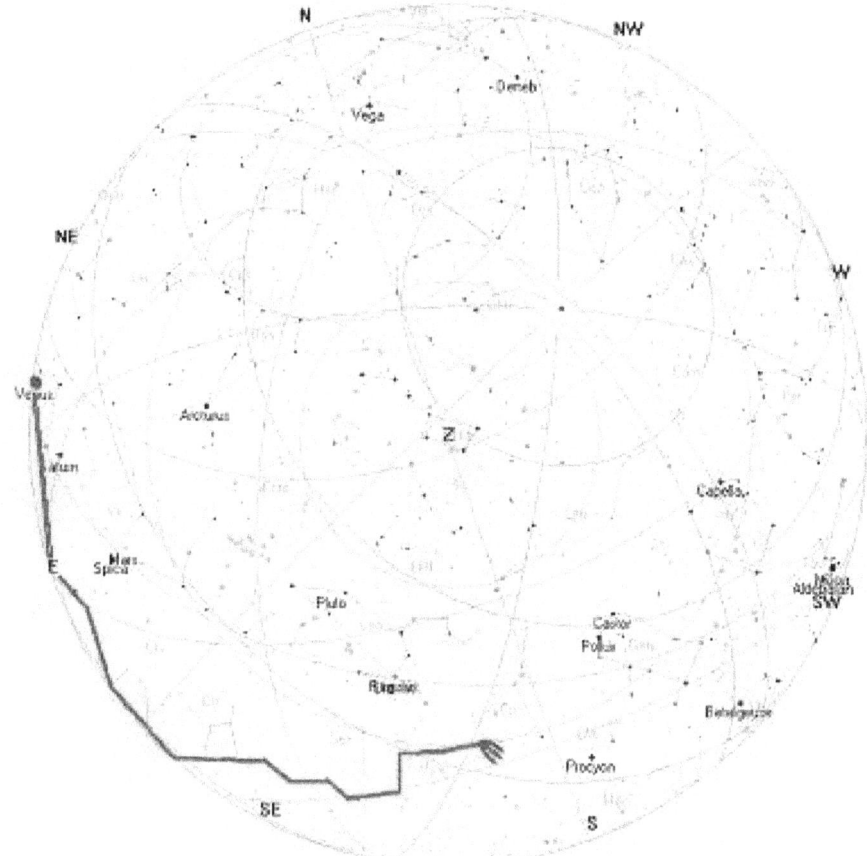

9/21/10390 BC

As in the text of the Fourth Division of the book of Am Tuat, Venus is behind the serpent in this star configuration. The Fifth Division, below, shows the 3-headed serpent united with Venus as a head on its tail.

---

[315] Photograph by Francis Dzikowski, ©Theban Mapping Project, reprinted with permission.

Upper Register – Part 3

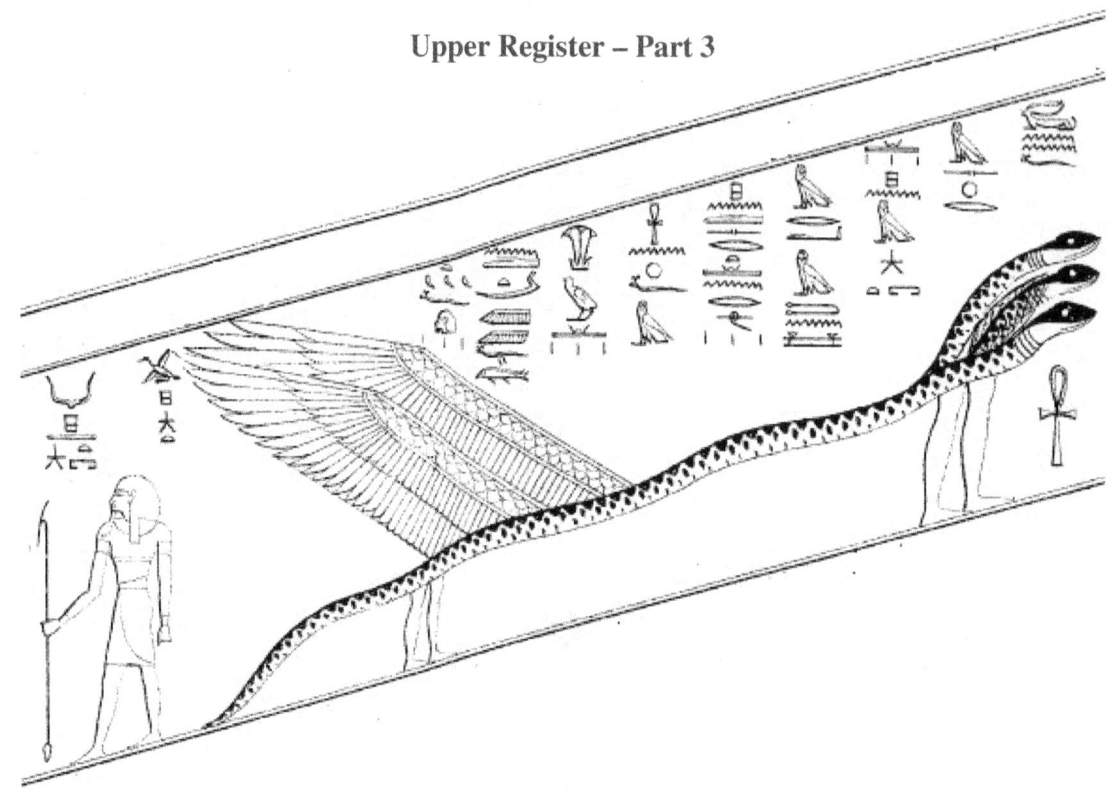

Above the serpent:

Unn ef em skher pen em tuat em ra em then uat pen tesert en
is he in designs this in Tuat in action in this path this holy of
He is in this design, in the Tuat, in action, in this path of this holy

Restau ankh ef em hau net temati ef khat
abode of the dead live he in addition to of two wings his the dead
abode of the dead he lives. In addition to the pair of wings of his body without life,

aah ef tep khemt pa pen sba up ta tuat
limbs his heads three fly this door open earth other world
his limbs, and three heads fly[316] this open door of the earth[317] of the Other World

In front of serpent:

ankh
alive.

---

[316] See this flying serpent illustrated in the image on the next page.
[317] The constellation Hydra apparently comes through an open door from the earth into the horizon. Once it has completely ascended the horizon door, it apparently flies into the Tuat sky of the Other World.

Upper Register – Part 4

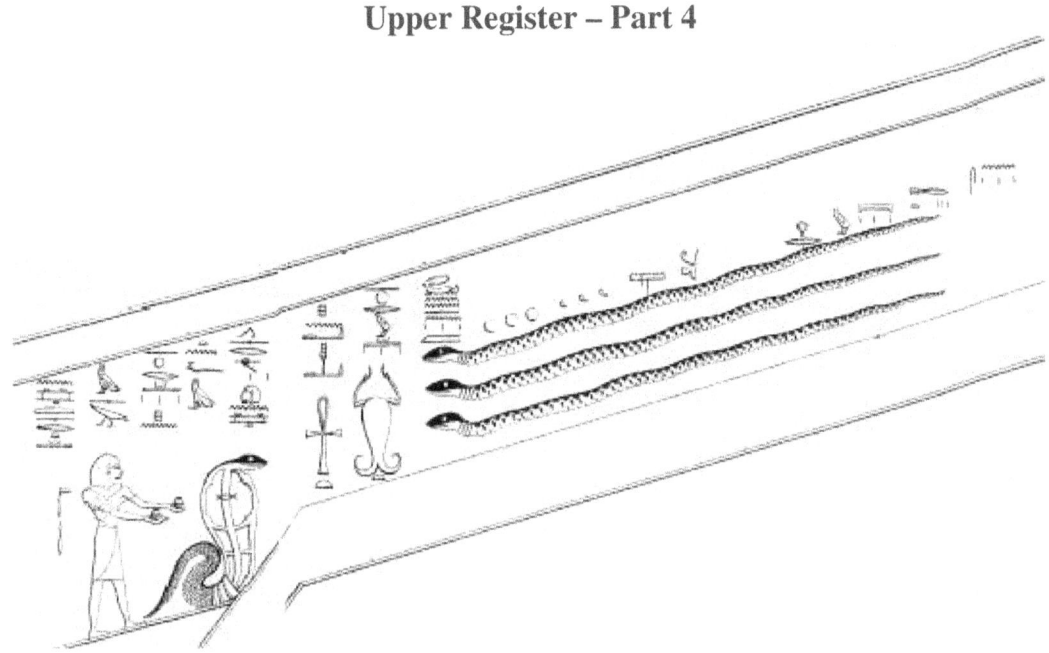

Above the man making offerings:

unn	*sen*	*em*	*skheru*	*pen*	*aha*	*s*	*restau*	*tep*	*en*	*uat*
are	they	in	designs	this	stand	she	abode of the dead	beginning	of	pathway

They are in this design. She[318] stands at the beginning of this path of the abode of the dead.

ef	*em*	*skher*	*pen*	*em*	*seshem*	*en*	*uat*	*tesert*
he	in	designs	this	as	guide	of	path	holy

In this design, he[319] is the guide of the holy path.

Behind the man making offerings to the upright serpent:

neter aa
god great
The Great God.

In front of the three serpents is the goddess Serqit:

Serqit   *ankht*
scorpion goddess   a living person or thing
The living Scorpion Goddess.[320]

---

[318] This may be referring to Scorpio.
[319] This may be referring to Apep/Hydra.

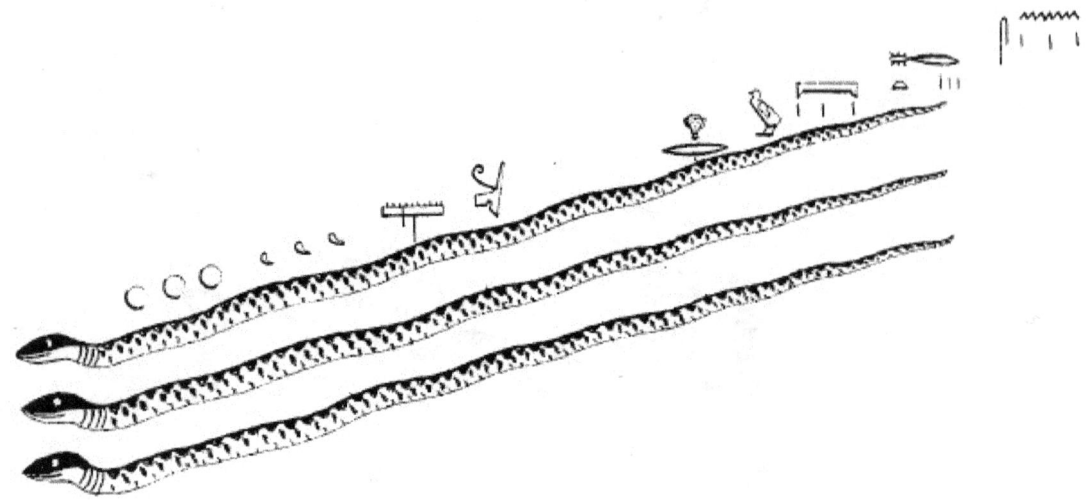

Above the three serpents:

sen	khat	her	en	hebs	au	heru
their	bodies	who are over	in	covered over	flesh	days

The flesh of their bodies which are above are covered over in the daylight.[321]

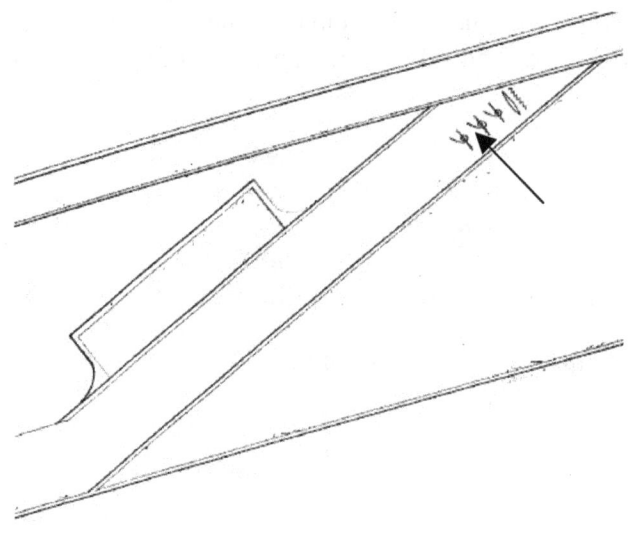

Written at the uppermost end of the canal:

en	restau
to	the abode of the dead

---

[320] Scorpio Constellation
[321] Stars are not visible during the hours of daylight

Upper Register – Part 5

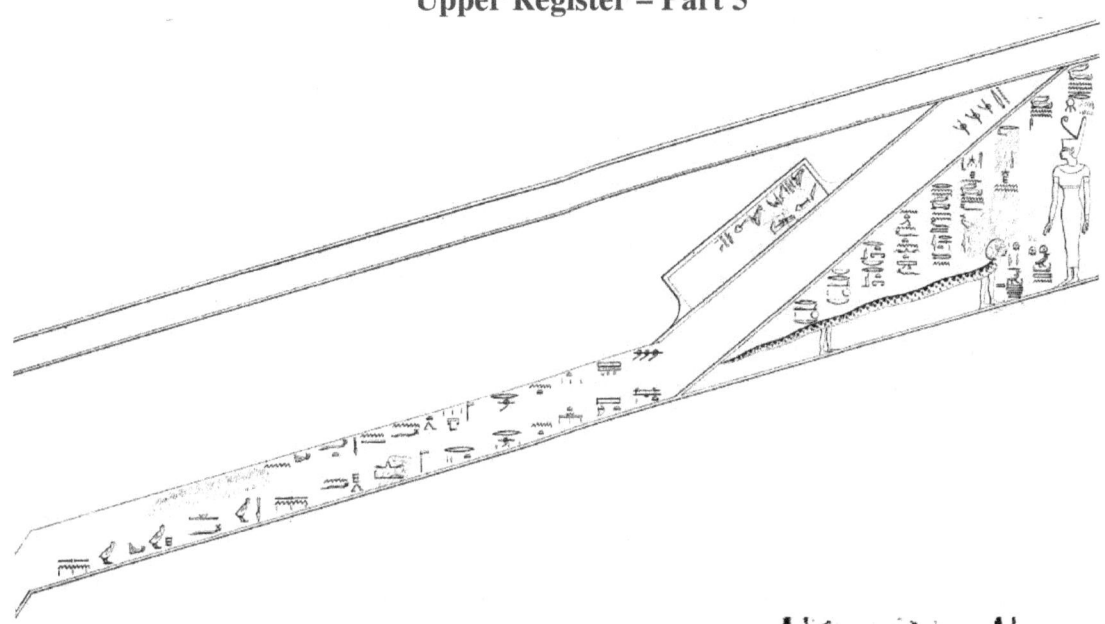

Written on the open door:

m	s	tes	sma	ta
in	her	door	edge of the road	

Tes	sma	Amen
To divide	to unite	Amen

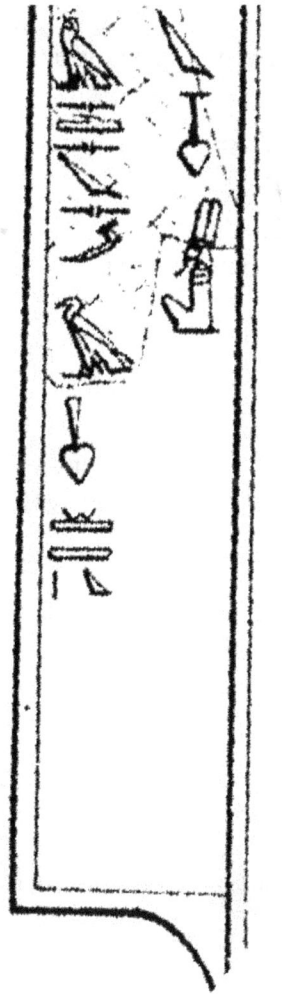

The canal below the open door

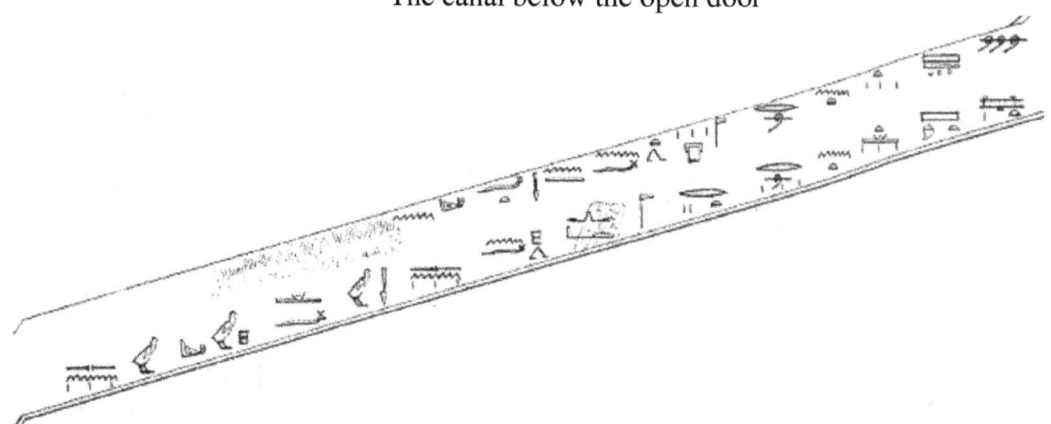

Written across the top:

Antht   shetat   neter stau neteru   sa[323]   *ai   en   ef   en   ta*
Ropes hidden divine tow   gods   fortified gateway to come to   him   in   earth
Hidden divine ropes tow gods to come to his fortified gateway in the earth,

kheru Ef   t   setchem   en   [remainder of this line of text damaged]
voice his thou hear   in
his voice thou hear in

Written across the bottom:

Way secrets of   restsau
Way of secrets of   the entrance to the corridors in the other world
The way of secrets of the entrance to the corridors in the Other World,

ruti   neter
two leaves of a door divine
two leaves of a door,

nt   ap   en   ef sen   kheru ef   pu   setchemu   sen
not travel in   he they voice he this   hear   they
he does not travel in, his voice this they hear

---

[322] Image from Lefebure, Seti I.
[323] Budge, EHD, 633B, *sa*: a wall, a walled building, fort, castle, fortified gateway

From Lefébure 1886 drawing from tomb of Seti I
The absence of color makes red and black text indistinguishable.

Above the goddess:[324]

Unn s   er uben sba pen
Is   she near rising star this
She is near this rising star.

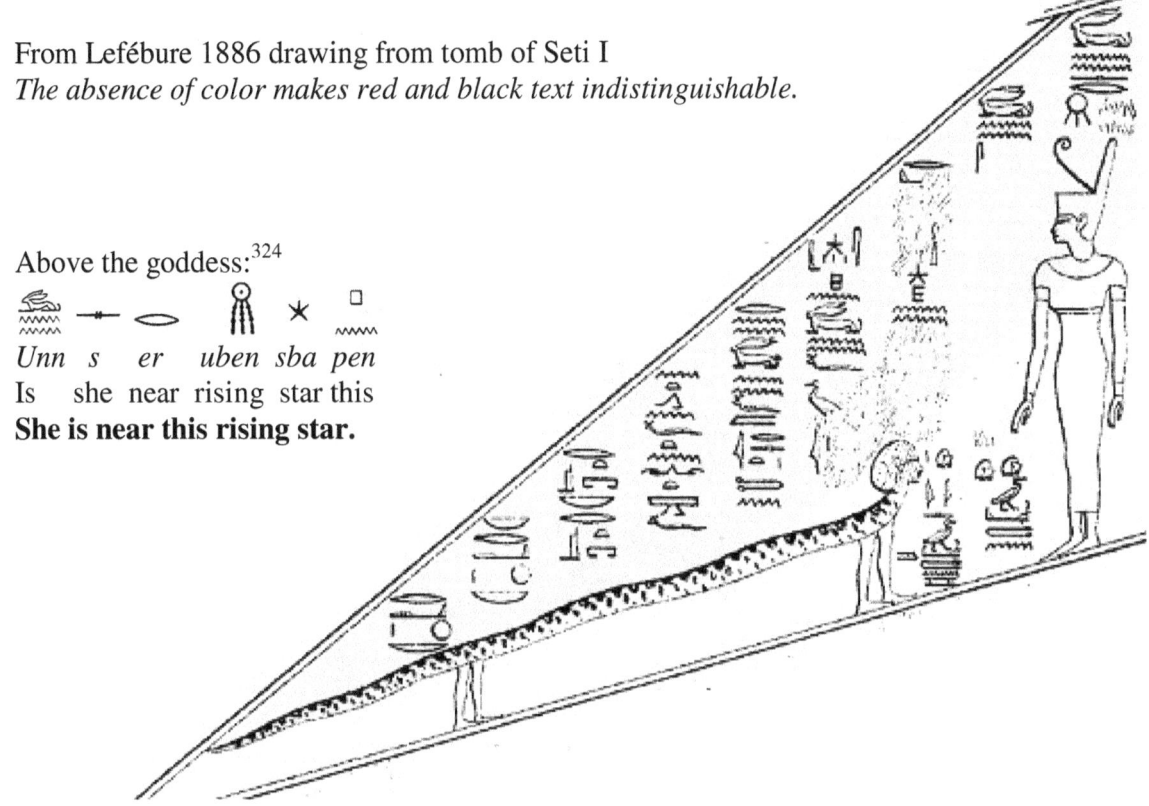

Unn ef em ar uat ten nt shem en ef er s-t neb ra
is he to go up paths this not go to his entrance place each every day
He is to ascend the paths. This does not go to his entrance place each and every day. [325]

Unn s er bu en nu ai sba pen
She is near place as hour comes door this
She is near the place, as the time comes, this door

unn ef geb er uat then nt ai en ef er s-t neb ra
is his earth entrance path this not to go to his entrance place each every day
is his earth entrance path; this not to go to his entrance place each and every day.

---

[324] This section was completed using text from the tomb of Amenhotep II
[325] The stars do not rise in the same place every day; therefore, if we know the position in which a star rises, we can determine the date that it rose at that position on the horizon.

In front of the human headed serpent with four legs in the tomb of Seti I:

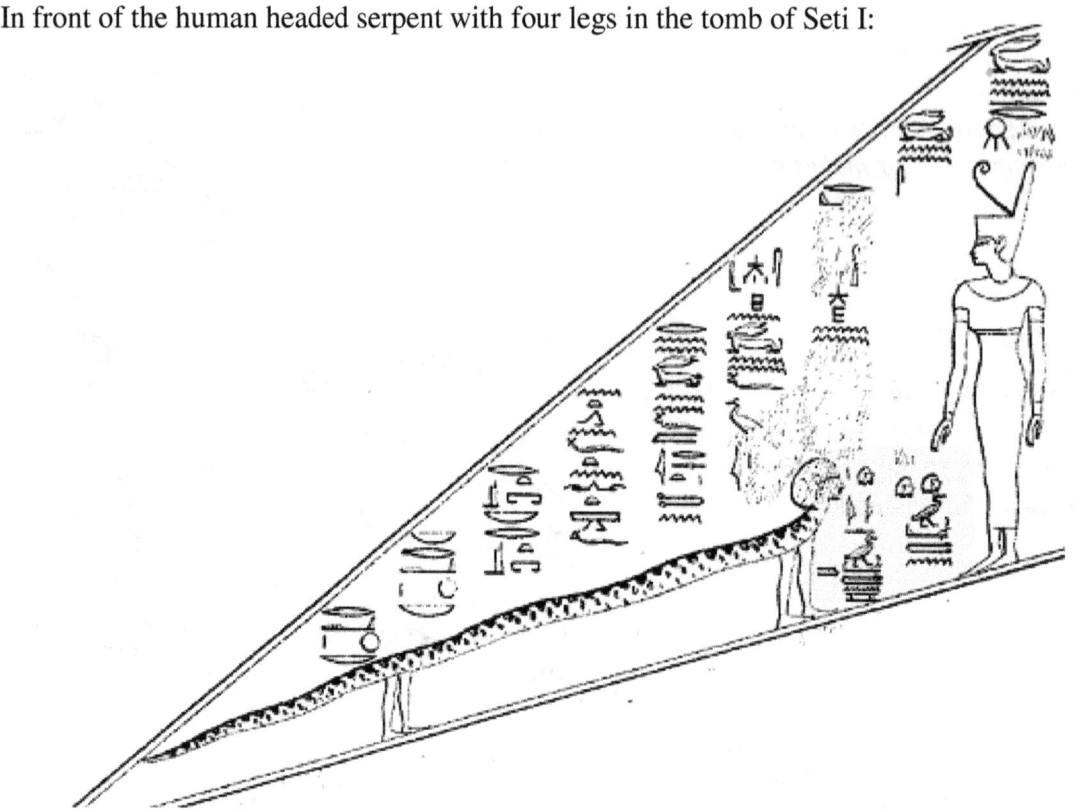

Tepui	sa	then
God with two heads	guard	this

The god with two heads that looks both ways guards this.

Tepi	s	sa	em	then	m[326]
He who is over	her	guard	in	this	canal

He who is over her guards in this canal.

---

[326] Budge, EHD, Vol I, A List of Hieroglyphic Characters, cxxvi, ▭, *m*: canal, any collection of water

The same text from the tomb of Amenhotep II in more complete form:

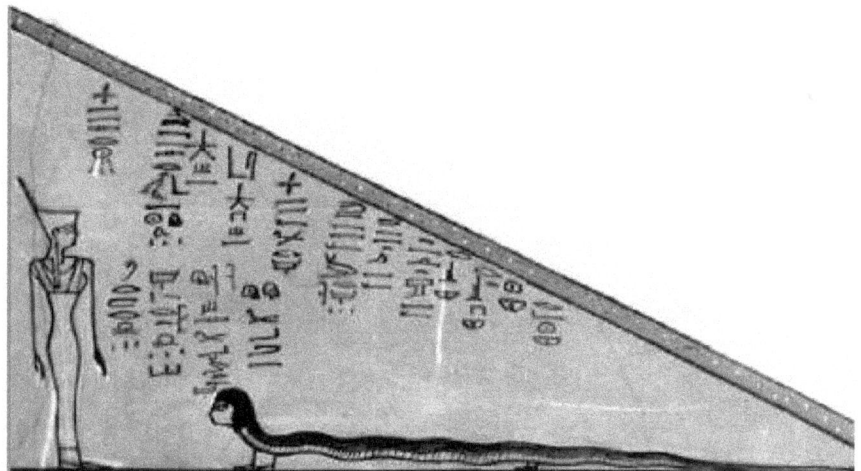

(Photograph by Francis Dzikowski,
©Theban Mapping Project, reprinted with permission.)

In front of the goddess and over the human head of the serpent in the tomb of Amenhotep II, first the outer (black) columns, and then the inner (red) columns:

Ur   em   restau
Great in entrance to the corridors of the Other World
In the great entrance to the corridors of the Other World,

tepui¹   geb   Ath¹   en
gods with two heads earth pull   in
the earth gods with two heads pull in

uat   art¹   restau
path a serpent fiend in the tuat entrance to the corridors of the Other World
the path the serpent fiend in the Tuat entrance to the corridors to the Other World.

aa   pen   s   sa   m   ten   uat
he who is over this she guard   in   this path
He who is over this she guards in this path.

164   FURTHER EXPLANATORY MATERIALS

Star Chart Illustrations of the Fourth Division

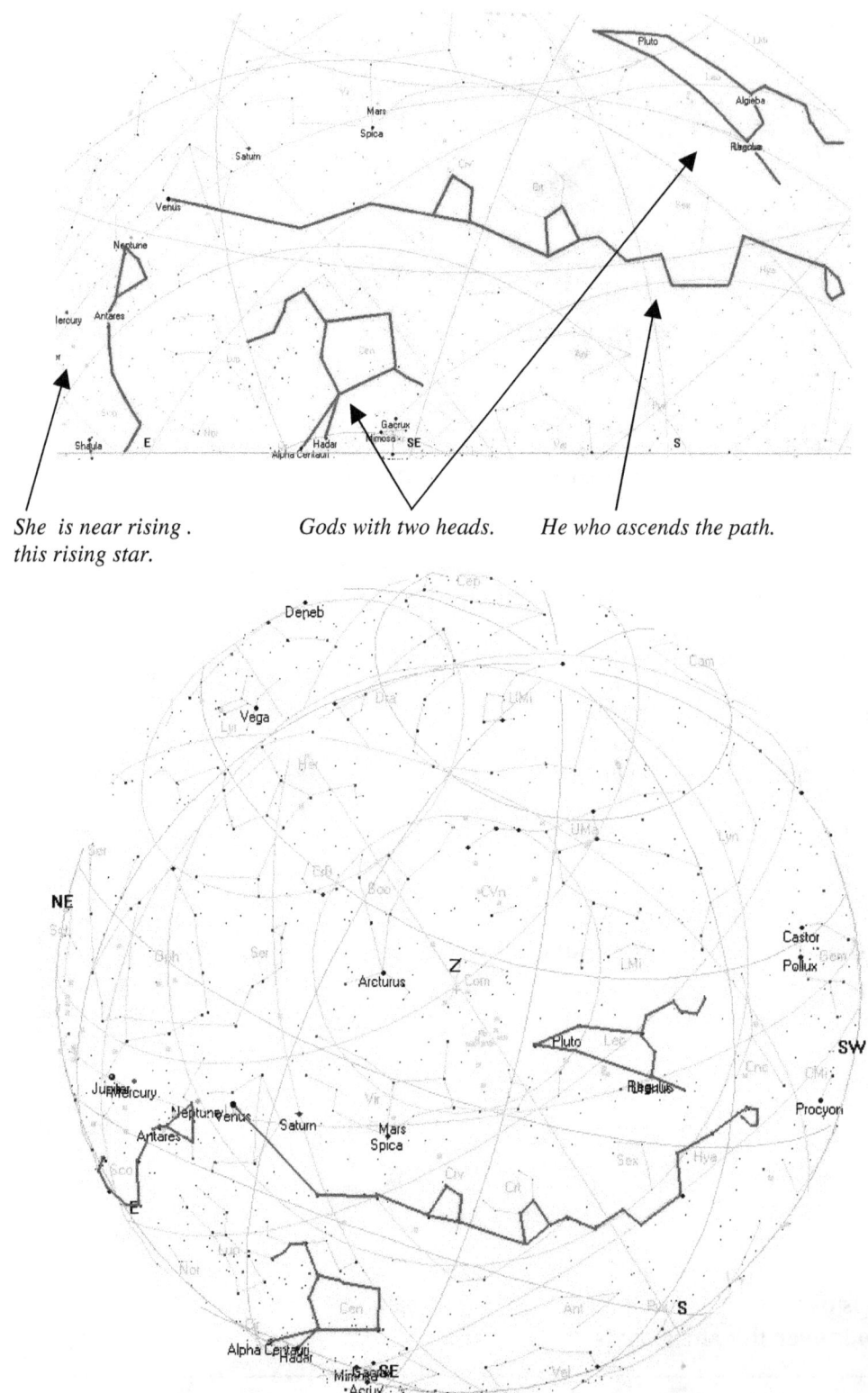

She is near rising. this rising star.   *Gods with two heads.*   *He who ascends the path.*

Straight Up Overhead View

The Middle Register

We have divided the middle register into 3 parts:

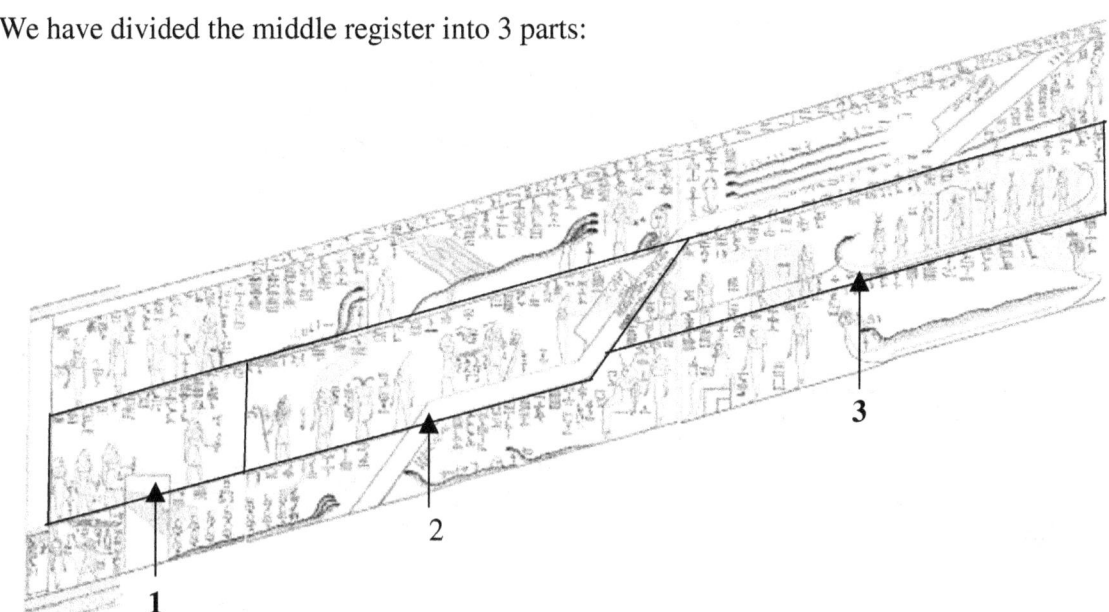

Middle Register – Part 1

Written over the people (each person carries the sign of life):

Unn	sen	em	er	tesert	net	aqiu	amen	net	tuat
are	they	in	doors	holy	of	those who enter	in hidden	of	Other World

They are in the holy doors of those who enter in of the hidden Other World,

net	sen	sa	en	pa	Neteru	em
which they	guard		to	fly	gods	as

which they guard, to fly as gods,

Seshemu	ef	en	sta	then	aq	en	ef	her	sen	em	en	teser
guides	him	to	tow	ye	enter	in	as	he	above them	among	as	holy

guides to tow him, as ye enter in, he above among them as holy.

In front of the people beginning with the woman:

Neb ankh	tch-metu	uat an	ankh seshem
Living Goddess	recite words	path brings	living guide

Middle Register – Part 2

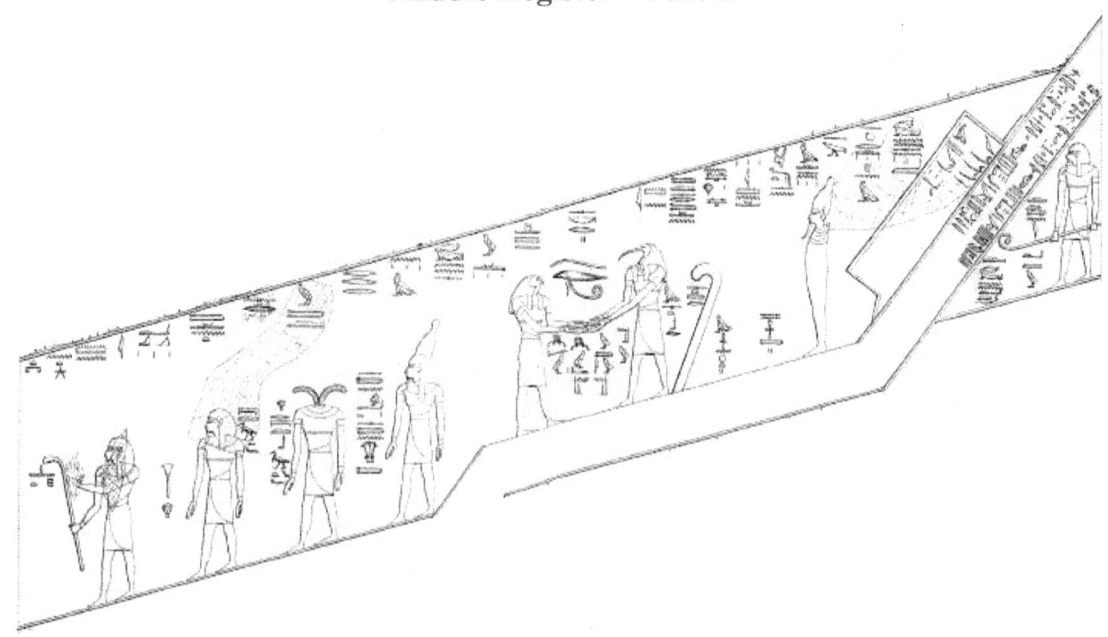

Across the top:

Unn sen em skher pen em seshem sen en tchet sen amen en uat
Are they in designs this to guide them in bodily form their hidden in path
They are in these designs to guide them in their bodily forms hidden in the path

Her uat th tesert en amen sekti sheta unn sen em er
above, path thy holy in hidden boat of Afu-Ra secret are their in doors
above, hidden in thy holy path, the secret boat of Afu-Ra are in their doors.

ut tesert net aq amen net Tuat
command holy to enter in hidden of the Other World
Holy command to enter in hidden of the Other World.

In front of the first figure:

Hotep
Reposed

In front of the second figure:

Utch   her
Green above

In front of the third figure:

pet   ba   tef[327]   heri   t   b   ba   ta   tef
heaven soul this celestial being   give   place soul earth this
This soul is a celestial being of heaven, give this soul a place on earth.

In front of the fourth figure:

s   then   hat[328]   s   then   hat[329]
she   to raise up   front of   she   to raise up   hall of a tomb
She to raise up front of, she to raise up hall of a tomb.

---

[327] Budge, EHD, 832B, *tef*

[328] Budge, EHD, 460A, *hat*: The front or forepart of anything, the beginning

[329] Budge, EHD, 465A, *hat*: tomb, sepulchre, the hall of a tomb.

Fourth Division – Middle Register

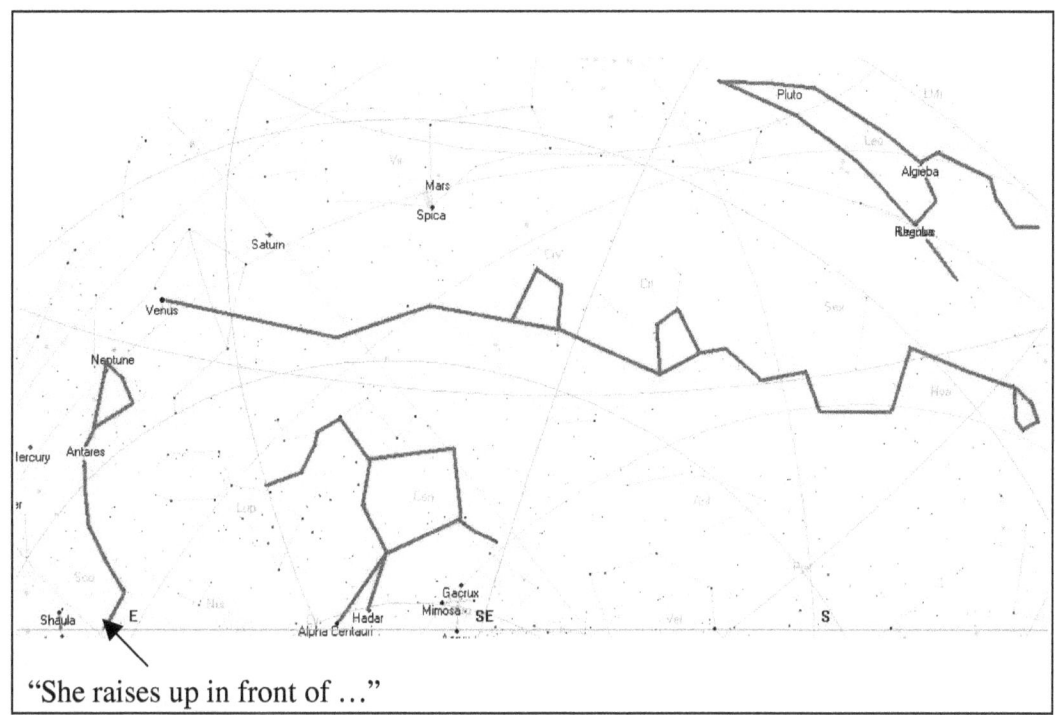

"She raises up in front of …"

Between the hawk-headed god and the ibis-headed god:

Aua[330]
gift
The open hand

aua   uthes
gift   raise up
raises up a gift.

uthes[331]
Lift up
Lift up [332]

uthesu
those who lift up
those who lift up

[330] Budge, EHD, 3A, *aua*
[331] Budge, EHD, 189B, *uthes*; see also Budge, EHD, 190A, *Uthesu*
[332] Horus and Thoth, supporters of the right eye of the Sky god

170 FURTHER EXPLANATORY MATERIALS

Behind the Ibis headed god:

em set Asar set sher³³³   e   ankhti³³⁴
to place Osiris place passage walled up at leaves of a door

to the place of Osiris, the place of passage walled up at leaves of a door.

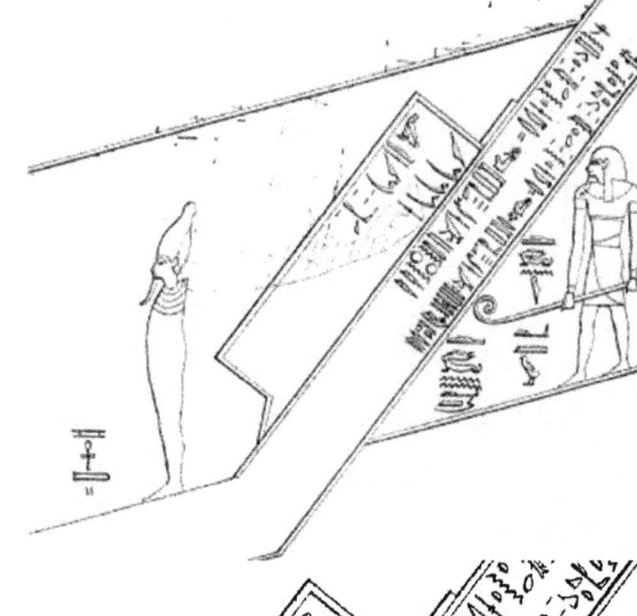

In front of the mummy of Osiris:

m³³⁵   ankhti
canal   living one

canal of the living one

Written on the open door:

M'tes-sma-ta³³⁶

Individually the symbols are:

metes   sma ta   tes
sharp   border or edge of a road   divide

---

³³³ Budge, EHD, 750A, *sher*: to stop up, to block, to wall up, to close to obstruct the passage.

³³⁴ Budge, EHD, 126a, *ankhti*: the two ears, i.e. leaves of a door

³³⁵ Budge, EHD, Vol I, 'A List of Hieroglyphic Characters', cxxvi, , *m*: canal, any collection of water

³³⁶ Budge, EHD, 291B, *m'tes-sma-ta*: Tuat IV, the door of the second section of Restau [questionable translation]

Written in the canal beneath door :

Staui	*net*	*khat*	*net*	*sekri*	*pet sha*	*ef*	*seshem*	*en*	*ma*
haulers	of	dead body	of	Sekeri	over sand	his	image of a god	to	perceive

Haulers of the dead body of Seker over his sand, the image of a god to see and

en	*ma*	*uat*	*net*	*aqt*	*khat*	*net*	*sekri*	*her pet*	*sha*	*ef*
to	see	path	of	entrances	bodies	of	Sekri	who is over	sand	his

to perceive; the path of the entrances of the bodies of Seker who is over his sand,

seshem	*sheta*	*en*	*ma*	*en*	*petr*
image of a God	secret	to	perceive	to	see

the image of a god, a secret to perceive and to see.

Middle Register – Part 3

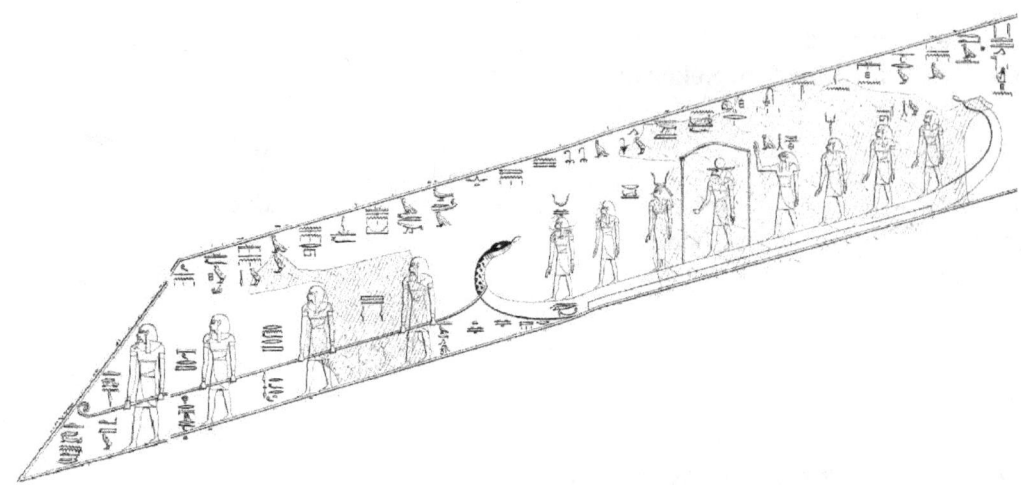

The text begins on the uppermost top right side, and reads to the left across the top:

Sqett	neter	pen	aa	her	sen	skheru	em	pen	an	sen
Travel about in a boat	god	this	great	above	these	designs	of	this	by	their

This great god travels about in a boat above in these designs of this, by their

ta	tepi	er	aa	ef	seshem	shu	em	nen	en	m	then
flames	over	entrance	boat	his	guide	his	by	this	in	canal	this

flames over the entrance, guide his boat by this, in this canal

n-t	Maa	ef	seshem	sen	tua	ef	en	sen	er	hau
not	See	he	image of a god	they	praise	he	in	their	entrance	nearby

his image unseen, they praise him in their entrance, nearby

Sen	kheru	ef	pu	setchem	sen
them	voice	he	belonging to	hears	them

them, a voice belonging to him they hear.

Nehs-iu
The two Utchats which were painted on the two sides of the front of the boat to keep a look out.

FOURTH DIVISION – MIDDLE REGISTER

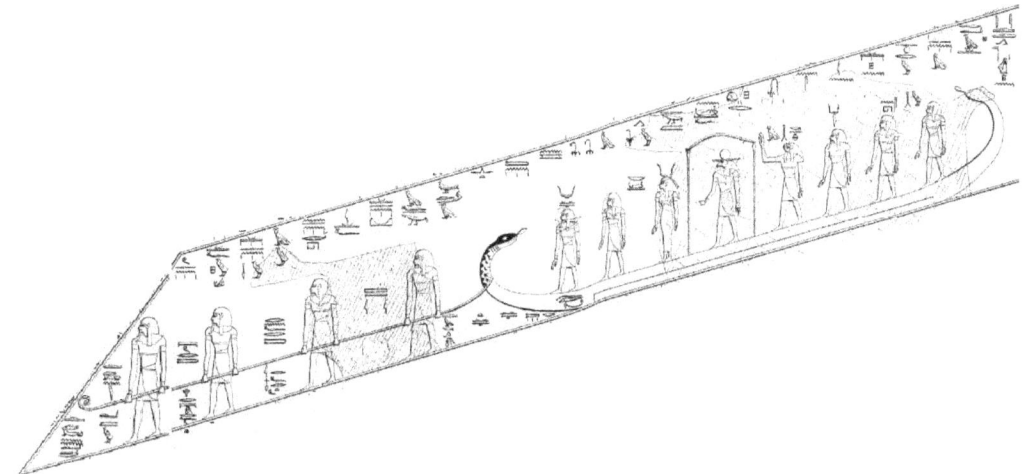

Beginning on the left side, on top of the rope held by the men towing the boat:

Tun	*shut*	*reth*	*ren*	*ef*	*reth*	*shtai*
stretch out	sky	rope	men[337]	name	his	mankind hidden one

Stretch out the sky rope, his name mankind hidden one.

Beginning on the left side, under the rope:

Tun	*na*	*maa*	*maat*	*u*	*heri*	*uar*	*ef*	*ar*
stretch out	this	give	truth	they	he who is over	measuring rope	his	rope of

Stretch this out, they give truth. He who is over his measuring rope. Rope of

Nefert	*shetat*	*mek*	*ai*	*uat*	*uat*	*k*
rope	hidden	behold	come	path	paths	thy

the hidden rope. Come behold the path. Thy paths,

op-uat	*neb*	*aa*	*af*	*heru*	*hekenu*	*ka*	*Shu*
opener of the way	master	boat	sun god of night	sky god	praise	double	sun god

opener of the path; boat master sun god of night. Praise the sky god, the ka of the sun god.

Nehes	*Hu*[338]
To wake	ka of Ra

Awaken the ka of Ra.

---

[337] Budge, EHD, 436A, *reth*: Tuat V, "men," i.e. the Egyptians in the Tuat. They were formed of the tears that fell from the eyes of Ra.

[338] Budge, EHD, 469B, *hu*: one of the 13 *kau* of Ra (*kau* is the plural of *ka*)

Lower Register

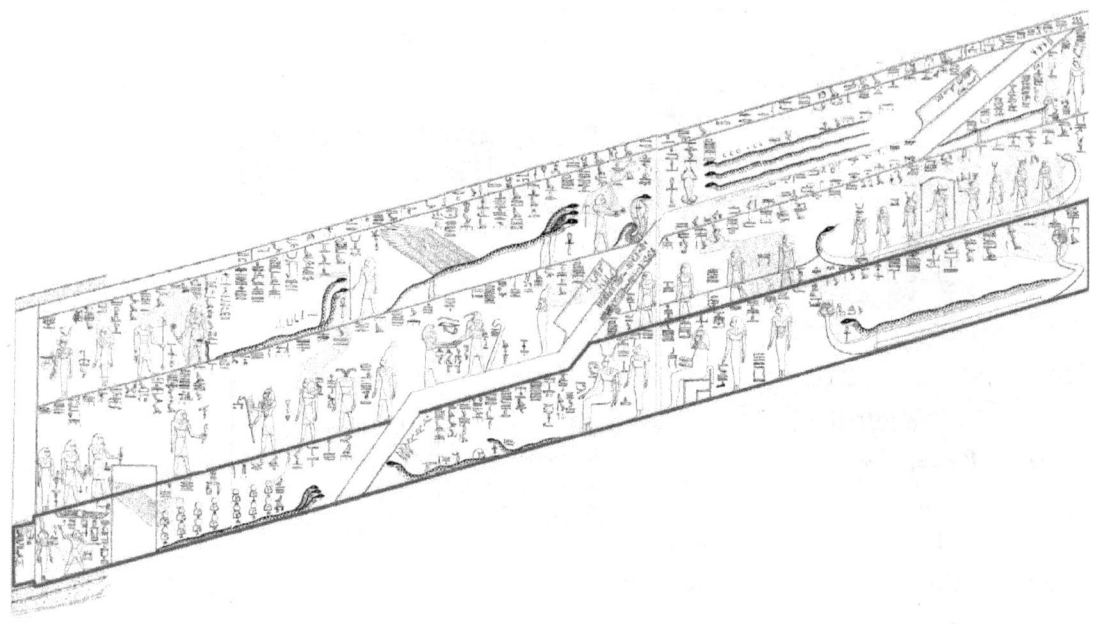

We have divided the lower register into 4 sections:

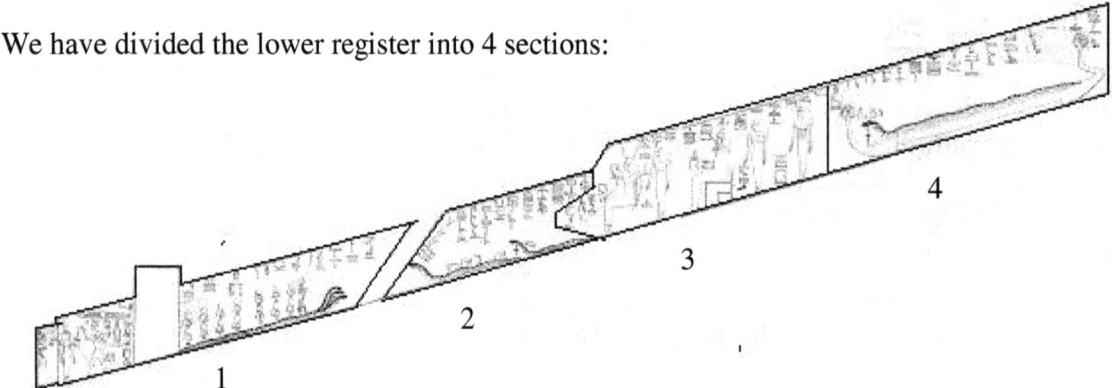

Fourth Division – Lower Register

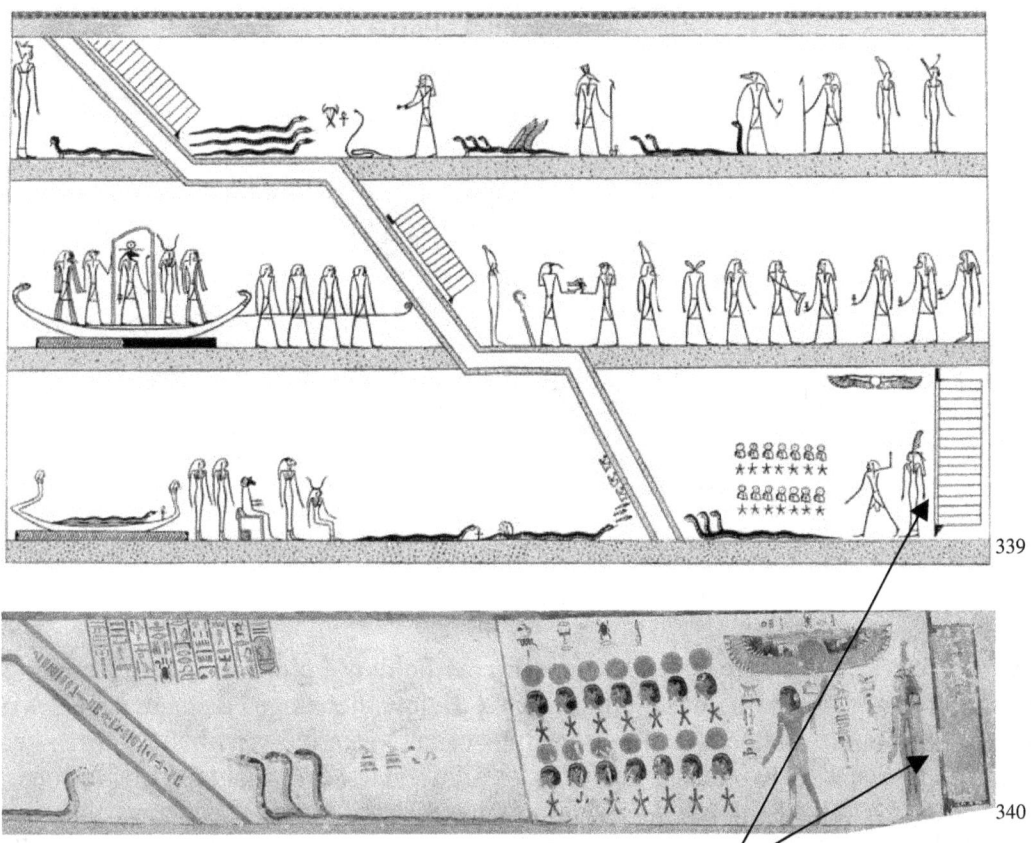

Written on the door is *The Door to Eternity*. It is open to the sky. The goddess is the double goddess of truth, Gemini. The man is Orion, Dweller in the Sky. The heads and circles and stars represent time. This is midnight, when Orion is on the horizon. The stars, heads, and circles are 14 in number, the number of hours for Hydra (from midnight) to complete its journey below the western horizon.

---

[339] Piankoff, *The Tomb of Ramesses VI,* Figure 77, between pages 254 and 255, from the tomb of Tuthmosis III.
[340] Hawass. *The Royal Tombs of Egypt,* page 119, from the Tomb of Ramesses VI.

Lower Register – Part 1

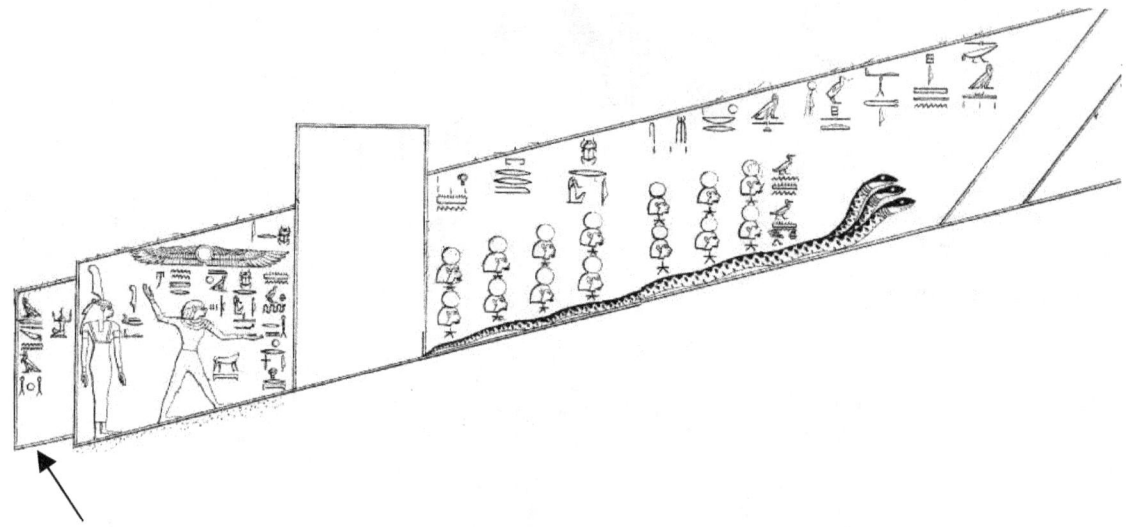

The door to eternity opens to a goddess and a man holding up one arm and extending the other arm forward. Above them is a winged disk. Below the winged disk are details written in hieroglyphic text. Farther up the ascending canal, over the length of a three-headed serpent, are fourteen disks, heads, and stars. Additional details in hieroglyphic text are written across the top of the canal. The following Skyglobe star chart shows the stars on 9/21/10390 BC at midnight, as if the observer is looking straight upwards into the sky. These images display the constellations of Gemini, Orion and Hydra.

Written on the door behind the goddess:

Metes	*en*	*neheh*
Door	to	eternity

The Door to Eternity

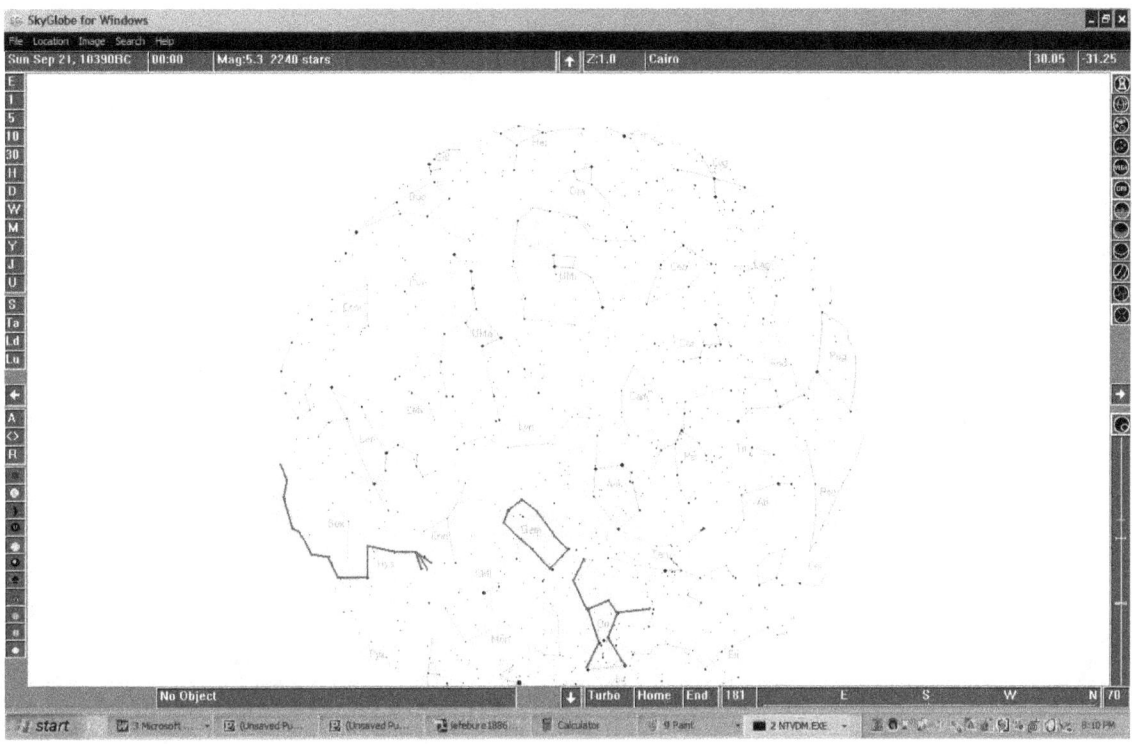

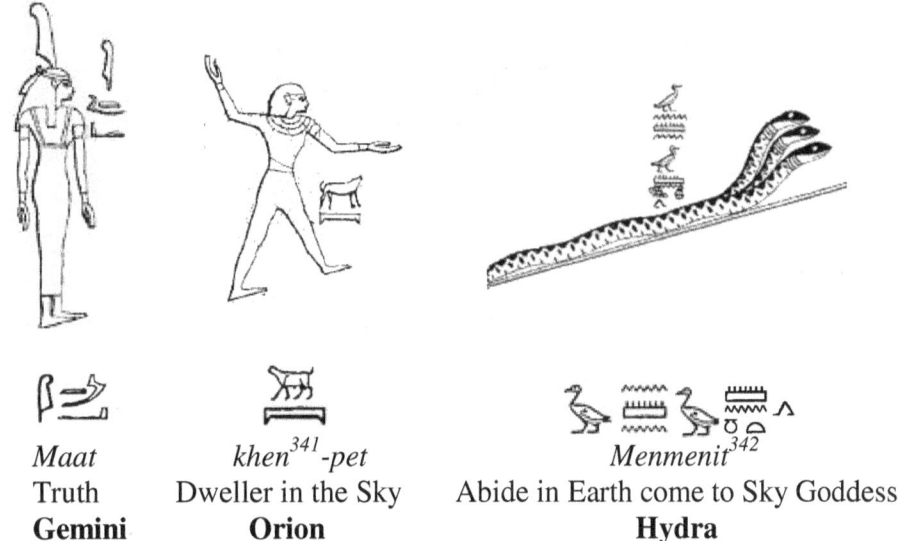

Maat	*khen*[341]*-pet*	*Menmenit*[342]
Truth	Dweller in the Sky	Abide in Earth come to Sky Goddess
Gemini	**Orion**	**Hydra**

Budge gives the word *Menmenit* as the name of the three headed serpent from the tomb of Seti I, who died 1279 BC. When the hieroglyphic text from the name of *Menmenit* is translated, it looks like this:

geb	*en*	*men*	*geb*	*en*	*men*	*nut*	*ai*
earth	in	abide	earth	in	abide	sky goddess	to come

---

[341] Budge, EHD, 573A, *khan*: he who is in, dweller in; also see 576 A *Khen-pet*: Tuat IV, a god
[342] Budge, EHD, 298B, *Menmenit*

Compare this with text from the tomb of Ramesses VI, who died 142 years before in 1137 BC. In this earlier version of the same text, the name of the serpent looks like this:

The translation of the hieroglyphic text in the serpents name is:

Ani[344]	menmen	ta	aua[345]
to remove	to move away	earth	to travel

The hieroglyphic words near the serpent are descriptive of the idea connected with it. Both the Seti I and Ramesses VI versions seem to suggest that the serpent travels away from the earth. This makes sense, because the serpent constellation appears half-way visible above the horizon of the earth when Orion is standing erect and Gemini is behind, as shown in the next illustration.

---

[343] Hawass, Zahi A. *The royal tombs of Egypt: the art of Thebes revealed.*

[344] Budge, EHD, 7A, *ani*: to remove, to put aside

[345] Budge, EHD, 32A, *aua*: to travel, to go on a journey

FOURTH DIVISION – LOWER REGISTER

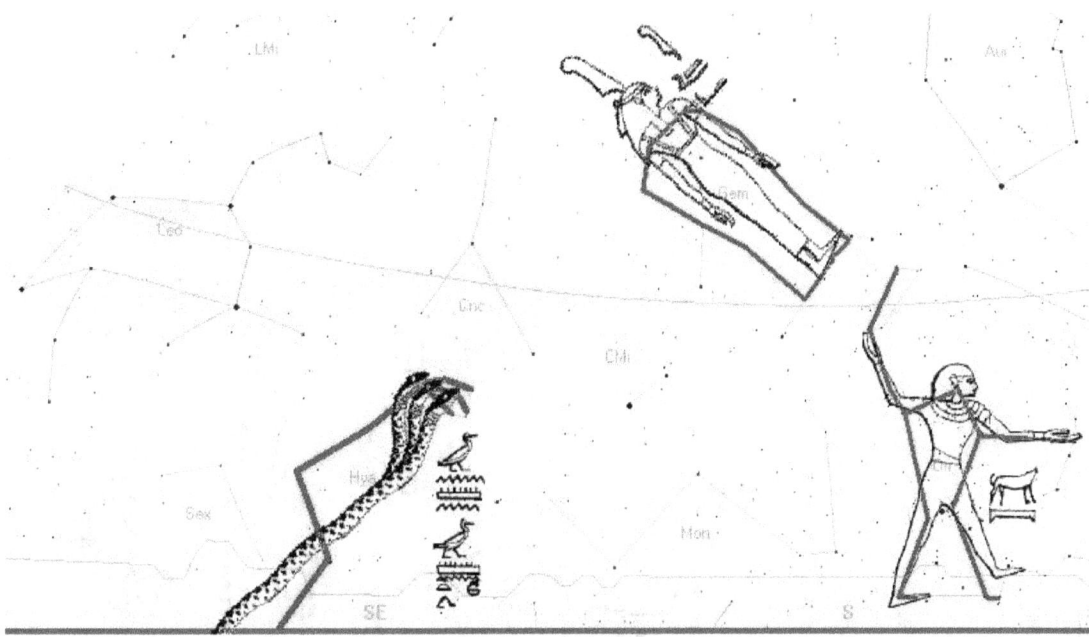

Skyglobe Star Chart showing the sky of Cairo on 9/21/10390 BC at 12:00AM

The duration of the journey of the serpent from its position as illustrated above, until it descends below the western horizon is 14 hours (12:00 AM to 2:00 PM). It is likely the 14 heads with disks and stars refer to the transit time of this constellation. The line at the bottom of the illustration is the horizon.

180　　　　　　　　　FURTHER EXPLANATORY MATERIALS

The Multifaceted Design: Encrypted Meaning

This is the drawing in its complete form with both images and text.

The Images

The names of these celestial beings are easier to recognize when they are separated from the accompanying text. The goddess Maat (Truth) is the constellation Gemini. The god Khen-pet (The Dweller In The Sky) is Orion. The winged disk is Khepera. Khepera represents an idea that is difficult draw because it is an abstract concept. It is the personification of the Creative Forces. i.e., On-Going Change; the transformational and evolutionary process of the universe; the manifestation of everything - - here presented in its symbolic manifestation representing its creation of the positions of the stars.

The Text

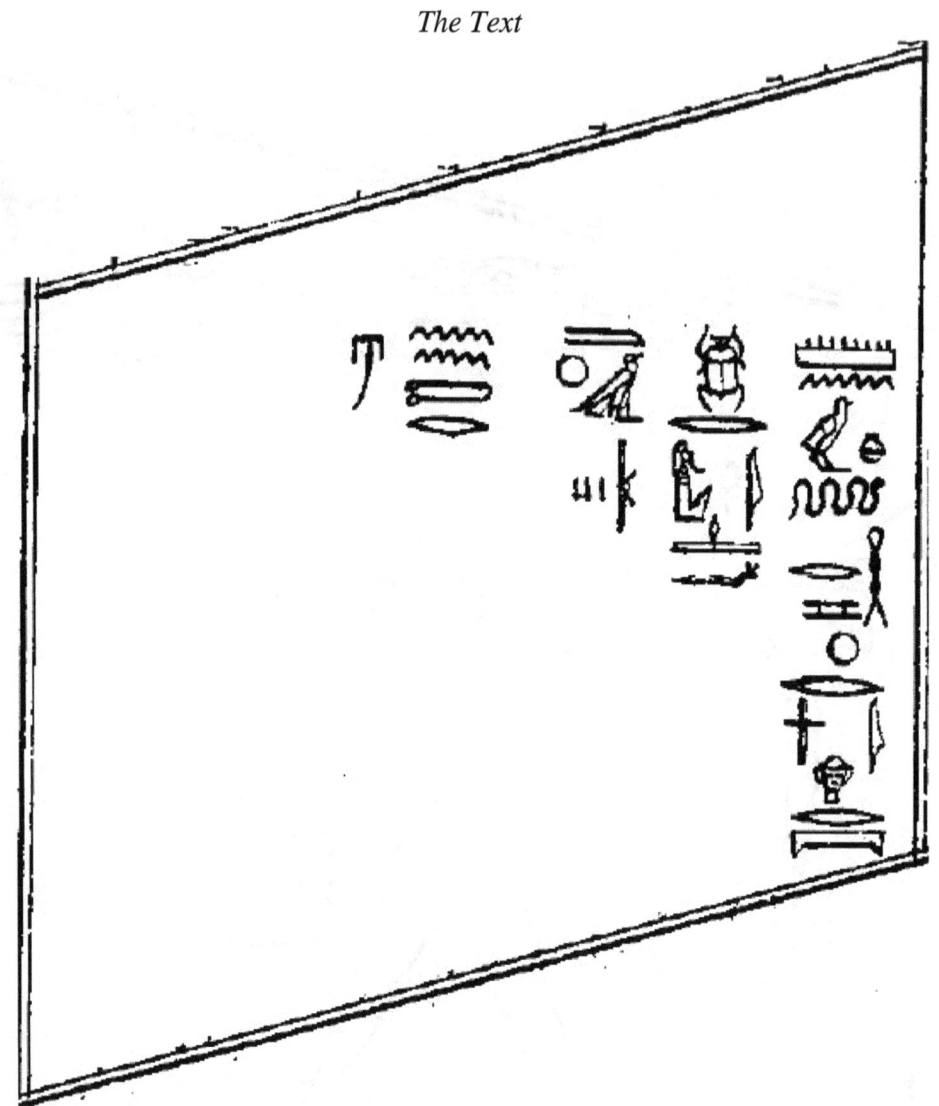

Above, the text is easier to recognize when the accompanying illustrations of the entities and their titles have been removed. It is to be read from right to left.

menu[346]   *hefau*   *her*   *m*   *kher*   *ami*

commemorative building of colossal scale serpent over canal through which it is in

The serpent over the monument, through the canal which it is in,

---

[346] Budge, EHD, 298A, *menu*: , ; monument, monuments, temples, commemorative buildings of a colossal scale, obelisks, palaces, walls, etc.

Fourth Division – Lower Register

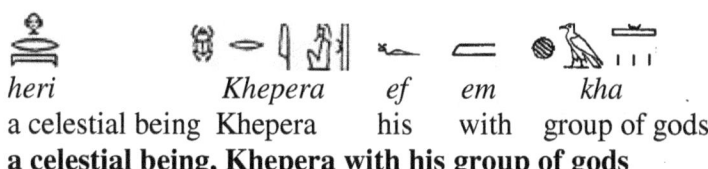
heri	Khepera	ef	em	kha
a celestial being	Khepera	his	with	group of gods

a celestial being, Khepera with his group of gods

en	neter	stuit[347]
of	divine	radiance

of divine radiance

The Text Above the Three-Headed Serpent

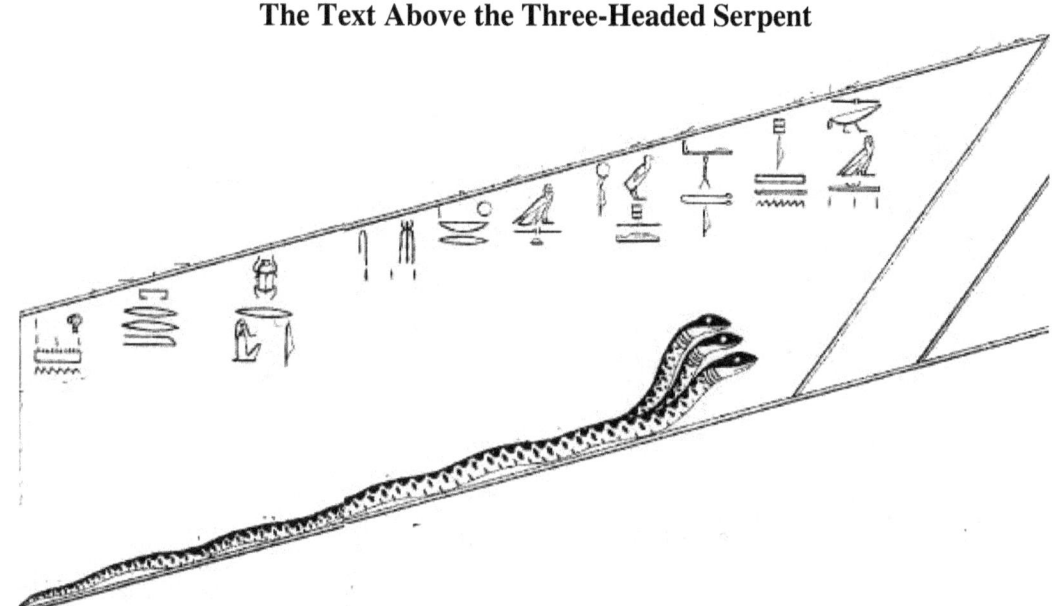

Across the top of the canal, reading from right to left:

Seshem	pa	sheta	na	het[348]	au	pest	am	set	ra
Guides	this	secret	journey	canal	come	to shine	within	it	every day

Guides this secret journey canal, come to shine within it everyday,

Mes	Khepera	perr	herui khemt[349]
births	Khepera	come forth	three headed

births Khepera, come forth three headed serpent,

---

[347] Budge, EHD, 708B, *stuit*: radiance,

[348] Budge, EHD, 516B *het*: canal, stream of water,

[349] Budge, EHD, 494A: see the use of *herui* in *herui senu* = two-faced, hence *herui-khemt* = three-faced

Lower Register – Part 2

The Name of the Canal

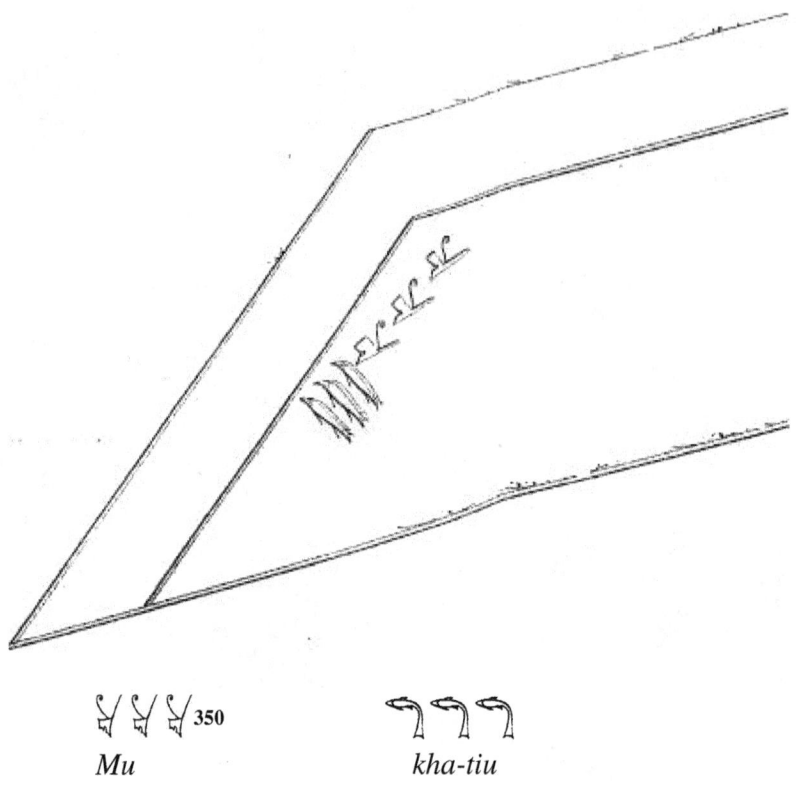

    𓈗𓈗𓈗 350

    Mu   *kha-tiu*

Watery mass of sky   the dead in general

The water of the bodies without life

---

350 𓈗𓈗𓈗 = 〰〰〰, see Budge EHD, cxxvi, A List of Hieroglyphic Characters, 〰〰, *mu* 🦉𓃀, water, watery mass of the sky

Text Above The Serpents

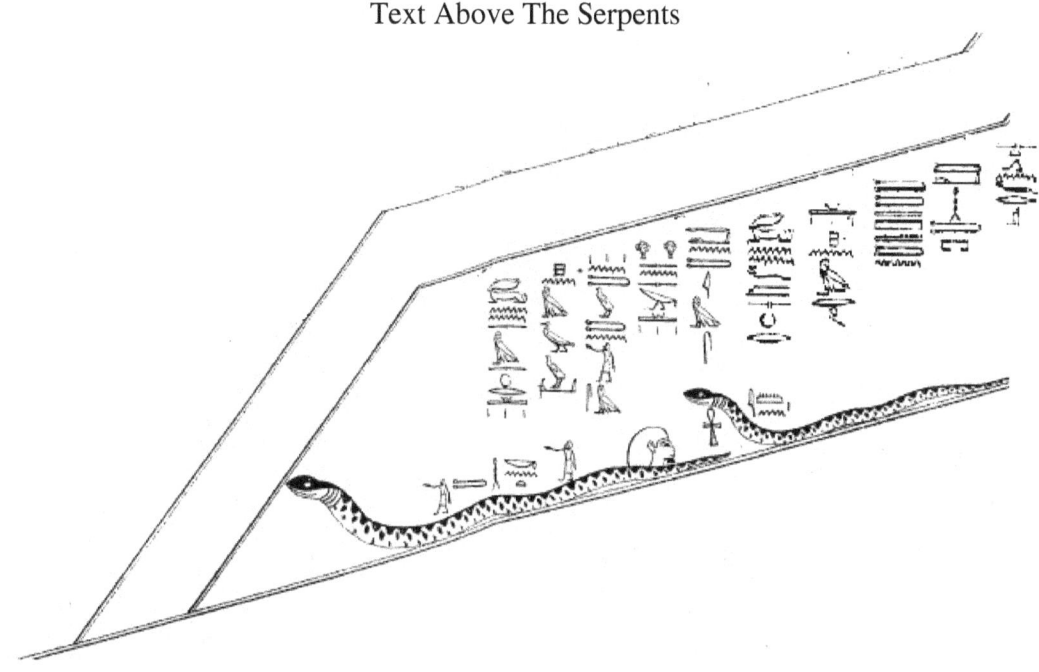

Unn	s	em	s	skher	pen	em	sa	neth	uten
are	they	in	their	designs	this	as	guardians	of	image

They are in their designs as these guardians image,

a	sem	herui-senu[351]	sen	shemu	aa	net	ames
praise	image	two-faced	they	guides	great	which	to conduct

praise two faced image. They are the great guides that conduct.

Unn	ef	em	skher	pen	em	rutt	ta	shetat	neth	aht
is	he	in	designs	this	like	ground	earth	hidden	of	chamber

He is in these designs like the ground of hidden earth chamber.

Set	ai	en	ef	er	s-t
they	come	to	his	entrance	place

They come to his entrance place.

---

[351] See also Budge, EHD, 831B; see also same page: *Tepui (Tchatchaui);* The god with two heads that looks both ways guards this.

Text Over the Body of the Serpents

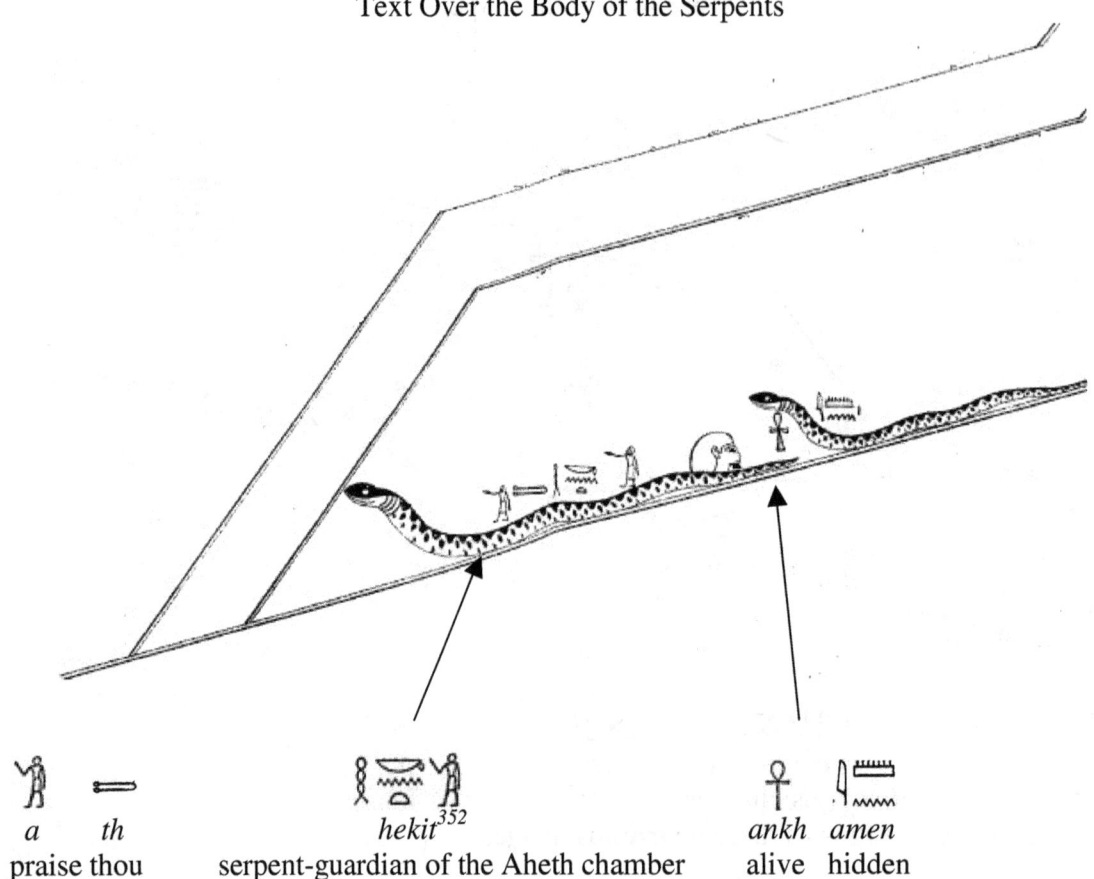

a	*th*	*hekit*³⁵²	*ankh*	*amen*
praise thou		serpent-guardian of the Aheth chamber	alive	hidden

---

³⁵² Budge, EHD, 515B, *heknit*: Tuat IV, a serpent-guardian of the Aheth chamber, ; *heknit*: a serpent-fiend with two faces

Lower Register – Part 3

Ra ankh ef em kheru neteru eru then
every day live he with voice gods words this
Every day alive with his voice gods words, daily this

tesit   upt   em   sep tepi   geb   per
high ground apex[353] of   primaeval time earth house
high ground, the apex of primeval time earth house,

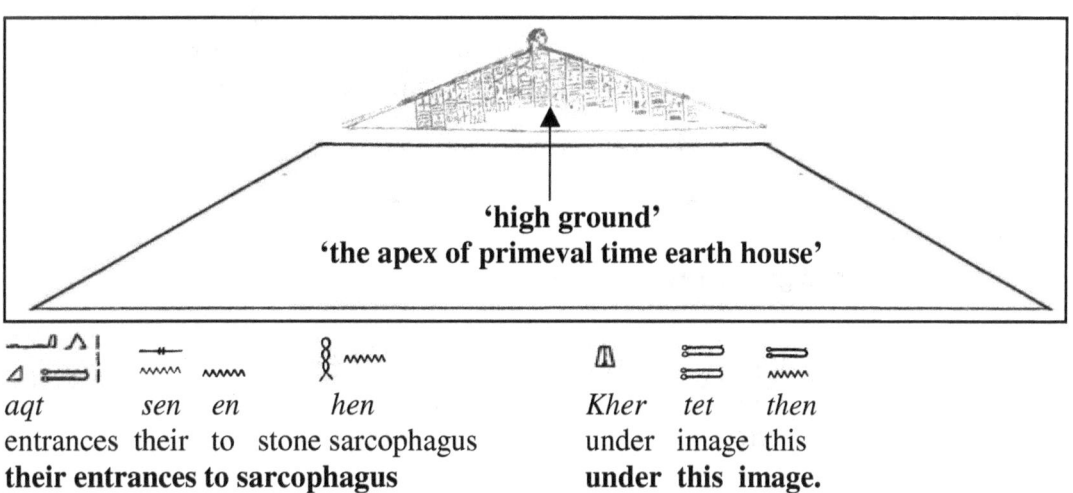

'high ground'
'the apex of primeval time earth house'

aqt   sen   en   hen   Kher   tet   then
entrances their to   stone sarcophagus   under image this
their entrances to sarcophagus   under this image.

---

[353] Budge, EHD, A List of Hieroglyphic Characters, page cxiii, Number 30,31,32; *up*: crown of the head, apex. Also see Budge, EHD, 163A, *upt*: the crown of the head, the top of the head

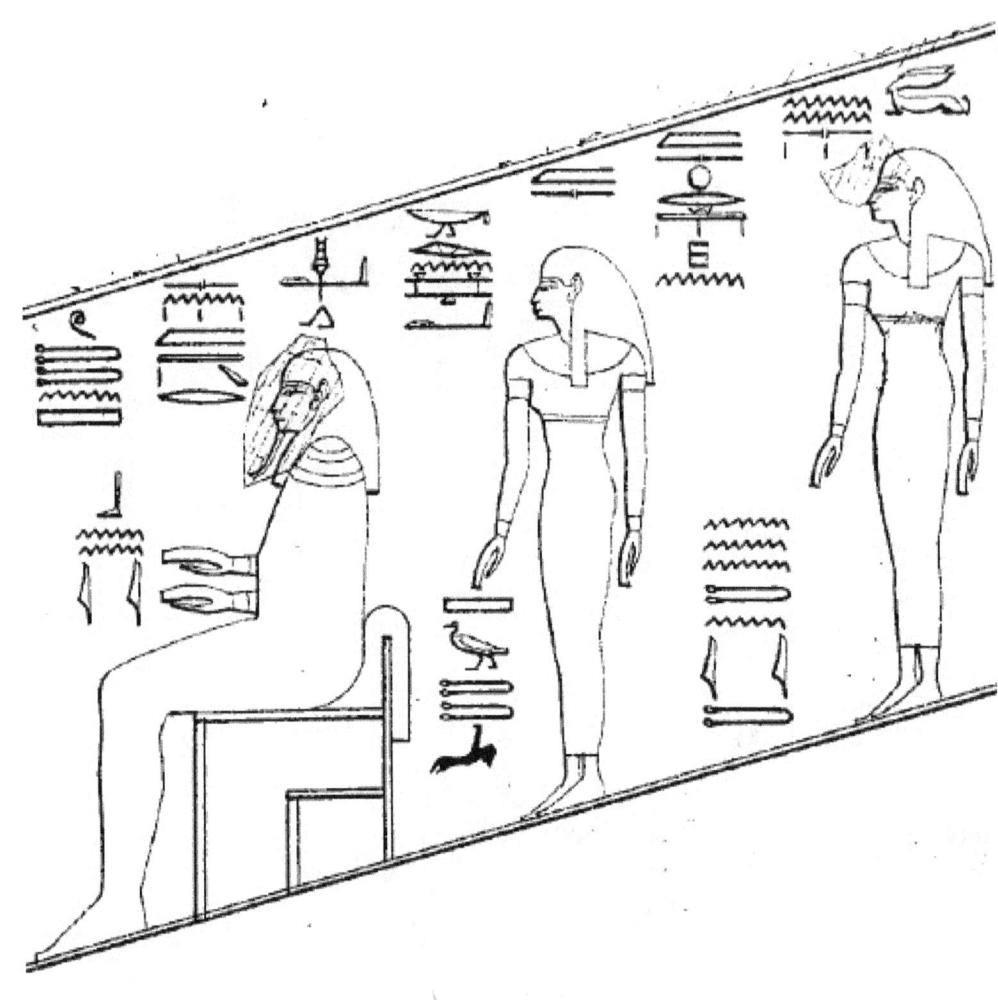

Unn sen em skher pen em seshem maat en uat aha sen em ta
are they in images this to guide something seen in path stand they near earth
They are in images, this to guide, seen in the path they stand near the earth

ru tet nesh
go away image hover over
the image hovers over and goes away.

| *Beni*[354] | *shatt*[355] | *Muthenith*[356] |
| a god | secret | a goddess |

---

[354] Budge, EHD, 217A, *beni*: a phallic god

[355] Budge, EHD, 722A, *shat*i: ⌇ \\ = ⌇ | , *sheta*

[356] Budge, EHD, 296A, *Muthenith*

Lower Register – Part 4

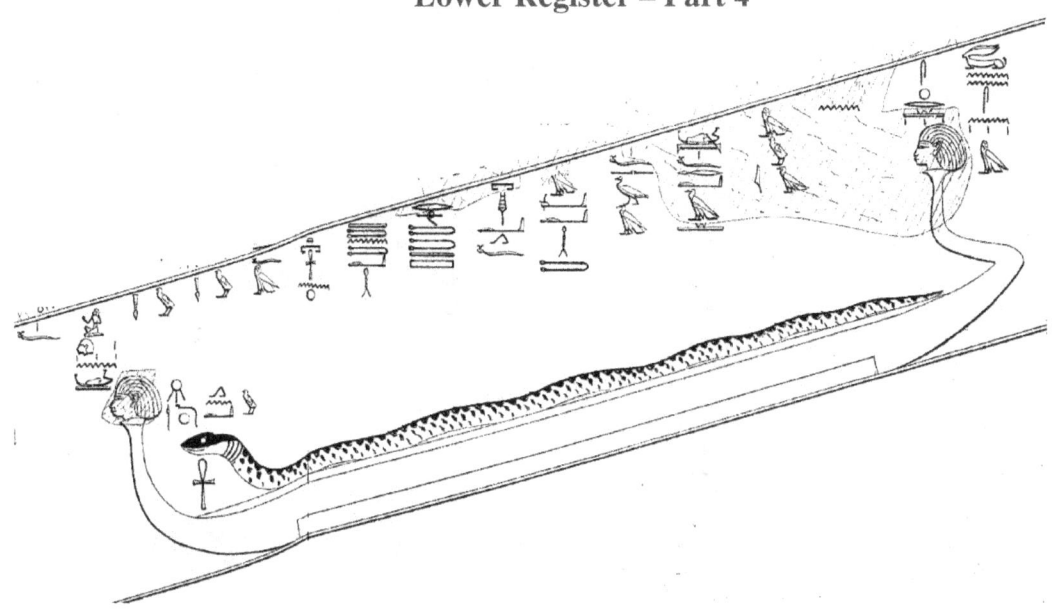

unn	sen	em	skher	en	em	uaa	ef	aa
are	they	in	images	of	with	ship	his	great

They are in images of, with his great ship

ef	sa	aht
he	guard	chamber

he guards the chamber,

ef	restau	tet	ta	shetat	neth	aht
his	entrance to the corridors	image	earth	hidden	this	chamber

his entrance to the corridors image, this hidden earth chamber.

ankh	ef	em	kheru	kheru	sa,
live	his	upon	word	word	I

I live upon his words.

tepi	en	uaa	ef	hetcht	ai	en	au
beginnings	of	boat	his	bright and shining	to come	to	travel

The beginnings of his boat, bright and shining to come, to travel.

DISCUSSION OF THE FIFTH DIVISION OF AM TUAT

In the tomb of Seti I, the illustrations of the Fourth and Fifth divisions are on opposite walls of the descending corridor.

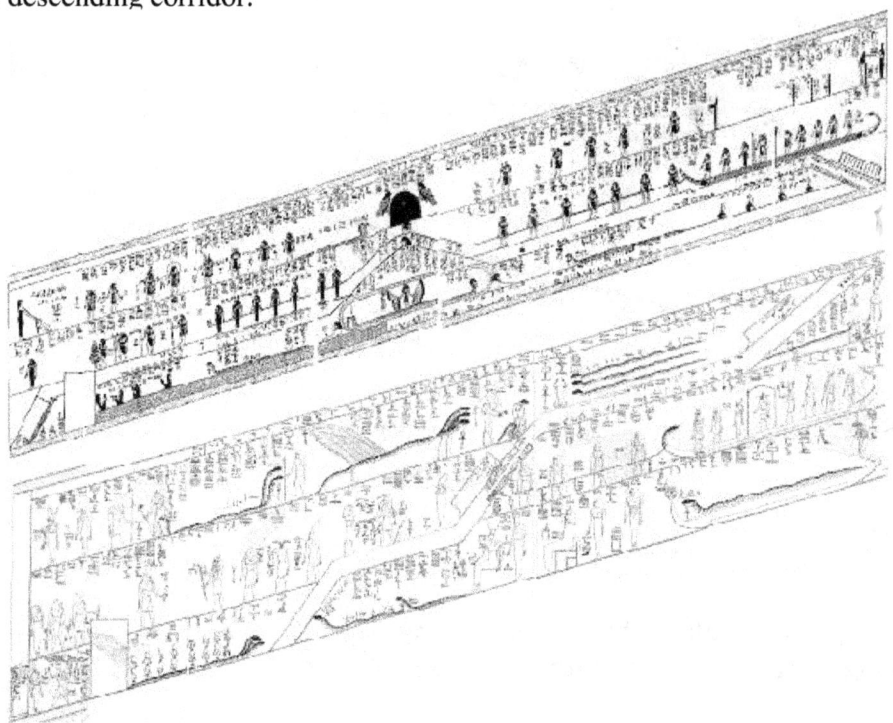

However they are intended to convey the idea of one continuous design, and where the Fourth division ends, the Fifth division begins.

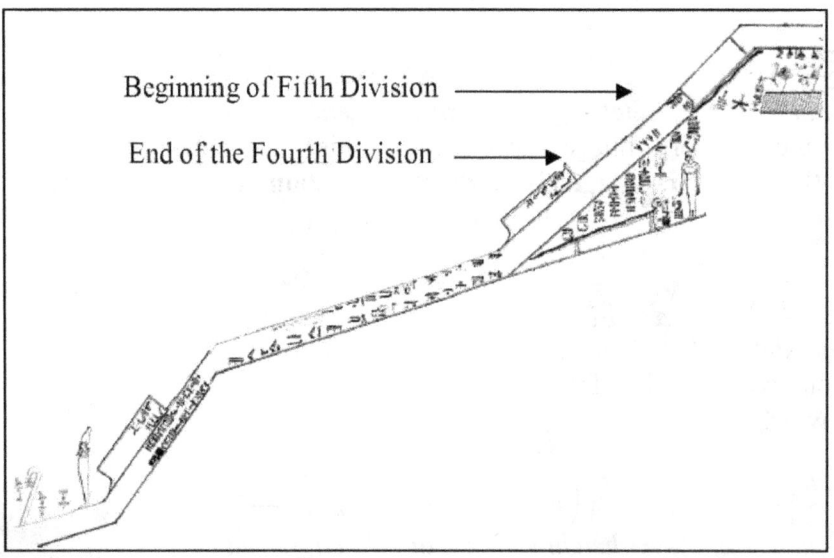

The lower horizontal arrow points to the end of the fourth division. The upper horizontal arrow points to the beginning of the fifth division and a walled-shut door.

The texts tell us that this image is to be spread out.

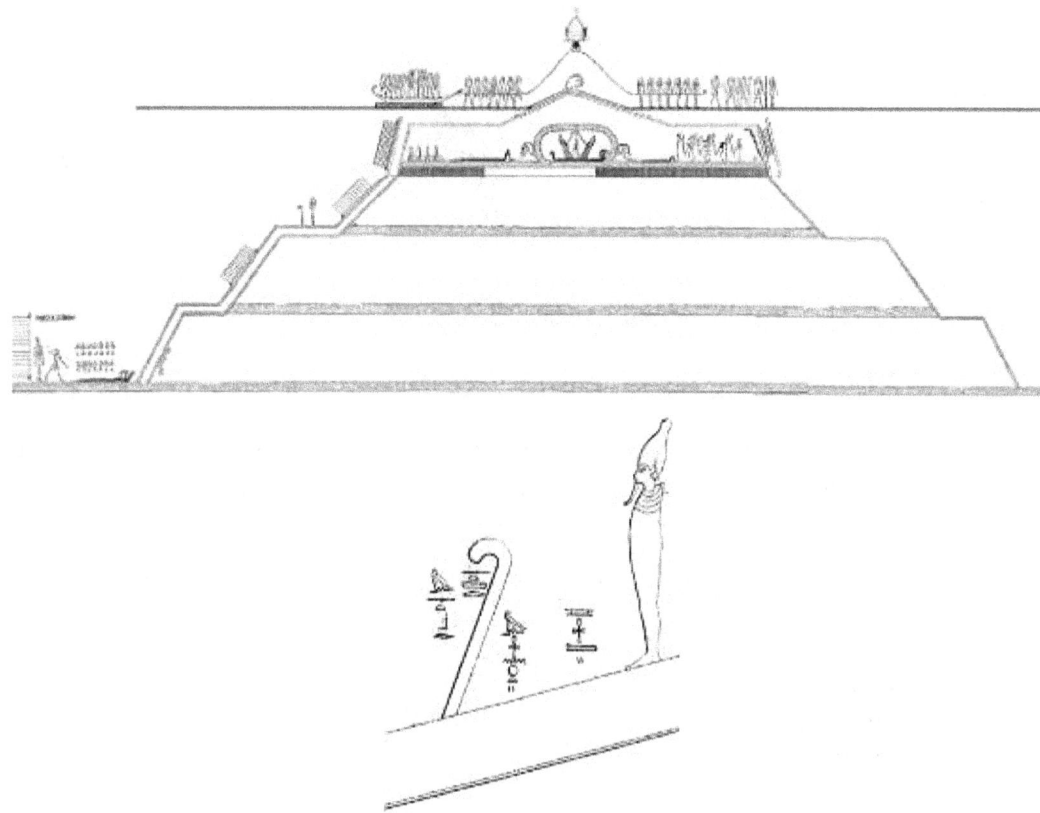

Traveling upward in the canal, toward the end of the Fourth Division, in front of the mummy of Osiris is written:

em	set	Asar	set	sher[357]	em	ankhti[358]
to	place	Osiris	place	passage walled up	at	leaves of a door

To the place of Osiris, the place the passage is walled up at the leaves of a door,

m[359]	ankhti
canal	living one

the canal of the living one.

---

[357] Budge, EHD, 750A, *sher*: to stop up, to block, to wall up, to close to obstruct the passage.

[358] Budge, EHD, 126A, *ankhti*: the two ears, i.e. leaves of a door

[359] Budge, EHD, Vol I, A List of Hieroglyphic Characters, cxxvi, *m*: canal, any collection of water

The Fifth Division Begins with a Sealed Door

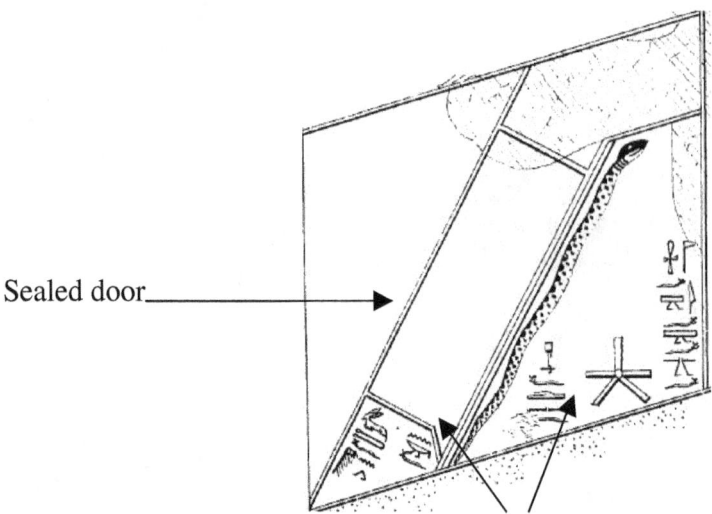

The serpent and the star in this image represent the constellation Serpens and the bright star Vega on the west side of the sky as part of the stellar scene over giza on September 21, 10390 BC.

Written below the *blocked or walled up* door in the canal:

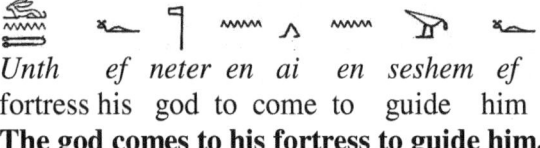

Unth — ef — neter — en — ai — en — seshem — ef
fortress — his — god — to — come — to — guide — him

The god comes to his fortress to guide him.

Written below the serpent:

uba — ef tes
to open, make a way or passage — he self

To open, to make a way or passage himself.

written near the star:

Neter ankh — Af[360] — shem — ef — shem — sebi — ef
God living — a serpent hostile to Ra — to travel — he — goes — to lead — him

The living serpent god travels--he goes to lead him.

The use of the word fortress is of interest when one considers information about the death and burial of Osiris, from the Shabaka Stone.[361]

---

[360] Budge, EHD, 43B, *Af*:

[361] "ANCIENT EGYPT : The Memphis Theology of the Shabaka Stone." *ANCIENT EGYPT : The Memphis Theology of the Shabaka Stone*. N.p., n.d. Web. 13 Sept. 2014. <http://www.maat.sofiatopia.org/memphis.htm>. #41.

The Shabaka Stone

The text of the cosmogony from Memphis is found on a rectangular slab of black granite, preserved in the British Museum and commonly called the Memphite Theology. The text includes the division of the kingdom between Horus and Seth, the slaying of Osiris (father of Horus and son of Geb) by Seth, the rescue of the body of Osiris from the Nile at Memphis, and the burial of the body of Osiris, beginning with column 8:

(8) And Geb made Horus King of Lower Egypt in the land of Lower Egypt, at the place where his father was drowned (9) which is the "Division-of-the-Two-Lands" (probably near Memphis).
(11a) Geb's words to Horus: "Go to the place in which your father was drowned."
(11b) Horus: Lower Egypt.
(17c) --- the burial of Osiris in the House of Sokar.

The story of what happen when Osiris died:
(18c) --- Isis and Nephthys without delay,
(19) for Osiris had drowned in his water. Isis [and Nephthys] looked out --- his drowning.
(20a) Horus speaks to Isis and Nephthys: "Hurry, grasp him ---."
(21a) Isis and Nephthys speak to Osiris: "We come, we take you ---."
(20b) --- and brought him to
(21b) --- the earth
(22) at the royal fortress, to the North of ---.

The Great Throne (Memphis) that gives joy to the heart of the gods in the House of Ptah is the granary of Tenen, the mistress of all life, through which the sustenance of the Two Lands is provided, (62) owing to the fact that Osiris was drowned in his water. Isis and Nephthys looked out, beheld him, and attended to him. Horus quickly commanded Isis and Nephthys to grasp Osiris and prevent his drowning. [*i.e., submerging*] (63) They heeded in time and brought him to land. He entered the secret portals in the glory of the Lords of Eternity, in the steps of him who rises in the horizon, on the ways of Re at the Great Throne. (64) He entered the palace and joined the gods of Tenen Ptah, Lord of Years. Thus Osiris came into the earth at the Royal Fortress, to the North of this land to which he had come. His son Horus arose as King of Upper Egypt, arose as King of Lower Egypt, in the embrace of his father Osiris and of the gods in front of him and behind him.

In the Osiris myth, the dead body of Osiris was in Nun, the great celestial waters, in which his grave was.[362]

---

[362] Reymond, *Mythical Origin of the Egyptian Temple*, page 108-109.

The throne of Osiris elevated into Nun atop a stepped megalithic stone pyramid

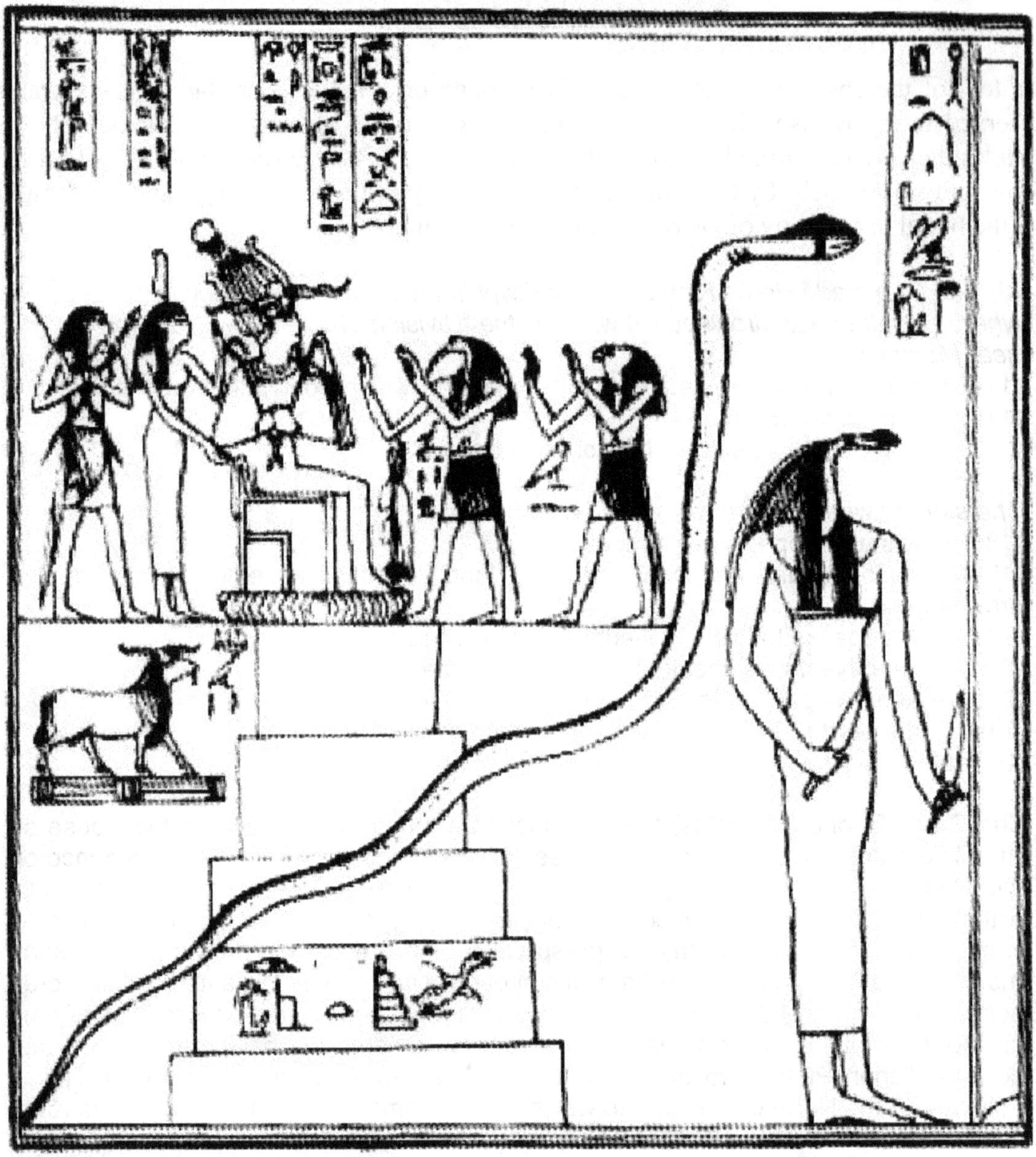

The hieroglyphic inscription on the stone block reads: "The Throne of Osiris"

The Symbology of the Fifth Divison

You've probably heard the phrase "A picture speaks a thousand words." This has never been truer than in the artwork of the ancient Egyptians. The picture below, from the tomb of Seti I, is a perfect example.

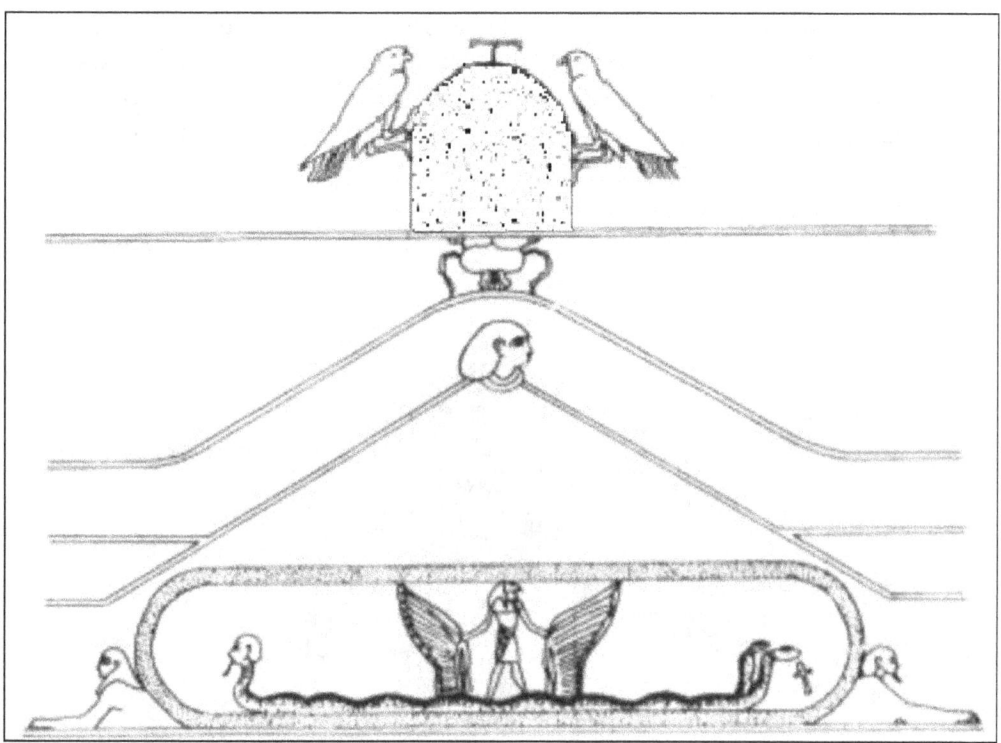

The Explanation of this Illustration

The symbol at the top of the dome is an Egyptian hieroglyph that means 'night.'

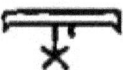

The domed shaped object represents a meridian. It is filled with stars.

The two birds represent the place where two meridians meet over one point.

Meridians

Meridians are imaginary lines in the sky. A meridian is closely tied to the idea of time and space.

You can trace out the meridian yourself by pointing your arm north. If you swing your arm up directly over your head and down again to the south, this marks a line dividing the sky into eastern and western halves. Facing south, everything to the left of the line is rising; everything to the right is setting. The meridian is different from celestial markers like the ecliptic because it is completely local, and varies from one observer to another. Only observers standing at exactly the same longitude will mark out the same meridian.

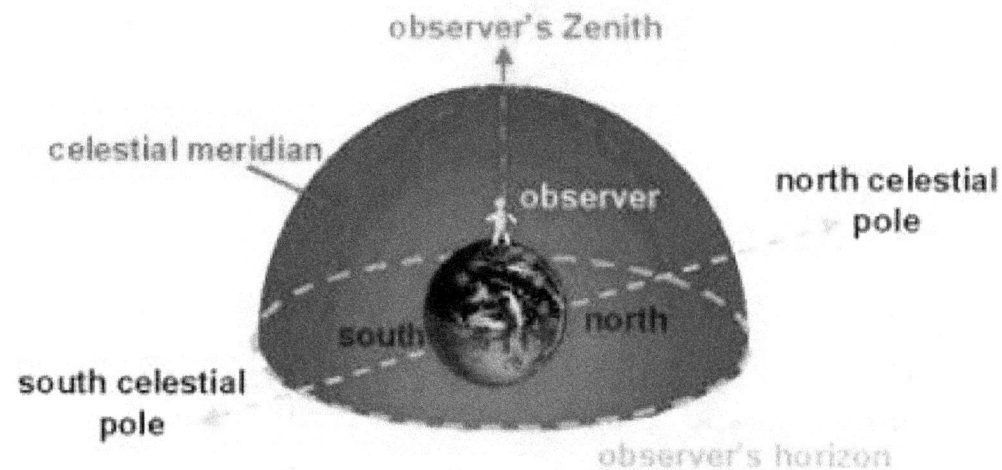

[363]

---

[363] http://astronomy.swin.edu.au/cosmos/Z/Zenith

The place where two meridians meet marks a specific place. The ancient Egyptians imagined that lines of the meridian were held in place by the power of the god Kheper, the great creative power of the universe, who is represented by the beetle.

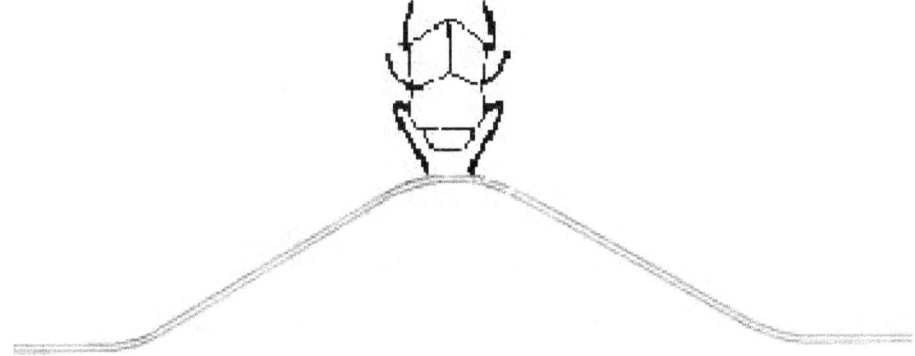

Egyptian hieroglyph for the word "top" is a head.

Below, the beetle Kheper (partially concealed behind the dome) holds the **meridian** above the **top** of a pyramid.

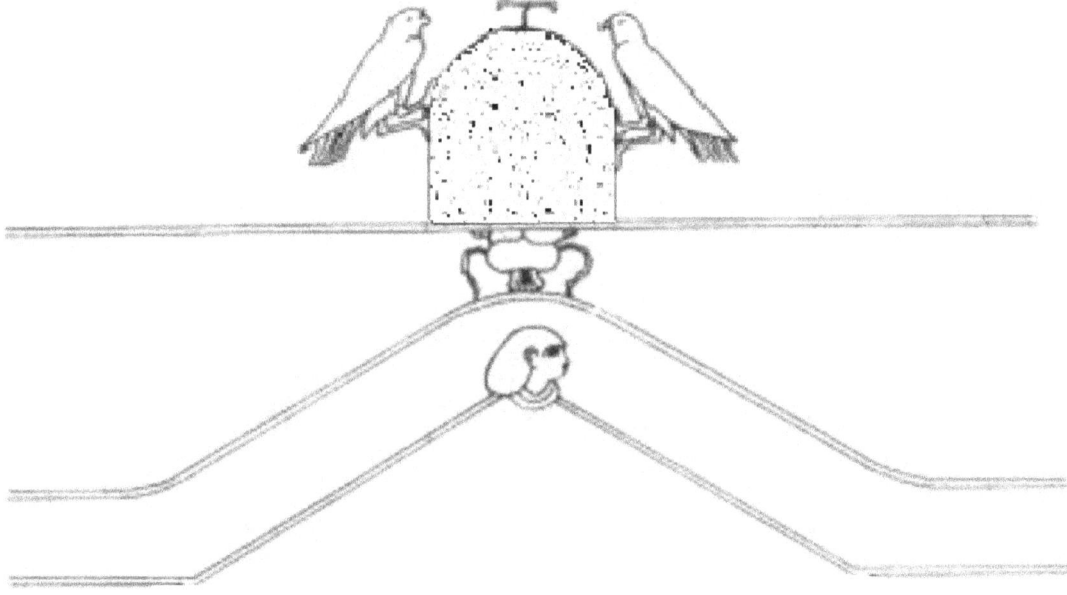

The Pyramid is Aligned with Specific Star Constellations

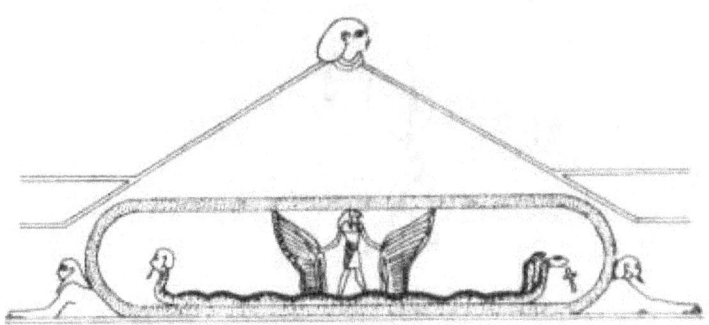

The oval is the Egyptian hieroglyph ⬭ '*horizon*.' At the center is a multi-headed winged serpent with the head of a god at its tail. This is a drawing of the constellation Hydra at a time when the planet Venus was behind it.

Below is a stellar view of the Constellation Hydra with the planet Venus behind it.

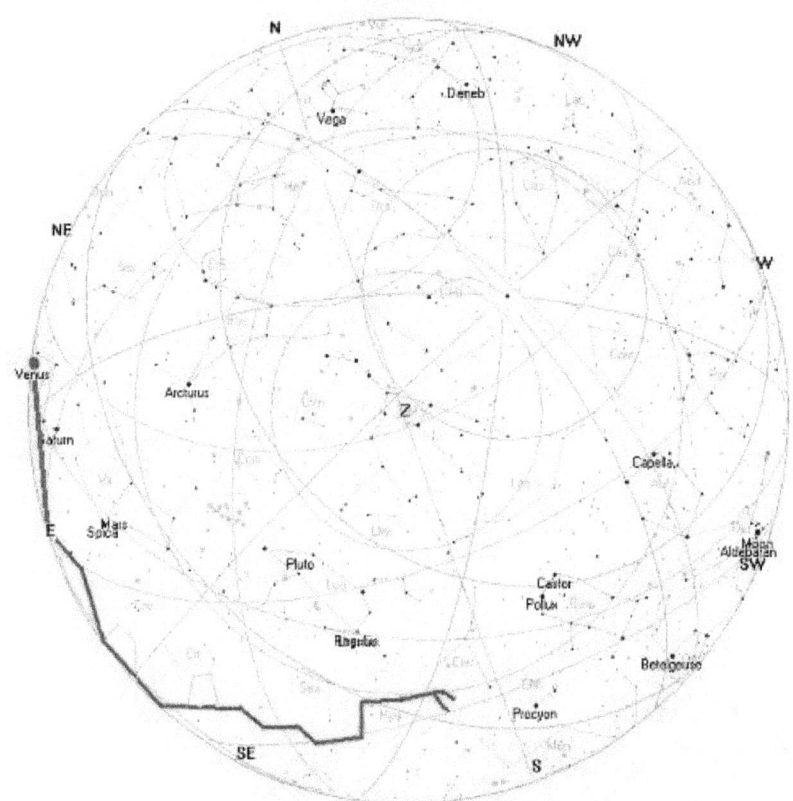

The section below is an illustration of two lion god constellations, one at the East and one at the west of the horizon.

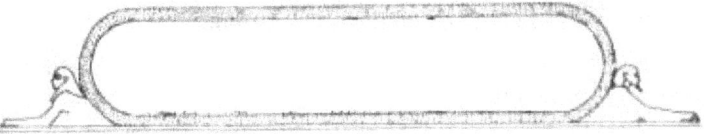

Below is the sky image they record.

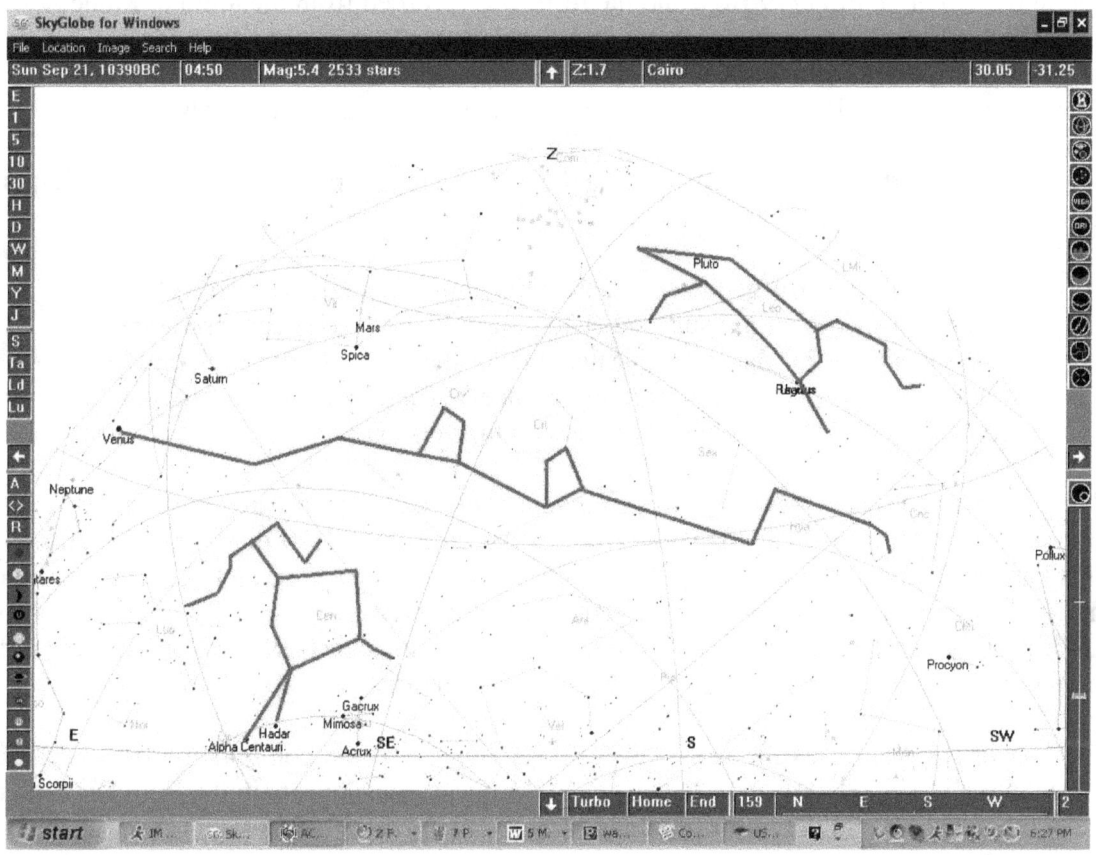

Taking all the above information together, the tomb drawing is pointing to a specific place, date and time – that is Sunday, September 21, 10390 BC at 4:50 a.m. The place is Giza, Egypt.

Seker and the Trapezoidal Mound

The ancient Egyptian book of Am Tuat is an ancient sacred text, recorded in the tombs of several great pharaohs from Egypt's distant past. Fortunately, multiple copies of *Am Tuat* historically recorded from several different tombs make possible a comparative study in an effort to understand its original meaning.

In this instance, the first record we have of *Am Tuat* comes from the tomb of Tuthmosis III (1425 BC), the second comes from the tomb of his son, Amenhotep II (1353 BC), the third from the tomb of Seti I (1279 BC), and the forth was recorded from the tomb of Ramesses VI (1137 BC). This allows a study of the same ancient book, transcribed by several different scribes, over several generations. Errors in copying, variations in spelling, and other interesting idiosyncrasies can help teach us about the language and the beliefs.

The story told by the *Am Tuat*, representing the movement and positions of the constellations at night, goes something like this:

> At nightfall, the two goddesses of truth (Gemini constellation) go in front of the boat of the nocturnal sun god (Leo constellation). The goddesses are the first to appear in the sky. After them, the god of evil (Apep/Hydra constellation) begins to make an appearance. (The book of Am Tuat tells us that he appears at precisely 120 degrees on the horizon.)

Using the Skyglobe star mapping software, we can precisely reconstruct that time, when the first star of Hydra appears at (or very close to) the position of 120 degrees on the horizon. This happens on September 21, 10,390 BC. On that date, Hydra appears to come from out of the earth as it enters the sky from the horizon, as described in *Am Tuat*. By 2:30 AM, Hydra has moved above the horizon and seemingly taken flight, hence illustrations of a winged serpent in the texts. Then comes the appearance of Centaurus (the second lion god).

The text of *Am Tuat* uses the word "Seker" in reference to the combination of these three constellations - Leo, Hydra, and Centaurus. Their illustration appears in the Fifth Division of the book of Am Tuat in the following images.

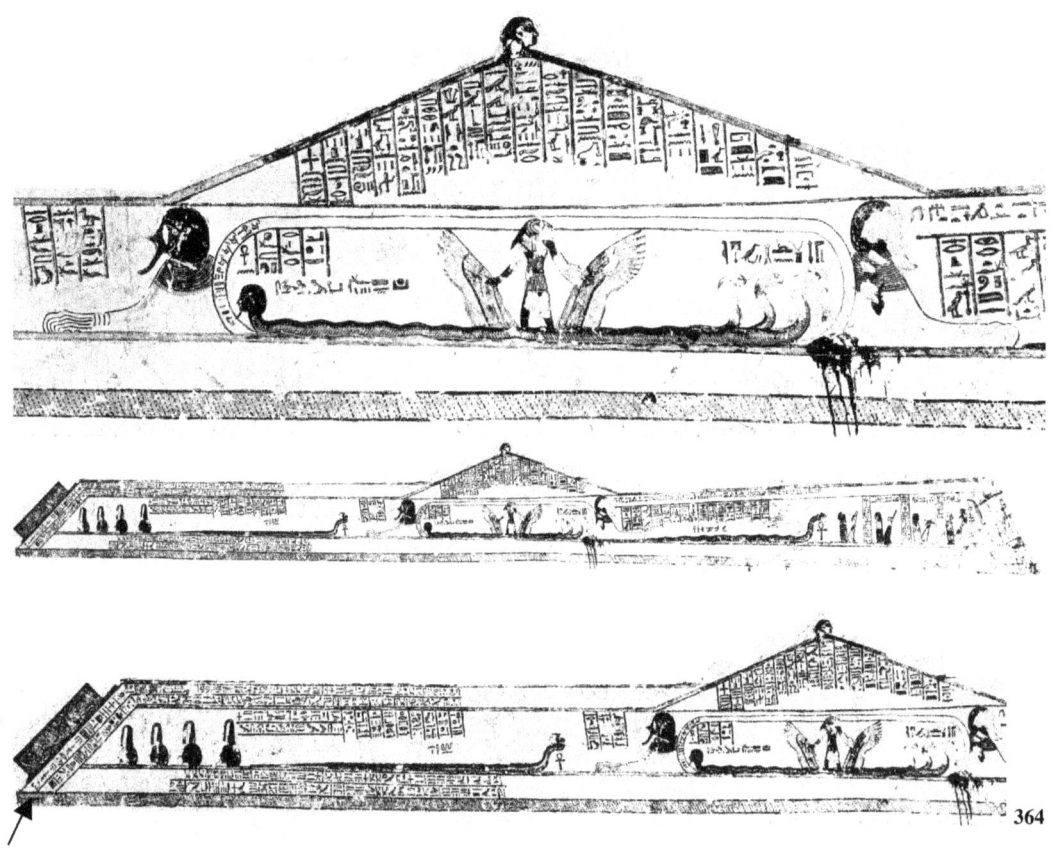

This passage with an open door is not inside the pyramid. It is a path outside the pyramid. It represents the path in the sky traversed by the constellation Hydra (Apep) to its highest position over the top of the mound to which was added an apex that completed the form of the pyramid.

The constellations of the two lions and the serpent are positioned together above a trapezoidal mound in the *Am Tuat*, with an image of a pyramid above them. The flying Hydra/Apep serpent is within an oval representative of the horizon, with the lion constellations positioned one on the east and one on the west of the horizon. The constellations were in this position around 4:40 AM on September 21, 10,390 BC.

---

[364] Piankoff, *The Tomb of Ramesses VI*

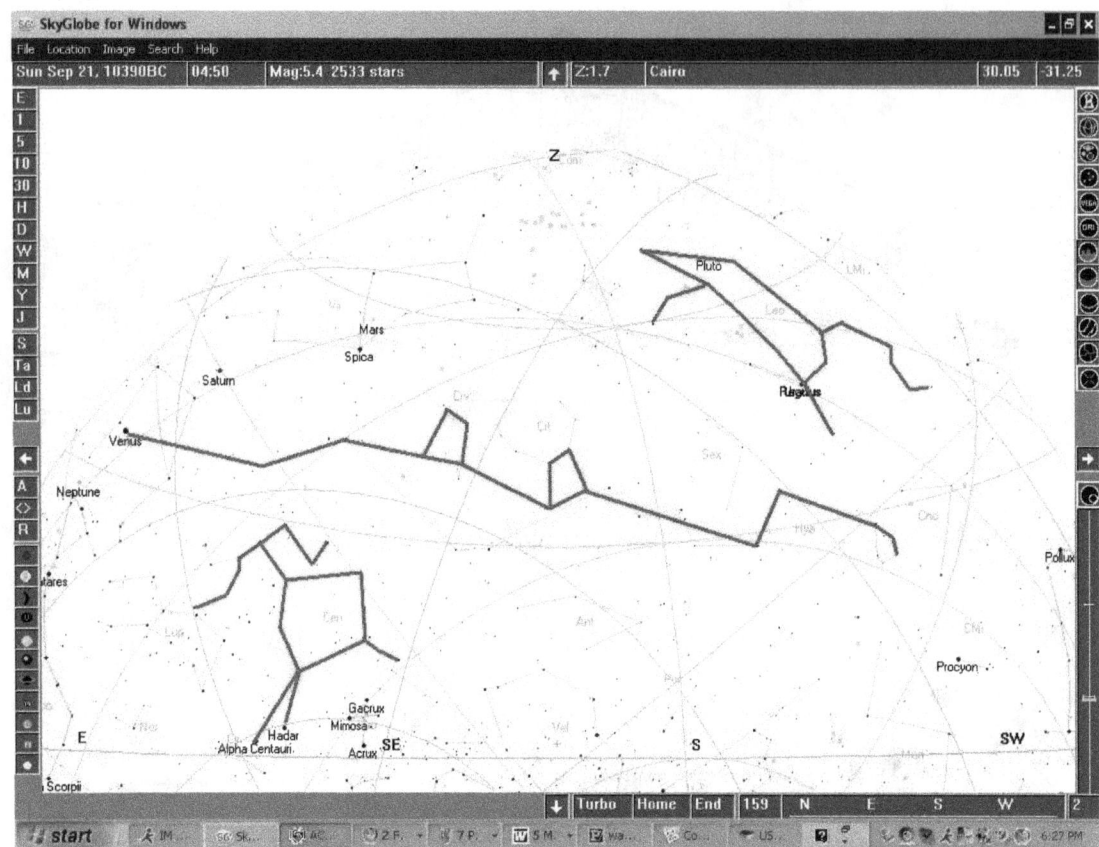

Image from Skyglobe for Windows

Text inside the Fifth Division, across the uppermost top near the doorway, explains that Seker is above the place of the throne of the earth (arura). It also explains that the god of evil (Apep) does not come from a hole in the ground.

The text inside the Fourth division explains that the guide (Apep, a.k.a. Menmenut) leads the way through canal (celestial water way, i.e. night time sky) outside the walls, but does not enter in. The story is of a scene that takes place in the sky on this particular date. Gemini appears first. Hydra then appears and makes its way up into the sky apparently from the earth and takes flight and hovers over the arura in-between the constellations of the lions on the east and west side of the horizon. The arura seems to refer to the size of the square flat surface of the top of the trapezoidal mound, to which later was added the apex.

Seker and the Trapezoidal Mound

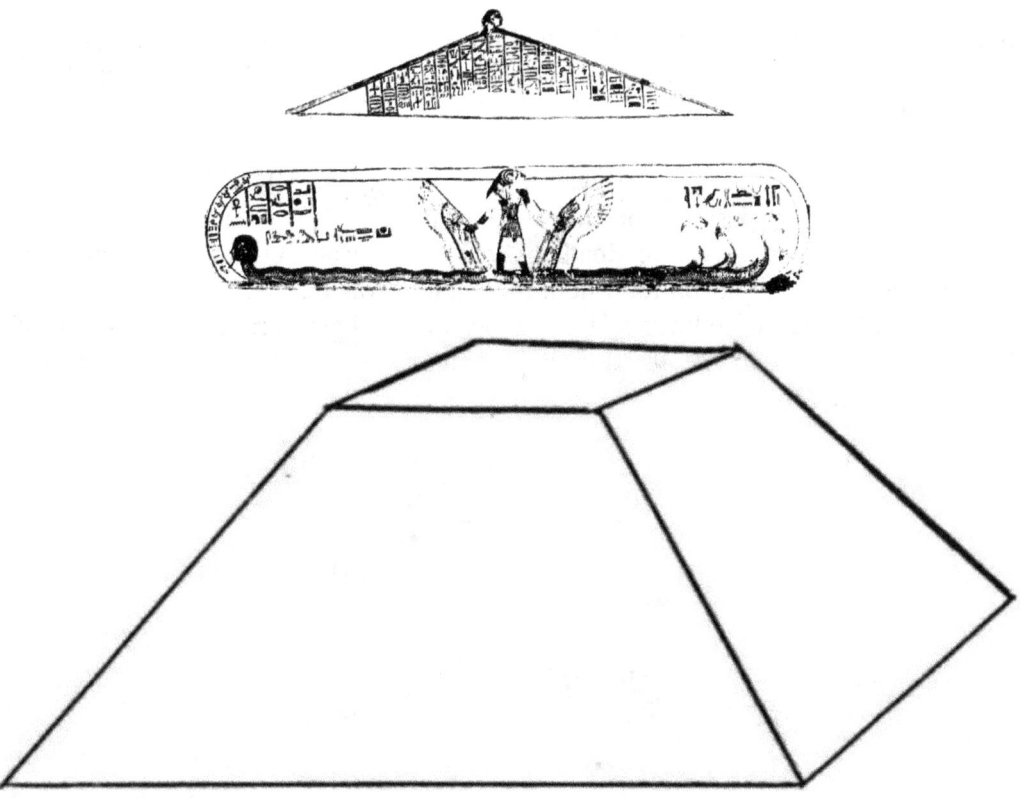

We think that originally there was a megalithic, trapezoidal mound at Giza. This was rediscovered when the first people entered the Nile Valley, after it resurfaced from a 250,000-year submergence beneath the sea.

THE EDGAR CAYCE FACTOR

Up to this point, we have focused mainly upon ancient Egyptian texts and astronomy. Now we can review the material that tells us about the location of the Hall of Records from the Cayce readings.

Edgar Cayce was a psychic and healer who lived from 1877 to 1945. He was recognized for his ability to cure health issues from a trance state. But his readings eventually became deeper when he began to give Life Readings, expounding on not only the factors affecting the current lifetime of the person for whom the reading was being given, but also the factors from previous lifetimes of relevance to that person in their current life. Many of these readings reached back into the far distant past, and many clues can be found embedded within them, with careful study.

An Illustrated Look at Some of the Highlights from the Cayce Readings

The Hall of Records lies just beyond the Sphinx. [365]

---

[365] *...lies just beyond that enigma that still is the mystery of mysteries* (Cayce reading 2404-2, text, #38)

It is along the causeway that leads from the sphinx to the pyramid, in a pyramid of its own.[366]

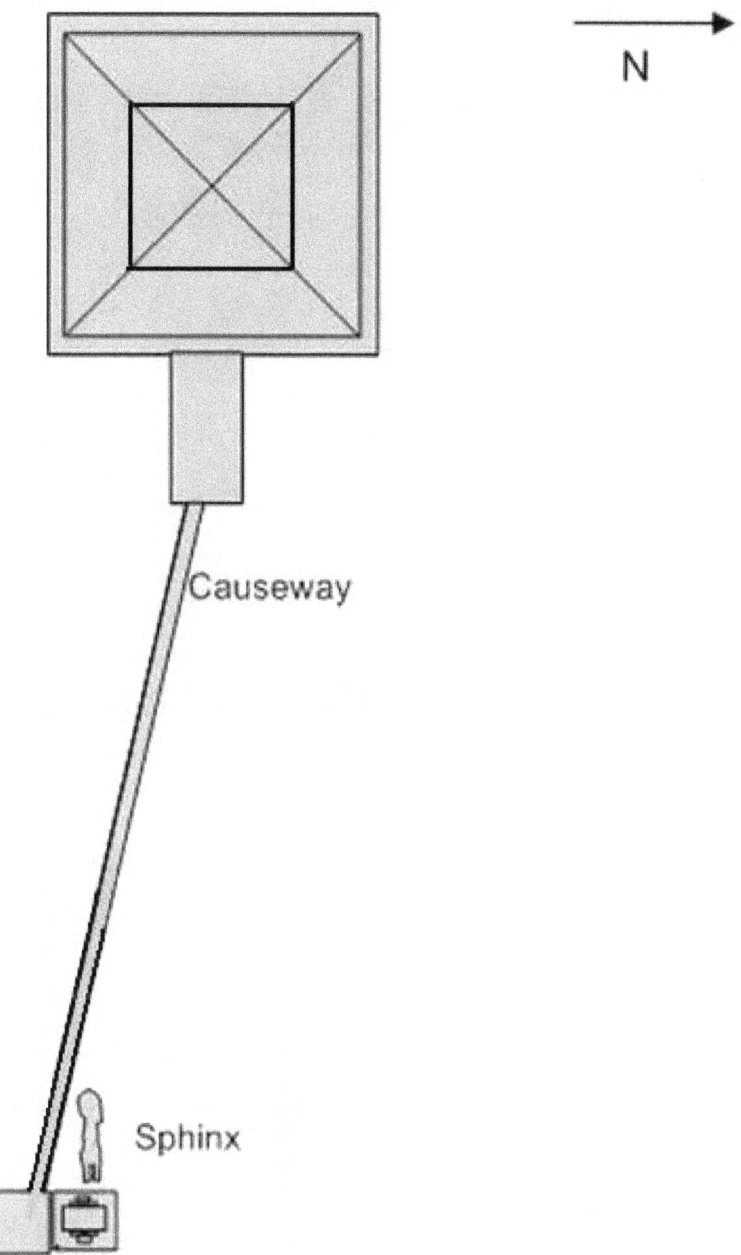

---

[366] 2012-1, 31. ...*in the place of the records that leadeth from the Sphinx to the hall of records, in the Egyptian land; 14-86-1,29. ...the records that are yet to be discovered, or yet to be had of those activities in the Atlantean land, and for the preparation of data, that as yet to be found from the chambers of the way between the Sphinx and the pyramid of records; 2329-3.36. (A) In the Tomb of Records, as indicated. For the entity's tomb then was a part of the Hall of Records, which has not yet been uncovered. It lies between - or along that entrance from the Sphinx to the temple - or the pyramid; in a pyramid, of course, of its own.*

The Hall of Records is still covered.[367]

The upper portion of the middle pyramid where the Hall of Records is located still retains its original casing stone covering.

---

[367] 2012-1, 24. *The entity was among those that aided in the actual building of some of these buildings that still remain, and in the preparation of that one yet to be uncovered - the hall of records*

It is built upon a mound [368]

This is a photo of Khafra's pyramid. It was built in two separate sections. First, the lower ¾ part was constructed. Later, the top ¼ was added. (See page 225 for more information)

---

[368] 5748-6 17.*When there was the entrance of Arart and Araaraart, they begin to build upon those mounds which were discovered through research. With the storehouse, or record house (where the records are still to be uncovered), there is a chamber or passage from the right forepaw to this entrance of the record chamber, or record tomb. This may not be entered without an understanding, for those that were left as guards may NOT be passed until after a period of their regeneration in the Mount, or the fifth root race begins.*

The position of the Hall of Records lies as the line of light falls between the paws of the Sphinx.[369]

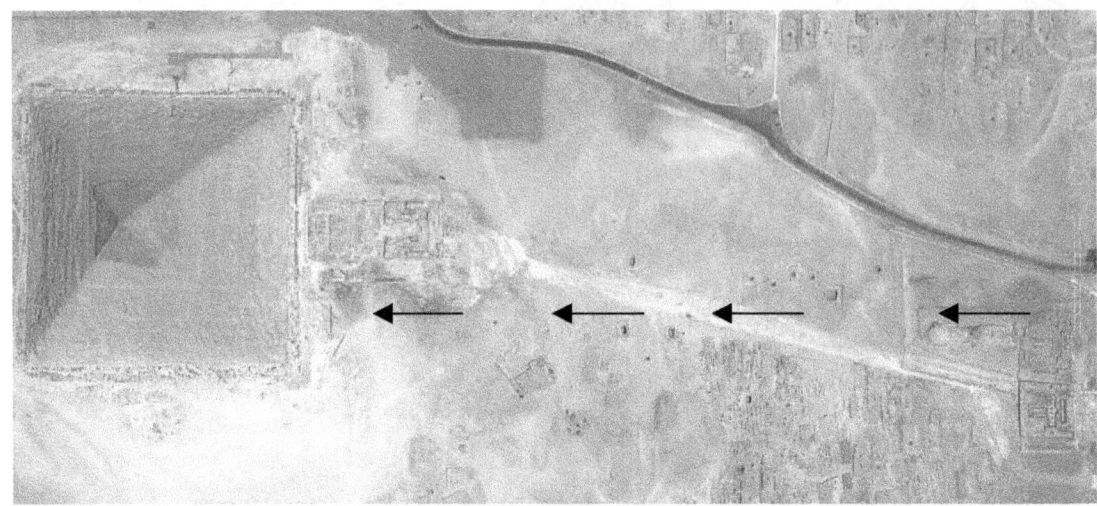

The light from the sun rising in the East would fall along a line indicated above by arrows.

---

[369] ...*this in position lies as the line of light falls between the Sphinx paws* (Cayce reading 0378-16, text, #11)

The Readings for Miss 993

When people came to Cayce for a reading they were assigned a number to protect their identity. In the life reading given for Miss 993, Cayce explained that she was alive during the time of Ra-Ta, the High Priest in Egypt, circa 10,500 BC, the time of the construction of the great pyramid at Giza. (We have underlined phrases for emphasis in the reading below.)

> 19. *In the one before this we find in that land where divisions arose, the land now known as Egypt.* The entity then among those of the household of the king, and an attendant with the priest in the temple that was called beautiful; coming under the influence of that priest, losing through the losing of self in that influence, gaining in gaining the knowledge of that being taught when the priest was returned to a partial power in the period. Then in the name Iskxe. In this experience the entity gained much in earth's forces, gained much in mental application, and this again brings much in the present experience of the entity.
>
> 20. In the one before this we find in that land known as the land of Og, now known as that of the American plateaus, or in north portion of now New Mexico, and such. The entity then among the peoples who first gave to those peoples the home and home's influence, making for that about which peoples came as those that would gain by the consolidation of strength; not in physical but in mental abilities. Then in the name Uzld. In THIS period the entity gained much, gaining much of the knowledge of the metals and the minerals of the earth and the usages same could be put for man's own use. In the one who brought to the entity this experience may the entity gain much in the present experience, and the entity will meet this entity on the 17th day of August 1929, at HOME. [GD's note: At the time we thought this might refer to Mr. [195].]

This reading goes on to explain that long before the great pyramid was created, the first of the pyramids was built.

> 21. In the one before this we find again in that land now known as Egypt. *The entity then among those that set up the first of the pyramids* that became more and more the monuments of endeavors and accomplishments of man. The entity then in the name Oual. In THIS experience the entity gained and lost. Gained through that given. Lost through that as came from aggrandizement of selfish motives.

When was civilization in this part of Egypt?

From Cayce reading 0341-009, TEXT:

> 4. As to that accomplished, we find this in one of the highest civilizations of this country in its present position, for we find this same country had been

submerged for nearly a quarter of a million years since the civilization had been in this portion of country,

So the first pyramid was submerged for nearly a quarter of a million years before the apex was added to the top.

From Cayce reading 5750-1 Page 4:
> *23. (Q) In which pyramid or temple are the records mentioned in the readings given through this channel on Atlantis, in April, 1932? [[364] series]*
>
> *(A) As given, that temple was destroyed at the time there was the last destruction in Atlantis.*
>
> *Yet, as time draws nigh when changes are to come about, there may be the opening of those <u>three places where the records are one</u>, to those that are the initiates in the knowledge of the One God:*
>
> *The temple by Iltar will then rise again. Also there will be the opening of the temple or hall of records in Egypt, and those records that were put into the heart of the Atlantean land may also be found there - that have been kept, for those that are of that group.*

There are three ingredients required to locate the Hall of Records:

1. The ancient Egyptian texts
2. Astronomy
3. The Edgar Cayce readings

It requires a study of all three to have all of the pieces to solve this mystery.

The RECORDS are ONE.

The Location of the Tomb of Osiris

Here, we bring together the ancient texts, the Edgar Cayce readings, and astronomy, to paint a compelling picture of exactly where the Tomb of Osiris may be found.

Ancient Texts

We begin by looking at lines 45 and 46 of text from the tomb of Amenhotep II as recorded in *Les Textes Des Tombes De Thouthmosis III et D'Amenhophis II*, recorded by Paul Bucher and published in 1932.

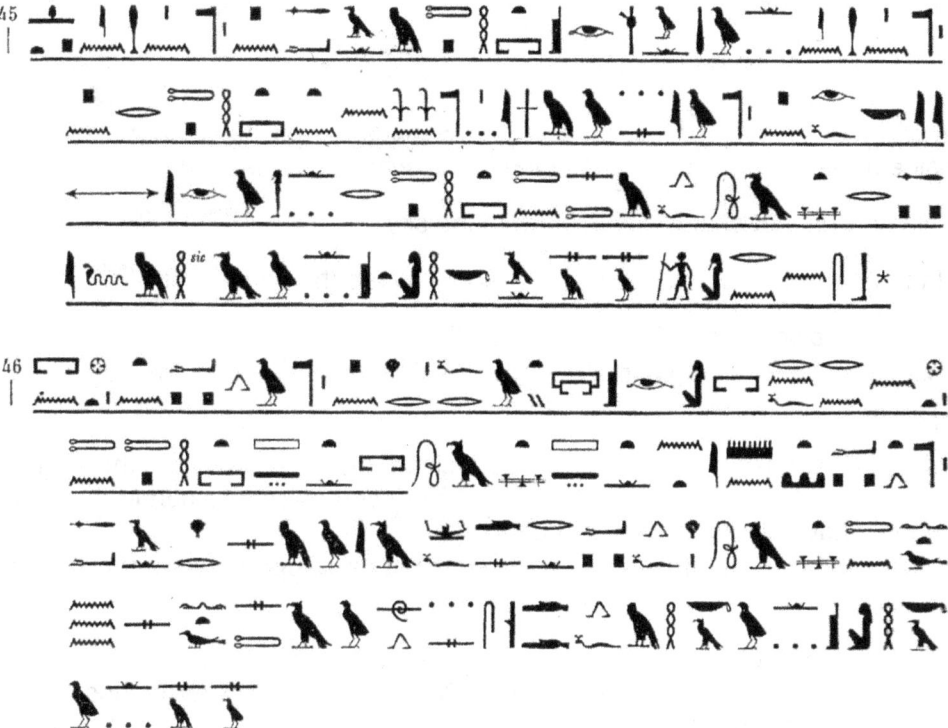

The following text is a translation of the underlined hieroglyphs above. (Bucher used the underline to indicate where the original hieroglyphs were written in red.)

> **Rest by the majesty of this great god in the storehouse of Osiris; Commands given by the Majesty of this god near this storehouse to these gods which are in this god. Come see his other forms near this storehouse. Turn back his way near Apep with beneficent spells, the place of god, the oldest word of power, name of the door to this sacred place that was created in primeval time. This god travels over it. Two leaves of a door, the entrance to a large building. Osiris house is the name of it, the name of the sacred place that was created in primeval time; this storehouse; secret house .**

'Apep' appears to be the name used for the constellation Hydra. It is said to be near the storehouse of Osiris. *'Other forms'* may refer to other star constellations near the house of Osiris that was created in primeval time. These ideas suggest the house of Osiris may be in a high place.

The Ancient Egyptian Coffin Texts

In support of this idea of targeting the chamber of Osiris in the northeast area of the top of the pyramid, we find the following in the Coffin texts:

1. At the stairway ... interred in it at the place where Osiris is. [370]

2. The chamber of Osiris, and those who are on (the steps of) the throne in the secret chamber. [371]

2. Lion-man of his open a path[372]

4. A path was shown ... Great One in hidden places ... yonder ... in darkness ... on his side asleep ... whose head is in the sky ... whose face is to the east. [373]

5. He sets on that seat which is north of the sky. [374]

6. In the realm of the dead you are the lion, you are the double lion.[375]

7. I will cause you to see Osiris in djedu. [376]

(It is possible to find Osiris in Djed, which is another name for the Giza necropolis.)

8. Osiris Onophris...a throne in the sky is given to you; see you are the king of the sky. A throne in the shrine is given to you. Your soul is established in djedu O god ... whom I have placed upon this great height. [377]

(Seems to refer to the throne of Osiris elevated on a high place in the sky, in the Giza necropolis.)

9. By what path did you go? ... By the great path ... which men do not know ... but upon which the foremost ones went that they might act as guides ... to the secret place of the sky. [378]

(The orbital path followed by the guides, who are star constellations, that lead to the tomb of Osiris, which is in the sky at the top of the stairs, or the pyramid.)

---

[370] R.O. Faulkner, Egyptian Coffin Text, Spell 399, vol. II
[371] R.O. Faulkner, Egyptian Coffin Text, Spell 572, vol. II
[372] R.O. Faulkner, Egyptian Coffin Text, Spell 649, vol. II
[373] R.O. Faulkner, Egyptian Coffin Text, Spell 584, vol. II
[374] R.O. Faulkner, Egyptian Coffin Text, Spell 585, vol. II
[375] R.O. Faulkner, Egyptian Coffin Text, Volume I, Page 1, Spell 1
[376] R.O. Faulkner, Egyptian Coffin Text, Volume I, Page 22, Spells 33-35:
[377] R.O. Faulkner, Egyptian Coffin Text, Volume I, Page 47 & 48., Spell 50
[378] R.O. Faulkner, Egyptian Coffin Text, Volume I, Page 110, Spell 118 cont'd

10. To know the paths to the sky. I have noticed the paths in the sky. [379]

11. Osiris ... whose place in the paths of the netherworld is hidden. [380]
(The burial place of Osiris is elevated high into the sky.)

12. Osiris...presides over the throne in the secret places of the netherworld...I am Osiris I have come to Rostau in order to know the secret of the netherworld into which Anubis is initiated; the House of the double lion; the earth-gods at the domain of Horus the elder. [381]
(The throne of Osiris is in Rostau; and Rostau is Giza. This may also be the house of the double lion.)

13. The gods who are in their primeval state ... those gods who are lords of the sky. [382]
(Stars and constellations)

14. The double lion has taken out the wig-cover for him, he has come with the word of Horus for Osiris ... wardens of the house of Osiris. [383]
(This refers to the double lions that are the wardens in the 5th Division of Am Tuat.)

15. The wardens of the mansion of Osiris rise up ... the great ones who dwell in the horizon even the wardens of *hm3tt* in the sky, who guard the roads ... I come forth to djedu and go all over his mansion ... the netherworld has been opened for me, the roads of the sky and on the earth have been opened for me. [384]
(This reveals the double lions that live in the horizon are the wardens in the mansion, or pyramid, of Osiris.)

---

[379] R.O. Faulkner, Egyptian Coffin Text, Volume I, Page 113, Spell 129
[380] R.O. Faulkner, Egyptian Coffin Text, Volume I, Page 186, Spell 237:
[381] R.O. Faulkner, Egyptian Coffin Text, Volume I, Page 189, 190, 191 Spell 241
[382] R.O. Faulkner, Egyptian Coffin Text, Volume I, Page 222, Spell 302
[383] R.O. Faulkner, Egyptian Coffin Text, Volume I, Page 231, Spell 312 cont'd
[384] R.O. Faulkner, Egyptian Coffin Text, Volume I, Page 232, Spell 312 cont'd

Edgar Cayce Readings

Edgar Cayce said the storehouse was built upon a mound. We believe that mound later became a pyramid.

Cayce Reading 5748-6, #17:

> *When there was the entrance of Araart and Araaraart[385], they began to build upon those mounds that were discovered through research. With the storehouse, or record house (where the records are still to be uncovered), there is a chamber or passage from the right forepaw to this entrance of the record chamber, or record tomb. This may not be entered without an understanding, for those that were left as guards may NOT be passed until after a period of their regeneration in the Mount, or the fifth root race begins. In the building of the pyramid...*

Even in these ancient times, archaeological research was unearthing very old monuments from an even earlier age. Upon one of these, the Tomb of Osiris (along with a storehouse of records) was constructed, high enough to appear to be among the stars to someone standing on the ground.

---

[385] Cayce gave the name Araaraart to the historical person referred to as Osiris.

Cayce said:

This entity is one that will be found in the North Corner of the Second Pyramid.[386]

"The entity, then, in the upper chamber of the northeast corner of the first pyramid builded[387], there placed by the grandson."[388]

---

[386] Khafra Pryamid

[387] This refers to the so called pyramid of Khafra, refer to page 209 with information about Miss 993.

[388] ECRS 341-8 Page 4, 17. In the one before this we find in the land of now Egyptian. Then in the second pharaoh [6/2/25 See 341-9 indicating that this particular period in Egypt was eleven thousand and sixteen (11,016) B.C.], or the ruler of that land [Ra Ta period], and the laws and the religions then just being established. The entity then assisted in giving much to these peoples. The foundation of the truth of the relations of earthly individuals with the High God of Heavens. The entity then in the name as called Araaraart. In this entity we find that the first temples of sacrifice were builded, and the offerings of blood were first made, and the monuments of the things afterward becoming a stumbling block, yet in the entity's day the means of representing to the peoples the approach to the indwelling of that not made with hands. The entity, then, in the upper chamber of the northeast corner of the first pyramid builded, there placed by the grandson, the king who afterward ascended to the throne in Egypt - Azorut. In the individuality and the personality exhibited from same in present plane, we find the desire of the study of all pertaining to laws and of reason of sacrifice, of the difference between sacrifice and mercy, and the innate force or urge to study this land and peoples

Egyptian Illustrations

The first illustration comes from the Greenfield papyrus. Written in hieroglyphs above the figure of Osiris enthroned at the top of a pyramid:

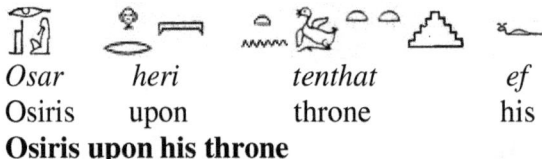

Osar	*heri*	*tenthat*	*ef*
Osiris	upon	throne	his

Osiris upon his throne

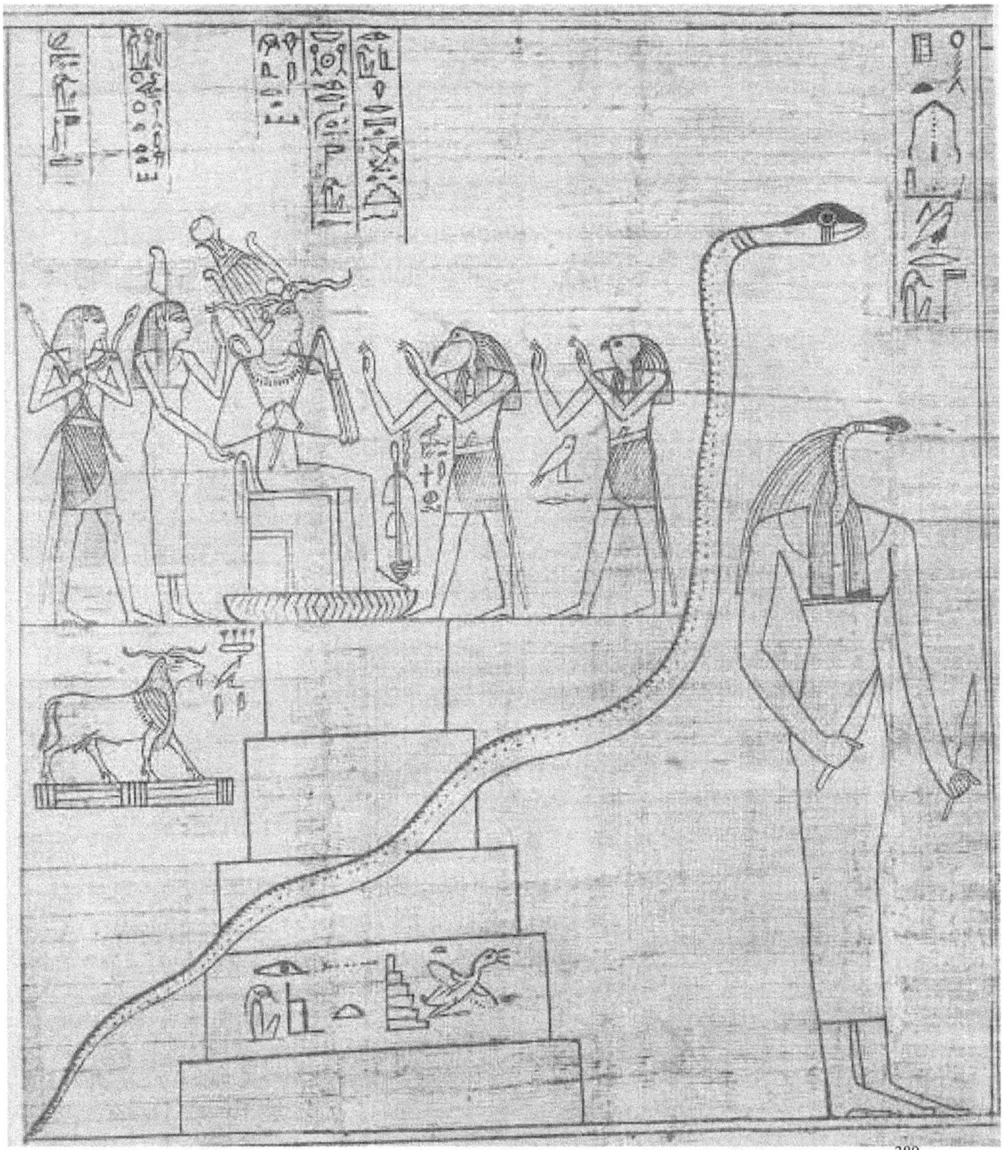

The hieroglyphic inscription on the stone block reads: "The Throne of Osiris." [389]

---

[389] Budge, *Egyptian Hieroglyphic Dictionary*, page 839B, *tentha-t*: throne

The Serpent Guardian of Osiris

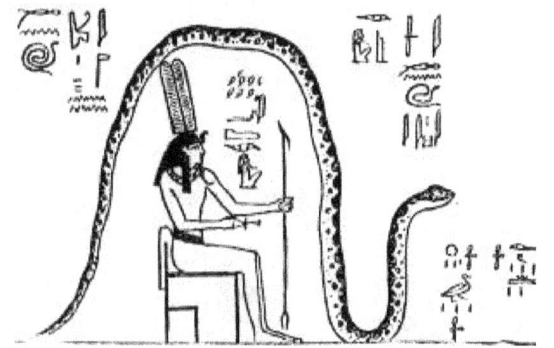

From the Seventh Division of the ancient Egyptian Book of Am Tuat [390]

Written inside the serpent:

    afi   Asar[391]
the flesh, *i.e.* the dead body   Osiris

Written behind the serpent:

an   neter   pen   en   Mehen[392]
of   god   this   in   serpent god

Written above the head of the serpent:

Asar   ami   Mehen[8]   Api
Osiris who is in   Mehen   a god in the Tuat[393]

Written in front of the serpent:

ankh-aru-tchefa [394]
serpent guardian of the body of Osiris[395].

Illustrating the body of Osiris in the embrace of the serpent god of the Tuat suggests that his body rests in a high place surrounded by the heavens.

---

[390] Budge, *Egyptian Heaven and Hell*, I, 149.

[391] Budge, EHD, 43A, *afi-Asar*

[392] Budge, EHD, 319B, *Mehen*, Tuat VII, a serpent-god who protected Afu-Ra in the Tuat.

[393] Budge, EHD, 42B, *Api[t]*

[394] Budge, EHD, 125B, *ankh-aru-tchefa*: a serpent guardian of Afu-Asar; see EHD, 43A, *Afi Asar*: the flesh, *i.e.,* dead body of Osiris

[395] See page 61 for an illustration of the protective serpent in Egyptian art.

218   FURTHER EXPLANATORY MATERIALS

The Serpent Aligned with the Apex of the Pyramid

The hieroglyphs of the serpent and the star ![glyph] are determinatives used in the an-cient Egyptian word *tchuat*: 'the period of culmination of a star.' [396] With this in mind, the following illustration may be showing the constellation of Hydra culminating above the pyramid tomb of Osiris.

Illustration found on a 21st dynasty coffin discovered in Thebes

---

[396] Budge, EHD, 904A, *tchuat*

[397] Clark, Robert Thomas Rundle. *Myth and Symbol in Ancient Egypt.* (London: Thames and Hudson, 1978) 171.

The Pyramidion of Amenhotep-Huy [398]

The scene on this ancient Egyptian artifact (the pyramidion of Amenhotep Huy) shows the mummified Osiris entombed within the upper portion of a pyramid. Accompanying the deceased Osiris are two couchant jackals and two utchats, symbolizing the solstices and the equinoxes.[399]

---

[398] Hornung. *The Quest for Immortality,* page 194.

[399] Budge. *The gods of the Egyptians*, Vol. 2, 264.

The Location of the Hall of Records

Ancient Illustration and the Edgar Cayce Readings

"This in position lies, as the sun rises from the water, the line of shadow (or light) falls between the paws of the Sphinx, that was later set as the sentinel or guard, and which may not be entered from the connecting chambers from the Sphinx's paw (right paw) until the TIME has been fulfilled when the changes must be active in this sphere of man's experience. Between, then, the Sphinx and the river."[400]

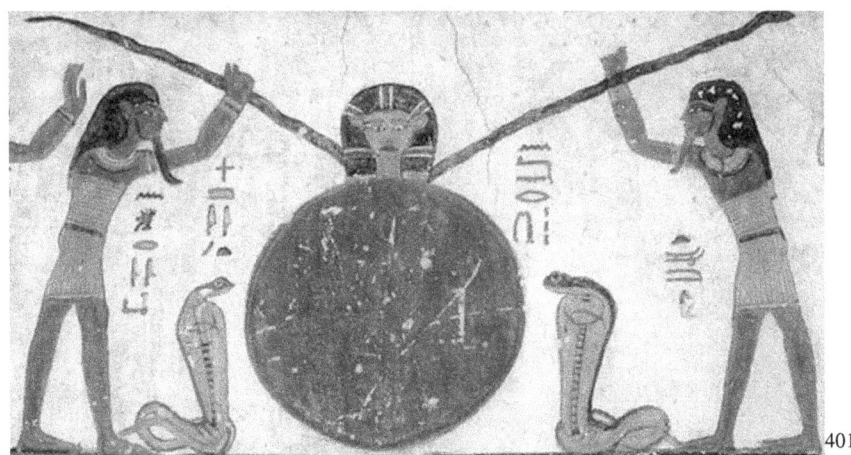

Sun rising on the summer solstice
aligned with the Sphinx from the tomb of Ramesses VI

Below shows the same alignment with a view of the pyramid of Khafra,
as seen from *between the Sphinx and the river* (Nile).

---

[400] ECRS 378-16, paragraph 11.
[401] Image from the Book of Aker in the tomb of Ramesses VI.

This image is from the tomb of Tuthmosis III. It illustrates the pyramid of Khafra with new construction at the top with a head at the apex. This head is the ancient Egyptian word *tep* or *tepi*, meaning '*top*.'

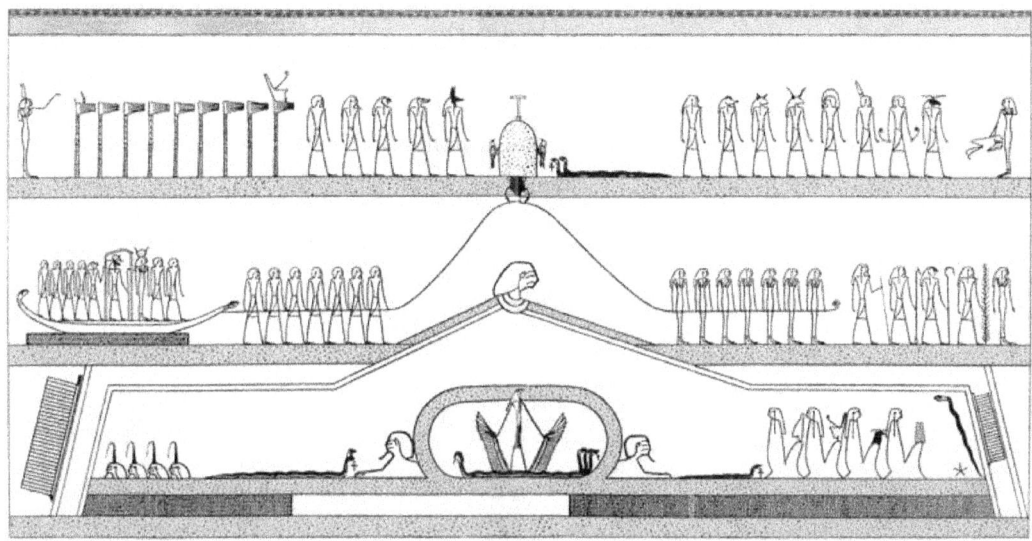

The ship being towed across the sky from East to West is a star constellation. So if East is on the left, we must be facing South. This indicates the perspective of the observer is the North side of the pyramid, looking beyond the pyramid into the sky. The dome shaped figure in the center at the top is a meridian marker.

> With the store house, or record house, (where the records are still to be uncovered), there is a chamber, or passage from the right forepaw to this entrance of the record chamber or record tomb.[402]

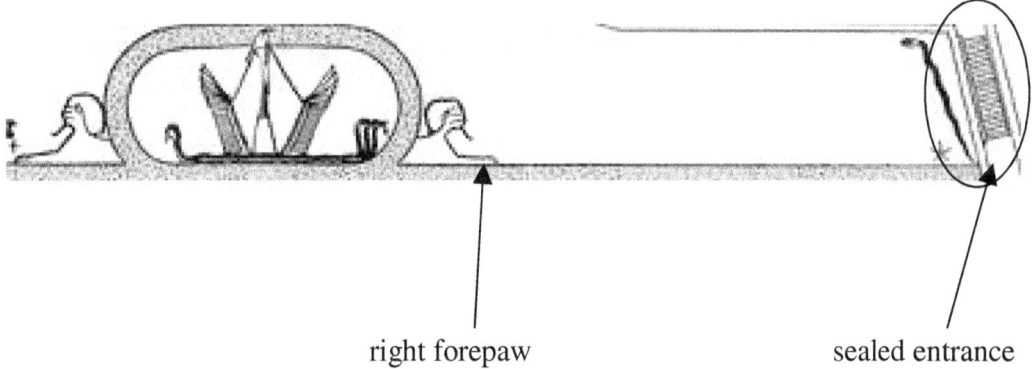

right forepaw   sealed entrance

---

[402] ECRS 5748-6, paragraph 17.

Ancient Egyptian Artistic License

We initially felt that the entrance to the Hall of Records was on the west side of the Khafra pyramid. Due to a new understanding, we have become convinced it is actually on the north side. Once again we find proof in three places: The Ancient Texts (*The book of Am Tuat, The Book of the Dead, and the Ancient Egyptian Coffin Texts*), the Cayce readings, and astronomy. The error in our original judgment was due to the fact that the ancient Egyptians drew two-dimensional images to illustrate three-dimensional space, as in the drawing below.

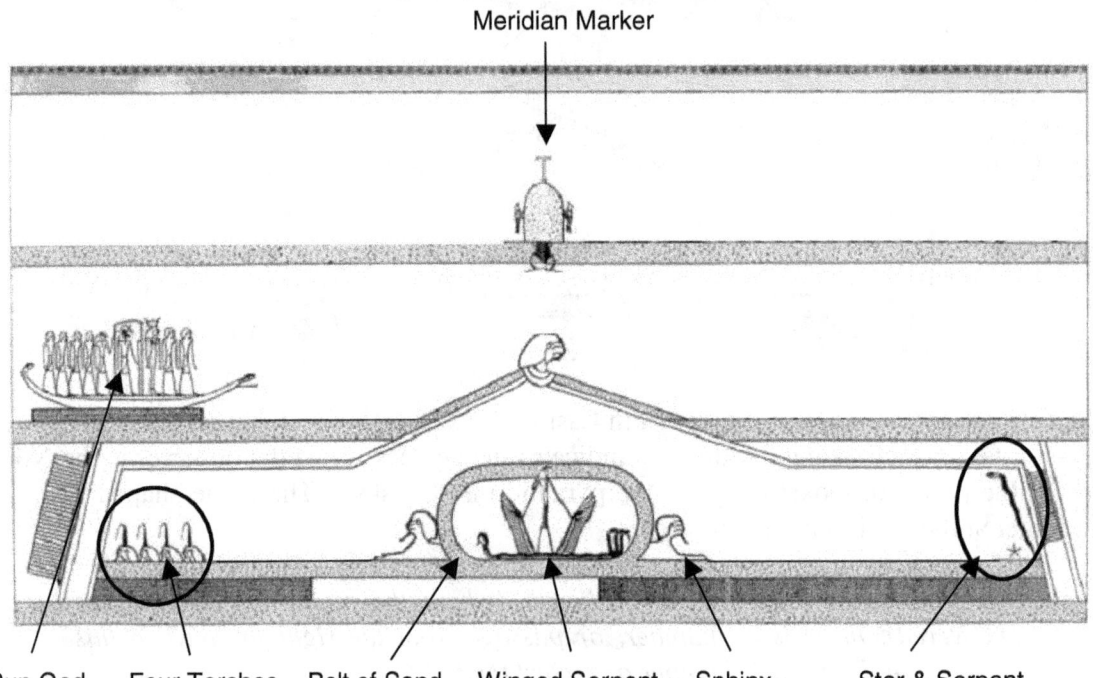

In the above drawing, the perspective shown is the southern sky, with the winged serpent (Hydra) and the Sphinx-Lion Gods in the East and the West (Centaurus and Leo). Refer to the panorama of the sky shown below for comparison.

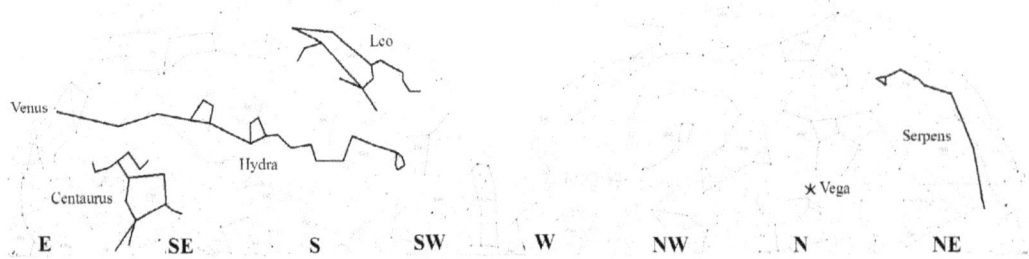

Panorama of the sky

The movement of the constellation of the Sun God of Night is from east to west along a meridian. This is indicated in the tomb image above by the meridian marker over the rope with which the Sun God is being towed.

Four torches on the left side of the tomb image were lighted for the Spirit-Soul in the tomb, as it is written in The Chapter of the Four Torches (Chapter CXXVII) in the *Book of the Dead* :

> Line 3: *"The fire cometh to thy Ka, O Osiris Khenti-Amenti."*
> Line 5: *"The fire cometh to thy Ka, O Osiris, Governor of those who are in Amenti."*
> Line 16: *"The four fires enter into thy Ka, O Osiris Khenti Amenti."*
> Line 32: *"It is an exceedingly great mystery of Amentet, and it is a type of the hidden things in the Tuat."*
> Line 47: *"I am the belt of sand round about the hidden coffer. I turn back the force of the blazing fire of the funerary mountain."*

Each of the sitting figures of the crown bearers on the right side holds one of the royal Egyptian headdresses.

Hedjet	Deshret	Shefit	Shuti
Upper Egypt	Lower Egypt	Power	Two plumes of a crown

Volume I of Budge's *Osiris and the Egyptian Resurrection* illustrates headdresses worn by Osiris, among which are those shown above. Additionally, the Seventh Division of Am Tuat illustrates Osiris wearing the Shuti[403]. All of this gives us the impression that this is the royal tomb of Osiris.

Looking toward the right side of the illustration, from the right forepaw of Leo (the Ka or double Sphinx Lion-God) we see a star before a standing serpent.

Comparing the actual position of stars and constellations in the night sky on September 21st, 10390 BC at 4:45 AM, the star Vega shines brightly (in the North) before the standing serpent image of the constellation Serpens (in the Northeast)! For this reason, we have reconsidered our former understanding, and now believe the entrance is on the north side, or the northeast corner. Our previous error was due to the position of the star and the standing serpent on the *apparent* west side of the image of the Fifth Division. What we learned by comparison with Skyglobe images of the sky at that date and time, is that the position of the star and the standing serpent were beyond the perspective of the observer facing south; so that it was necessary for the artist to record the images in this way above, although they were not in the field of view.

---

[403] See page 61 for an illustration of Osiris wearing the crown with two plumes.

Concerning the Hall of Records, the readings say:

"In the first of the pyramids built in the Valley of the Shadow, there still may be found unto this day portions of data as was preserved with the ruler, who afterward was worshiped as the representative of God made manifest in earth".[404]

Concerning the contents, the readings say:

"With the absence of the communications as is given, this was written on tables of stone and slate, with the characters of same." [407]

"(Q) Where are those records or tablets made of that Egyptian experience, which I might study?
"(A) In the Tomb of Records, as indicated. For the entity's tomb then was a part of the Hall of Records, which has not yet been uncovered ... begin with the interpreting of the tablets. For, remember there are thirty-two of these plates!" [405]

---

[404]ECRS 5748-4, paragraph 2: EC: *Yes, we have these here and the conditions surrounding same. As these were gathered in their tents and caves, each were given the portion of the fact as related to each group's conception regarding man's supremacy over the animal world, and how same was reached. As these were given, we find that each gave that conception in the way that was in relation to man's surroundings in the earth plane, so in this manner were the first laws as relating to the indwelling of the Higher Forces given to man. With the absence of the communications as is given, this was written on tables of stone and slate, with the characters of same. <u>In the first of the pyramids built in the Valley of the Shadow, there still may be found unto this day portions of data as was preserved with the ruler, who afterward was worshiped as the representative of God made manifest in earth. These will be found in the northwest corner or chamber of this mound.</u>*

[405] ECRS 2329-3, #36 (Q) Where are those records or tablets made of that Egyptian experience, which I might study?
(A) In the Tomb of Records, as indicated. For the entity's tomb then was a part of the Hall of Records, which has not yet been uncovered. It lies between - or along that entrance from the Sphinx to the temple - or the pyramid; in a pyramid, of course, of its own.
#37. (Q) Through what channels of the Association for Research & Enlightenment may the entity gain the most?
(A) As it begins it s further preparation and activity, seek through those channels for guidance - as it is felt that it is needed; or begin with the interpreting of the tablets. For, remember there are thirty-two of these plates!

CONCLUSION

The evidence from all of these sources supports the idea that the tomb of Osiris and the Hall of Records are high up, near a serpent figure in the sky, in a pyramid that was completed by building on top of a much older mound. So what we are looking for is a pyramid showing evidence of two different construction styles.

Mark Lehner, in his study of the pyramids, suggested that the bottom of the Khafra pyramid appeared to be built at one time and the top at a much later time, due to the extreme dif-ference in construction styles:

"**Only the upper quar-ter of the casing stone remains. Just beneath the lowest surviving course of casing stones, a band of regular stepped core stone is visible. The rest of the surface, down to the base, the greater part of the pyramid, consists of very rough, irregular loose stones. What is this lower band? Is it packing between the core and casing, exposed when the casing stone was torn away? That seems likely until, climbing the corners of the pyramid, one sees that this irregular masonry seems to continue for some depth into the pyramid body. The discontinuity might indicate different building styles, perhaps even a hiatus and then resumption of building."** [406]

This two-part aspect is unique to the Khafra pyramid. We believe that the portion at the top of this pyramid is the place we should explore to locate the Tomb of Osiris, and the associated Hall of Records.

---

[406] Lehner. *The Complete Pyramids*.

We think that originally there was a megalithic, trapezoidal mound at Giza. This mound was rediscovered later, when the Nile Valley resurfaced from a 250,000-year submergence beneath the sea and people entered back into the area. We believe these first people were the predecessors of the Egyptian Dynasties, and that they discovered the mound and built the apex on it. This became what is now known as the pyramid of Khafra, and its apex contains the Hall of Records.

They are the ones who wrote the book of Am Tuat to record the positions of the star constellations on the date of the completion of the construction of the apex.

Who will open the Hall of Records?

When asked about who it was that would open the Hall of Records, Cayce said there would appear three, "*two and a guide*," and he named them: *"Hept-supht, El-Ka and Atlan."*

Within the Cayce readings we find that *Hept-supht* was a priest who presided over the ceremony at the completion of Giza and the sealing of the Hall of Records. *Atlan* was either a brother of the Prince of Atlantis or the Prince of Atlantis, but *El-Ka* has remained unidentifiable...until now!

Consider this; in the Egyptian alphabet the hieroglyph for the letter "L" is a picture of a lion. When pronounced "L" and "El" sound exactly the same.

It was a listening stenographer wrote down the words and sounds that she heard from the sleeping Cayce. (It very well could have been "L-ka" that Cayce said.) The word "ka" more or less means *double*.

El-Ka may be a reference to the double-lion god AKER. If this is so, it may have been the *double* of the Sphinx Lion God that was connected with the entrance to the Hall of Records!

Most people are not aware that the ancient Egyptians portrayed the constellation we now call Centaurus as a sphinx. This can be seen in following image from the zodiac ceiling in the temple of Esne.

The ancient Egyptians were great astronomers, but so were the Greeks. The Greek king Alexander the Great conquered Egypt approximately 332 BC and the Greek's name for this constellation was Centaurus. This is how the name Centaurus supplanted the original Egyptian name, which was Lion-Man *(according to the ancient Egyptian Coffin Texts, spell 649)*[407]

It seems likely that the constellation of Leo was the Ka of the Lion-Man, (now known as Centaurus). Leo is the double lion god in the sky, facing west.

Also consider this: within the tombs of several kings of Egypt, whose names were Seti I, Ramesses VI, Amenhotep II, and Tuthmosis III, (in the Book of the Hidden Chamber also known as The Book of Am Duat) there are paintings (of the fifth Division) of a double sphinx lion god with a pyramid above it. And the forepaw of the sphinx lion god on the RIGHT (West) points to a sealed door! (See page 255)

Now let's consider what Cayce said:
> *With the storehouse, or record-house, (where the records are still to be uncovered), there is a chamber or passage from the right forepaw to this entrance of the record chamber or record tomb. This may not be entered without an understanding, for those that were left as guards may NOT be passed until after a period of their regeneration in the mount."*

It is not hard to imagine how easily Cayce's words could be misunderstood if the foregoing information was unknown. The reference to "passage" could easily be misconstrued to mean "tunnel." And since no one ever realized that there was a Sphinx constellation long before there was a Sphinx monument, it would seem self-evident that Cayce's words referred to a statue with a tunnel connected to its right paw. In this way the details were misinterpreted and the Hall of Records has remained concealed.

Cayce said: "*Thou hast shown us the pattern in the mount of our own conscious-ness.*" (Reading 254-101, #22.)

---

[407] as translated by R.O. Faulkner, *The Egyptian Coffin Texts,* Volume II

The *mount* is the mind. It is in our own consciousness that understanding happens after a period of rebirth of these ideas and concepts within our mind. *Regeneration* happens with recognition that star constellations are the guards. Then the tomb of Osiris and the Hall of Records may be entered.

APPENDICES

Appendix 1: Sphinx Chronology

This is an attempt to use the Cayce readings to show the development of the monument of the sphinx. With the theory that it was originally a monument of the face of councilor Asriaio,[408] and under it the body of a lion was later sculpted by excavation.

Reading 457-2, #11 describes a gathering of people in the area of land between two landmarks: (1.) *the facing of the sphinx* and (2.) *the holy mount*.

> *"...all gathered about that plat builded in the holy city between the facing of what afterward became the sphinx and the holy mount..."*

What is the "facing" of the sphinx?

Below are several statements from the readings that pertain to the face of the sphinx:

1. *the facing of what afterward became the sphinx*[409]
2. *the face, even as was given then, is the representation of this councilor*[410]
3. *this was later turned...so as to present...the lion with the man*[411]

Reading 194-14[412] explains how the body of the sphinx was created centuries after the face: There was a man, Arsha, who came into Egypt with the arrival of Araart and his people from the north, who invaded Egypt and took control. Arsha lived during both the first and second dynasties of Araart and hi son Araaraart.[413] During this initial period, there was the restoration of monuments that were discovered through archaeological research.[414] Monuments were pre-existent at Gizeh,[415] the remains of an ancient civilization.[416]

The next section of the same readings gives an indication that the time involved in the development of the monument of the sphinx took place over centuries. Construction of the Great Pyramid was begun at about the same time as the deluge of Atlantis[417] and was

---

[408] ECRS, 953-24
[409] ECRS, 457-2,#11
[410] ECRS, 953-024, #6
[411] ECRS, 5748-6, #17
[412] ECRS, 194-14, #19, Before that we find the entity was in the rule when the king in the Egyptian forces gave the greater knowledge of the indwelling of the divine in the then human forces in earth plane. The entity then was in the name of Arsrha and was the stone and the precious stone designer and carver for that entity, the ruler, Araaraart. [Ra-Ta period.] He arranged for the restoration of monuments that were being restored and builded in those places, being then the founder of now that mystery of mysteries, the Sphinx. He arranged for the restoration of monuments that were being restored and builded in those places, being then the founder of now that mystery of mysteries, the Sphinx.
[413] ECRS, 194-14, 28, (Q) What was the name of the ruler during this entity's sojourn in Egypt? (A) Araaraart.
[414] ECRS, 5748-6, #17, there was even then the seeking through the channels that are today called archaeological research.
[415] ECRS, 341-9, #5, monuments were unearthed and added to from time to time.
[416] See E.A.E. Reymond's *Mythical Origins of the Egyptian Temple*, translation of the Egyptian hieroglyphic text at the Edfu temple which supports Cayce's information of the ruins of an ancient civilization discovered and rebuilt by the first Egyptians.
[417] ECRS, 2067-1, page 4.

completed in 10,390 BC.[418] Upon its completion, there was the sealing of the Hall of Records,[419] *when all gathered between the facing of what afterward became the sphinx and the holy mount*.[420] The readings specify several hundred years passed after the deluge[421] before excavations were made to lie out the base of the sphinx. This indicates the lion body was added later, *under* the monument of the councilor! To accomplish this, channels were laid out and the stone was dug out to create the base *(the body of the lion)*. The readings explain that this was in the land above the place where the temple of Isis stood during the days of the deluge *(of Atlantis)*, which occurred centuries before *this excavation was begun!*[422]

The sculpting of the head-monument (of Asriaio the great Egyptian councilor) took place before the turmoil involving the priest Ra-Ta. Because of the ensuing chaos, the work (already in progress) on the monument had stopped[423]. Ra-Ta was banished to Nubia. Nine years passed and he returned to Egypt. Thereafter, the great pyramid was built. With the completion of Gizeh, there were ceremonies of dedication and the sealing of the Hall of Records. Centuries later the monument of the councilor was turned[424] into the sphinx by adding the body of a lion to it.

---

[418] ECRS, 5748-6, #7 & 8.
[419] ECRS, 378-16
[420] ECRS, 457-2, #11
[421] destruction of Atlantis
[422] ECRS, 195-14, #29 (Q) In what capacity did this entity act regarding the building of the sphinx?
(A) As the monuments were being rebuilt in the plains of that now called the pyramid of Gizeh, this entity builded, laid, the foundations; that is, superintended same, figured out the geometrical position of same in relation to those buildings as were put up of that connecting the sphinx. And the data concerning same may be found in the vaults in the base of the sphinx. We see this sphinx was builded as this:
> The excavations were made for same in the plains above where the temple of Isis had stood during the deluge occurring some centuries before, when this people (and this entity among them) came in from the north country and took possession of the rule of this country, setting up the first dynasty. The entity was with that dynasty, also in the second dynasty of Araaraart, when those buildings were begun. The base of the sphinx was laid out in channels, and in the corner facing the Gizeh may be found the wording of how this was founded, giving the history of the first invading ruler and the ascension of Araaraart to that position.

[423] 5748-6, #17 that which is now called the Mystery of Mysteries, this was intended to be a memorial – as would be termed today – to that councilor who ruled or governed, or who acted in the capacity of the director in the material things in the land. With the return of the priest (as it had been stopped)...
[424] 5748-6, #17 This was later (by Isis the queen the daughter of Ra) turned so as to present...the lion with the man...

Appendix 2: The Pyramid and the Positions of the Stars

The Cayce readings tell us that the Great Pyramid was constructed in 100 years, from 10,490 to 10,390 BC.

> *"(Q) What was the date of the actual beginning and ending of the construction of the Great Pyramid?*
> *(A) Was one hundred years in construction. Begun and completed in the period of Araaraart's time, with Hermes and Ra.*
>
> *(Q) What was the date B.C. of that period?*
> *(A)* **10,490 to 10,390** *before the Prince entered into Egypt."* [425]
>
> *"Then began* **the laying out of the pyramid and the building of same**...*This building, as we find,* **lasted for** *a period of what is termed now as* **one hundred years. It was formed according to** *that which had been worked out by Ra-Ta in the mount as related to* **the position of the various stars** *that acted in the place about* **which this particular solar system circles in its activity, going towards** *what? That same name as to which the priest was banished -* **the constellation of Libra,...**" [426]

Cayce tells us there was a great gathering of all the people for the ceremony of the completion of Gizeh and the sealing of the Hall of Records. In the surviving ancient Egyptian records from tombs and papyri, we can see that significant attention was given to the positions of stars and constellations when commemorating important events such as this one.

What were the positions of stars and constellations in 10,390 BC? How do we know what day and time? The dates of the solstices and the equinoxes were of particular interest to ancient astronomers. There are two solstices and two equinoxes during each year. If we begin our search here, our choices are narrowed down to 4 days from the total of 365 days in a year. Venus was in Libra that year on the Autumnal Equinox.

The funerary papyrus of the priestess Nesitanebetisheru (or Nesi-ta-neb-ashru) records an illustration of a *pyramid* and symbolism that may represent Gemini, Venus in Libra, and Hydra (see page 240 for more information). The fifth division of The book of Am Tuat records an illustration of a *pyramid* and symbolism that may represent the star constellations of Centaurus, Hydra, and Leo, along with Venus in Libra. In both cases, all of the illustrated star constellations were in the sky together, along with Venus in Libra, on September 21, 10390 BC, about 5:00 AM.

---

[425] Edgar Cayce Reading, 5748-6, paragraphs 7-8.
[426] Edgar Cayce reading, 294-151, paragraph 9.

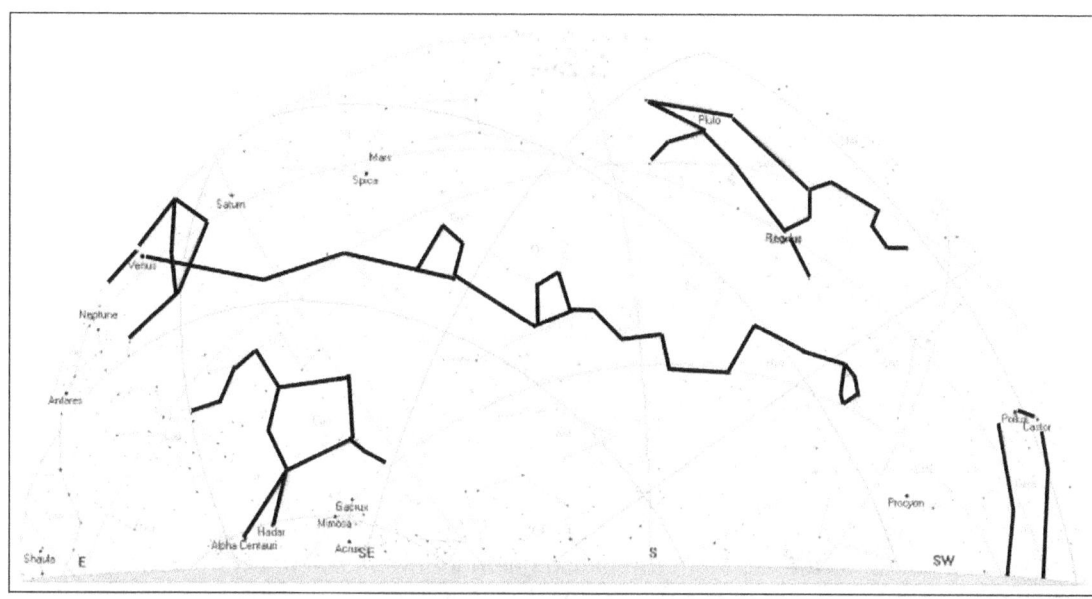

"In the administration of Egypt, the area between 29° 51' and 30° 06' North[427] was organized as a special district which did not belong either to the list of nomes (provinces) of Southern Egypt nor to that of nomes of Northern Egypt. The hieroglyph for this district is a rectangle, which is either empty or filled with water or fish. (17.24 miles)"[428]

As illustrated on the right, in the square Zodiac of Dendera, Egypt, the symbol of the Square of Pegasus, a grouping of stars, is also generally a rectangle, either empty or filled with water or fish.

In *Hamlet's Mill*, de Santillana and Dechend have presented illustrations of this symbolism occurring all over the globe.[429]

---

[427] Coordinates for the Pyramid of Khafra: 29.9761° N, 31.1308° E
[428] Computing Distances between Latitudes/Longitudes in One Step, Stephen P. Morse, http://stevemorse.org/nearest/distance.php
[429] De Santillana, *Hamlet's Mill*. Illustrations are located between pages 434 and 435.

Livio Catullo Stecchini explains the significance of the Square of Pegasus to the ancients:

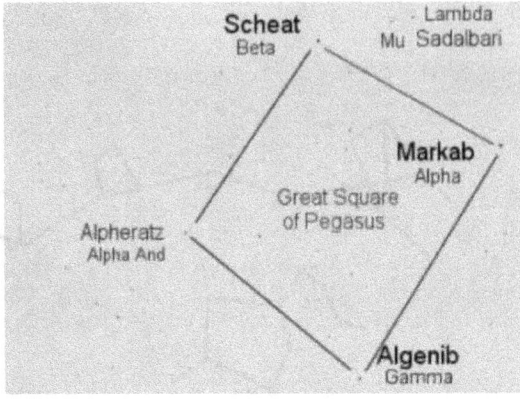

"There are in the sky four stars which are at a distance of about 15° from each other and mark a square with sides that run according to the celestial meridians or parallels; these four stars form the Square of Pegasus. In iconography this square was at times portrayed as filled with water or fish, because it was in the constellation of Pisces. The Square of Pegasus was considered the starting point in the mapping of the sky. The ancients; from the Sumerians to the Romans, in surveying land began by marking a square of a standard dimension and then proceeded to measure out of it in a checkerboard pattern. In cuneiform texts the name *ikū* is given to the basic surveying square, to a unit of land surface, and to the Square of Pegasus. The hieroglyph used to refer to the district extending for 15' from Memphis-Sokar to the apex of the Delta indicates that this district was considered the basic reference unit from which there started the mapping of Northern and Southern Egypt."[430]

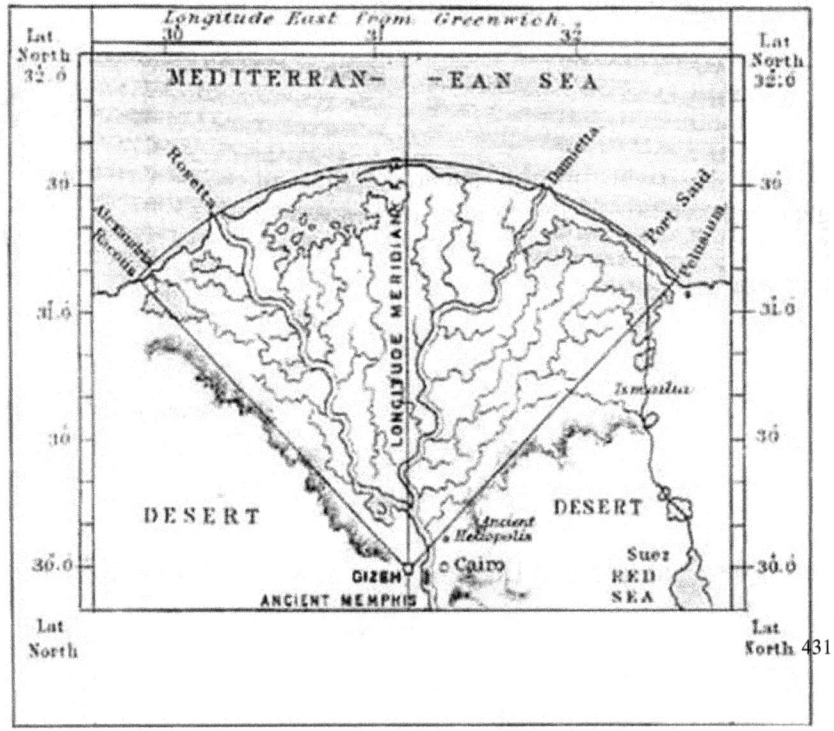

---

[430] Tompkins. *Secrets of the Great Pyramid*, page 297.
[431] Smyth. *The Great Pyramid*, plate II.

Above is an illustration from the papyrus of Ani. The great scales represent the constellation Libra. Thoth is associated with the scales. The ancient sky god Heru stands facing the tomb of Osiris. Osiris is upon his elevated throne located in the delta district (⌑) between 29° 51' and 30° 06' North in Egypt. The four sons of Horus stand upon the lotus, representing the four cardinal points of the compass, as the pyramids at Giza were also aligned. The constellation of Gemini is represented by the presence of the twin goddesses standing behind Osiris. Below, a star map of Giza on September 21, 10390 BC, about 5:00 AM, shows Libra and Gemini opoosite one another, as in the papyrus of Ani.

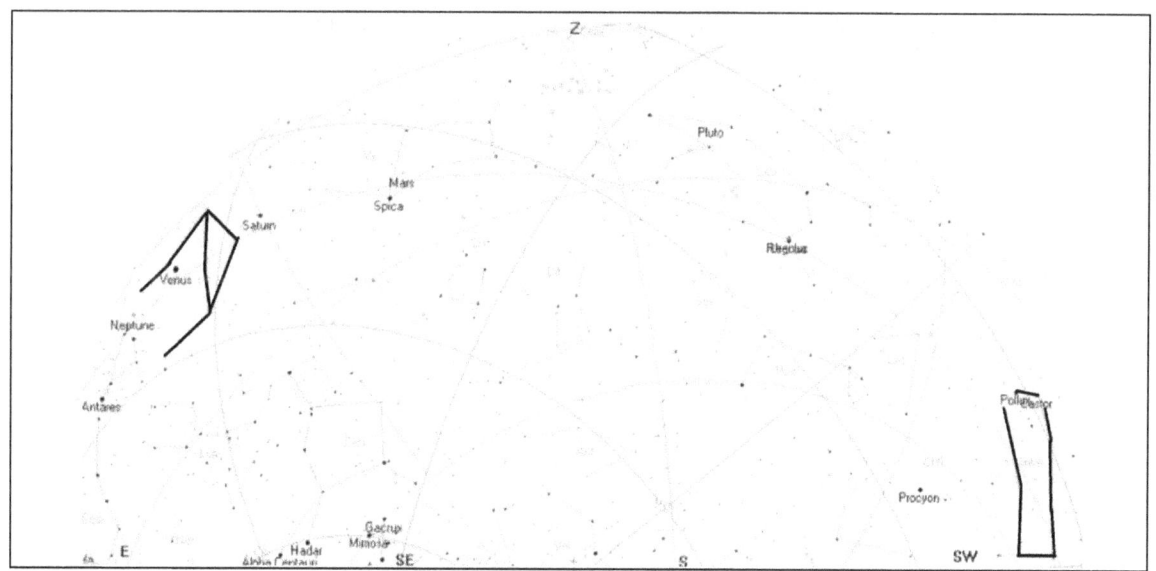

Libra and Gemini

APPENDIX 2

The Position of the Pyramid

Illustration found on a 21st dynasty coffin discovered in Thebes

Heka (god of magic) Heru (ancient sky-god).   A single funerary lily on a table near the throne of Osiris indicates this is his tomb at the top of a pyramid, with the culmination[433] of the constellation Hydra, accompanied by the constellation Gemini.

The interior is the sacred place from primeval time where his mummy rests, at the boundary that divides Upper and Lower Egypt, at the intersection of two meridians.

---

[432] Clark, Robert Thomas Rundle. *Myth and Symbol in Ancient Egypt*, page 171. Illustration found on a 21st dynasty coffin discovered in Thebes. Heka, God of magic (far left), stands with the goddess Maat behind the throne of Osiris. Funerary papyrus of the priestess Nesitanebetisheru, c. 950 BC. EA 10554/88, British Museum.

[433] Budge, EHD, 904A, *Tchua-t*: , the period of the culmination of a star; variant .

The goddess Nekhebit　　　The goddess Uatchit
Goddess of Upper Egypt　　Goddess of Lower Egypt

In the Egyptian Geodetic system, the Giza plateau was located (at latitude 30°00'30") within an intermediate geographic area that divided Upper and Lower Egypt, the area extending from 29° 51' to 30° 06' North.[434] That is why the pyramid is illustrated as the boundary marker between the goddesses of Upper and Lower Egypt.

 Dr. Eve Reymond, in her book *The Mythical Origin of the Egyptian Temple*, page 14, explains that ⊗ *niwt* is the determinative of the name of any sacred place that was created in the primeval age.

 Sir Alan Gardiner, in his book *Egyptian Grammar*, page 52, paragraph 60, explains that these symbols are used phonetically to express the sound of t.

When grouped together this way , the hieroglyphs are a phonetic compliment.

Wallis Budge tells us that this hieroglyph can be translated as *'interior.'*[435]
Ab

---

[434] Tomkins, *Secrets of the Great Pyramid*, Appendix, Notes on the relation of ancient measures to the Great Pyramid, page 291-300, Egyptian Geodetic System, by Livio Catullo Stecchini.
[435] Budge, EHD, page 37, *ab*

North South

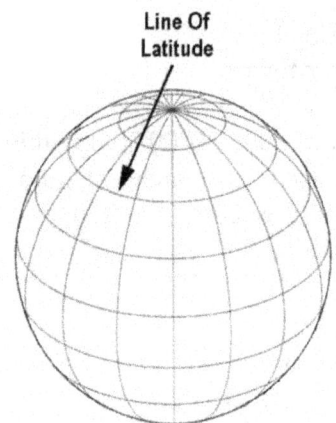

The vulture and the cobra represented the directions of north and south in ancient Egypt, because the vulture was the symbol for land that was located to the south of the Giza plateau and the cobra was the sign for land to the north. Imagine traveling down from the top of the globe, from north to south. Every time you travel across a line, you are at a different place of latitude. Imaginary lines of latitude extend horizontally around the entire Earth.

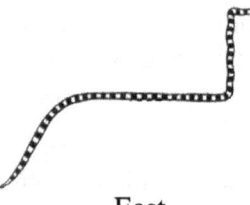 

East West

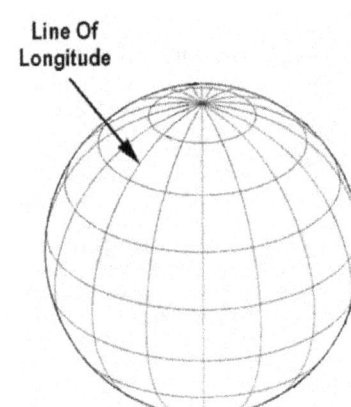

The serpent and the twins represent the star constellations Hydra and Gemini that move from east to west across the sky during the night. Imagine you are traveling around the globe. Each time you travel across a vertical line, you are at a different longitude. Imaginary lines of longitude extend horizontally around the entire Earth. These lines of latitude and longitude together can be used to locate any place on the globe.

The Pyramid and the Positions of the Stars 239

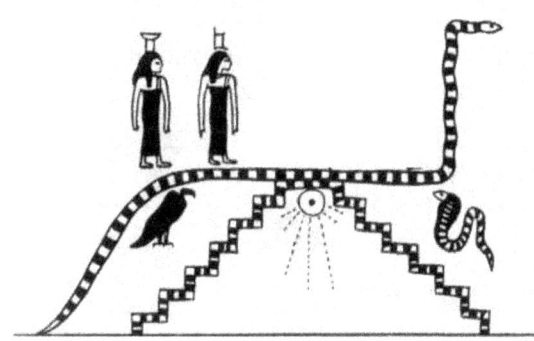

Now we can see that this illustration shows the intersection of meridians of latitude and longitude at the location of the pyramid, at the time of the culmination of Hydra, with Gemini.

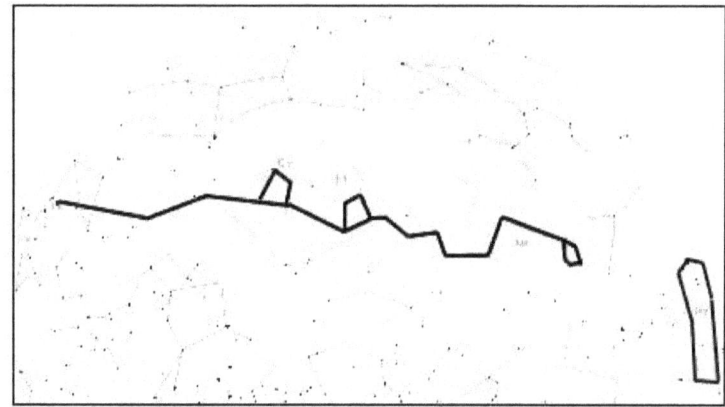

Gemini with Hydra at its culmination over Giza 9/21/10390 BC about 5:00 AM.

Below, a modern map of the Earth showing the same intersection of meridians.

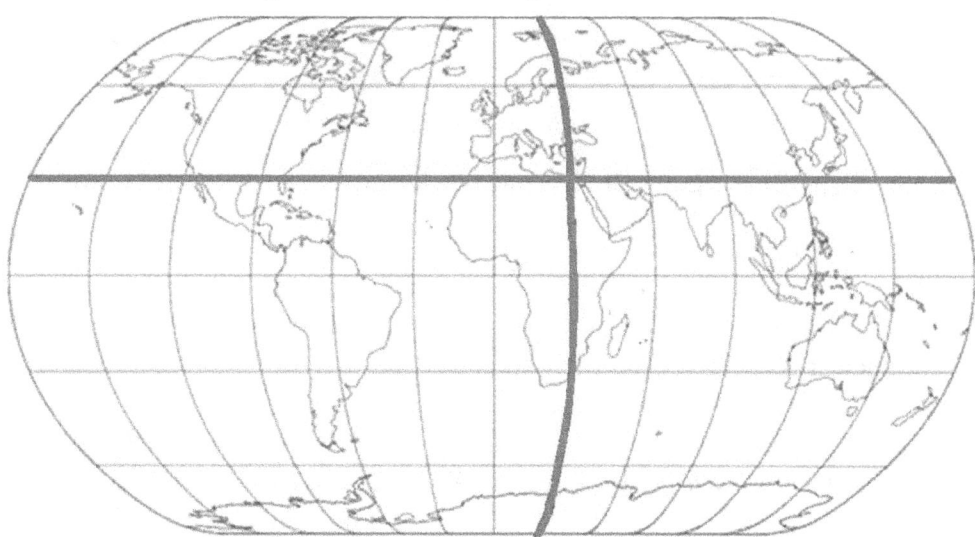

240   APPENDIX 2

The Throne of Osiris

Next we will look at the rich symbolism in this illustration, part of the Greenfield Papyrus from the tomb of Nesi-ta-neb-ashru, piece by piece.

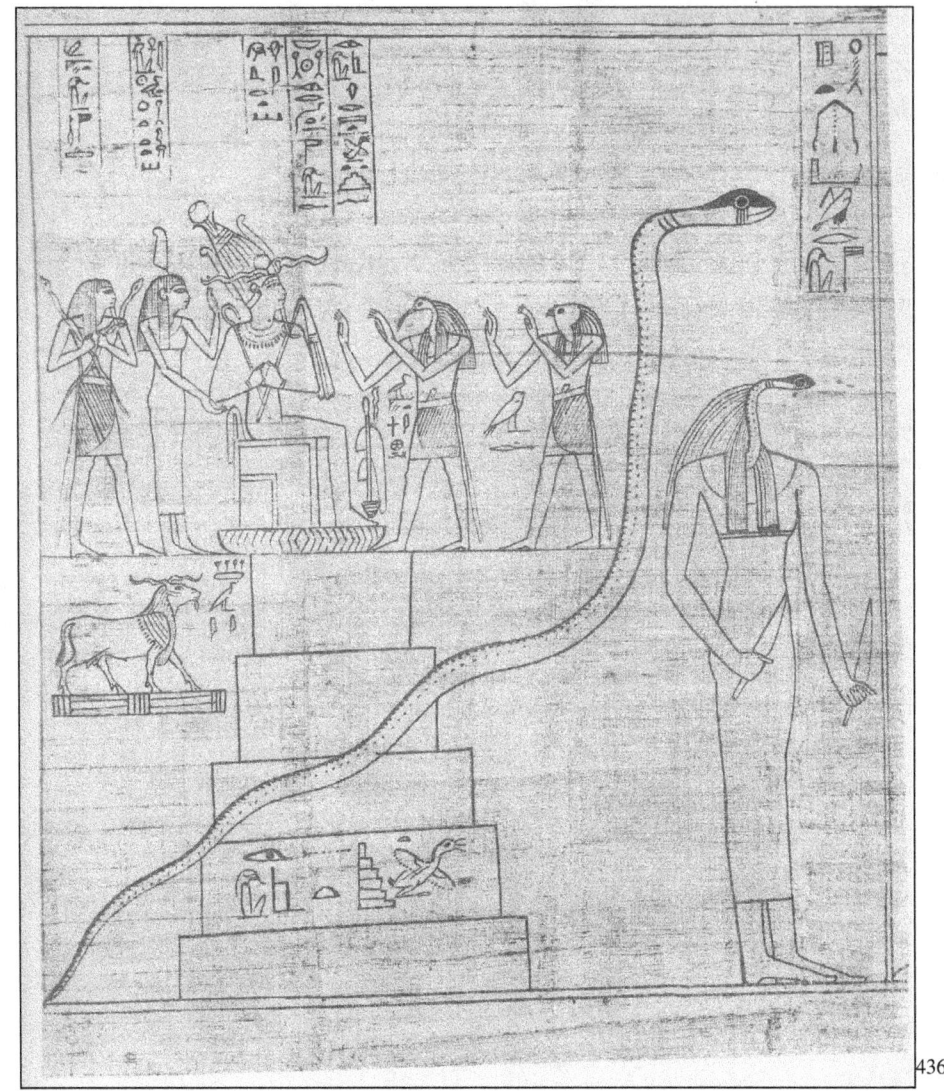

The hieroglyphic inscription on the stone block reads: "The Throne of Osiris." [437]

Written above the serpent:

hept [438]   her
embrace   ancient sky god
The ancient sky god embrace.

---

[436] Budge, *Osiris and the Egyptian Resurrection*, reproduced from the Greenfield Papyrus between pages 42 and 43.
[437] Budge, EHD, 839B, *tentha-t*: throne
[438] Budge, EHD, 479A, *hept*: to embrace, to hug, to take to the breast.

Written above Osiris:

Osar	*heri*	*tenthat*	*ef*	*Neb*	*heh*	*ar*	*tchet*	*neter*	*aa*
Osiris	upon	throne	his	Lord	forever	maker	eternity	god	great

Osiris upon his throne; lord forever, maker of Eternity, great god,

Heri ab　　*Aqertt* [439]
inside　　the "perfect land," the Other World
inside the other world.

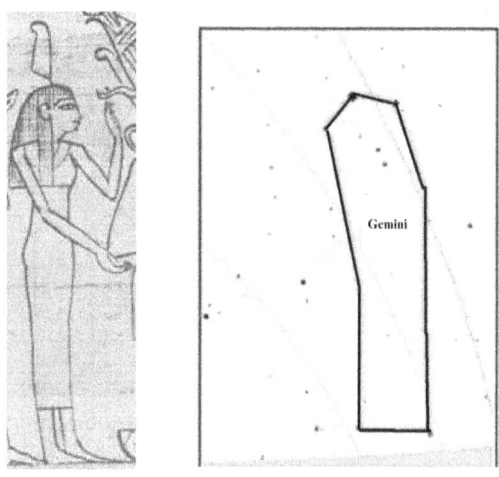

Written above the goddess with a feather *(Maat, i.e., the constellation Gemini)

Maat	*henut* [440]	*paut* [441]	*Amentt*
Truth	a kind of bird	primeval being	abode of the dead

The truth goddess, a kind of bird, a primeval being in the abode of the dead.

Written above the god holding two serpents:

Pehti	*neter*	*aa*
Strength	god	great

the great god of strength.

---

[439] Budge, EHD, 93B, *Aqertt*
[440] Budge, EHD, 490A, *henut*
[441] Budge, EHD, 230B, *paut*, see *pautiu*: primeval beings

The Soul of Osiris, incarnate in a Ram, as worshipped at Busiris, Philae, etc.

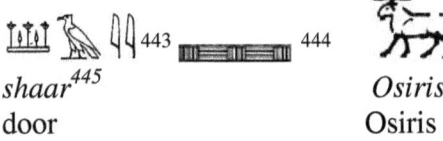

shaar[445]   Osiris
door   Osiris

The door to Osiris.

neb   hetem   Atef   imiut
lord throne crown worn by Osiris   sacred funerary ornament

Tomb of the throne of the lord of the Atef crown.

---

[442] Budge, *Osiris and the Egyptian Resurrection.*

[443] 𓏭 = \\, sign of the dual

[444] Budge, EHD, 416A, *re*: door: | ; ▦ = ◯ | = door = ▤

[445] Budge, EHD, 723A, *shaar*: ▦ , door, gate, prison.

In front of Thoth, if read from the top down it may be interpreted as *"Thoth who is in Tuat this;"* but may also suggest a double meaning or a play on words, as the ancient Egyptians were so fond of doing. If read from the bottom up, it very well could be interpreted as *"This Venus which is Libra."*

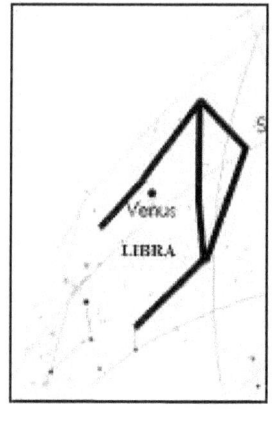

Tehuti	*ami*	*Tuat*	*tef*
Thoth	which is in	Tuat	this

Thoth was associated with the Great Scales, i.e. Libra.

Venus was represented by a 5-pointed star within a circle.

Venus in Libra

The complete text in front of the standing gods:

Tehuti	*ami*	*Tuat*	*tef*	*Her*	*aa*
Thoth	which is in	Tuat	this	ancient sky god	great

Thoth which is in this Tuat of the great ancient sky god.

APPENDIX 2

The five pointed star within a circle ⊛ and the scale pan ⌣ were also used in ancient Egyptian astronomical tablets as scientific notation for Venus in Libra with a scale pan (see illustration below.) Thoth was associated with the great scales that weighed souls in the balance near the judgment throne of Osiris. This idea of scales is associated with the constellation Libra. The implication seems to be an association of symbolism.

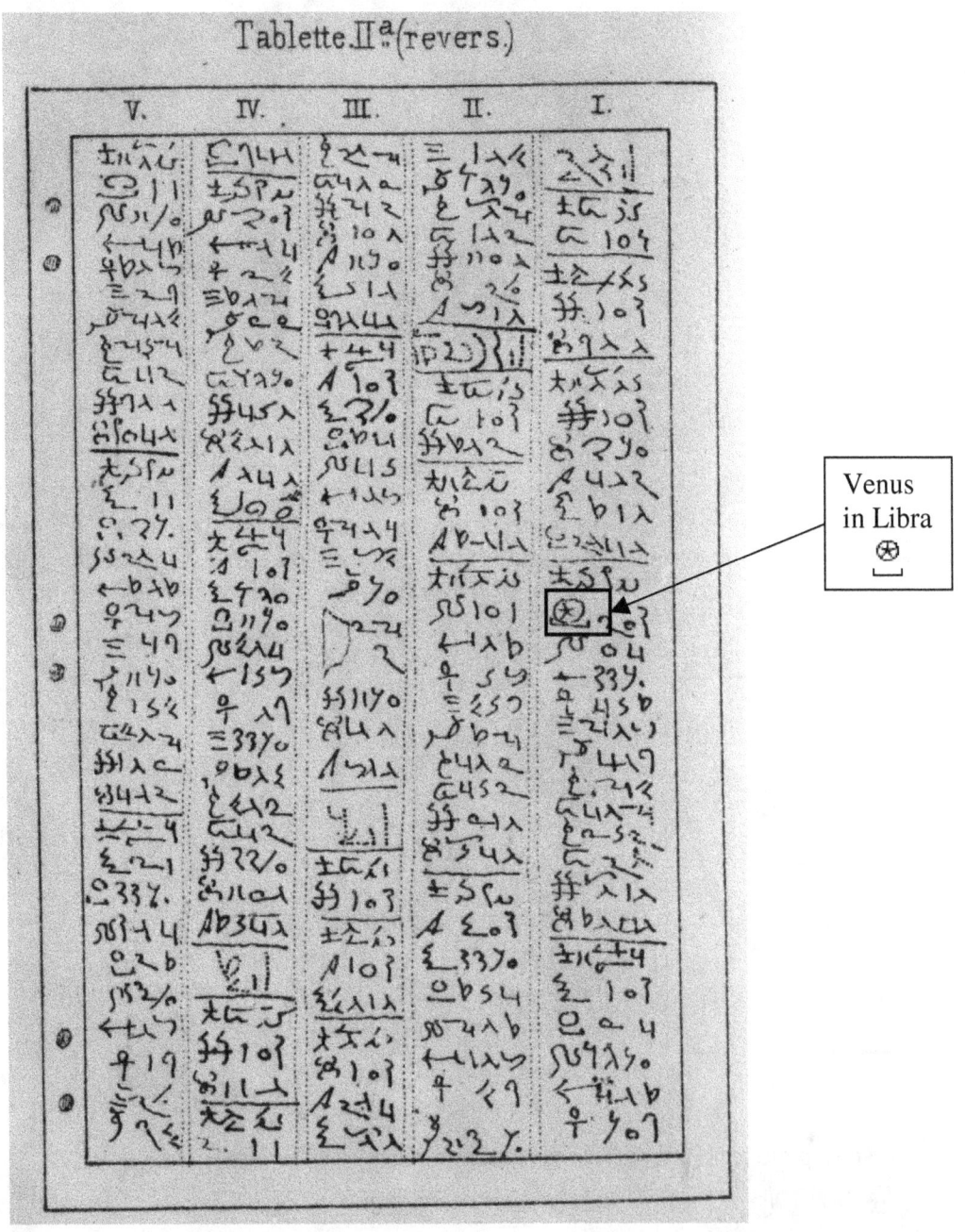

One of the Stobart Tablets

THE PYRAMID AND THE POSITIONS OF THE STARS 245

Gemini   Venus & Libra

Venus in Libra with Gemini over Giza 9/21/10390 BC about 5:00 AM

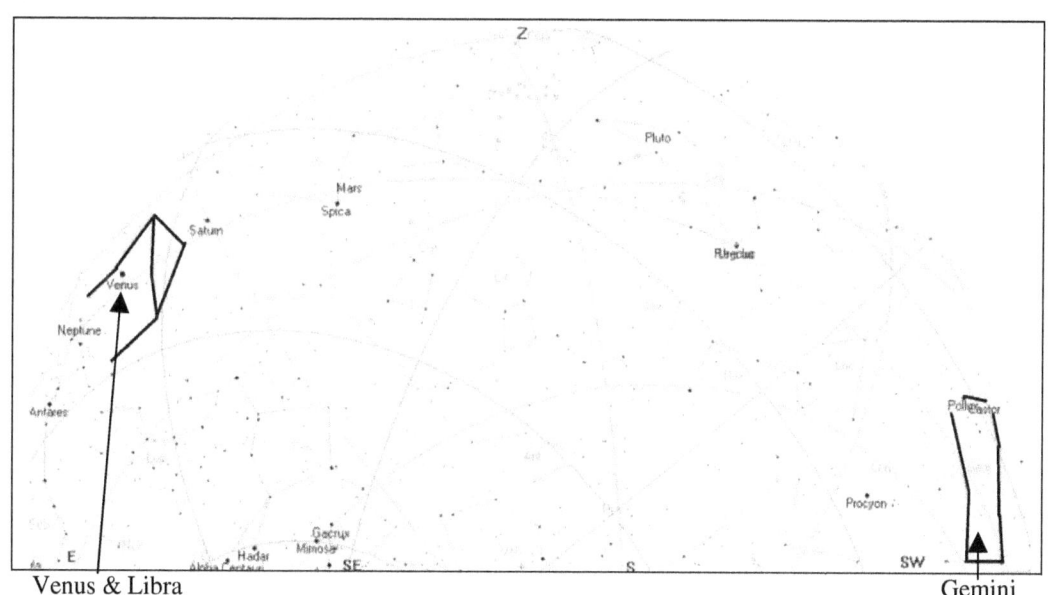

Venus & Libra   Gemini

This image from the tomb of Ramesses VI also shows another configuration of the same constellations during the same time. The god at the tail of the serpent is Venus. The lion on the left is Centaurus and the lion on the right is Leo. The winged serpent is Hydra.

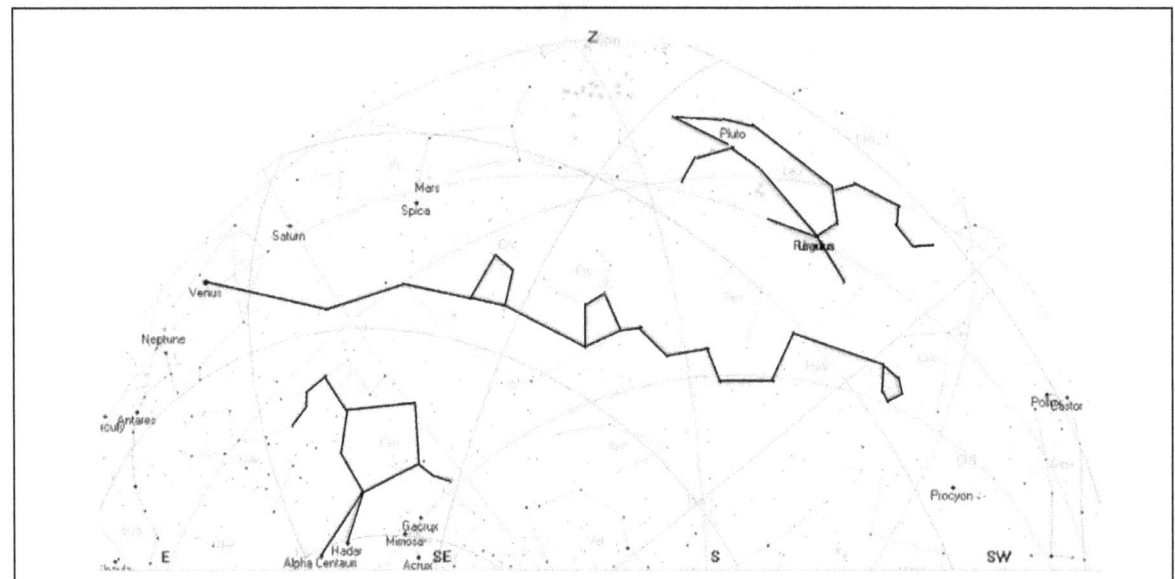

Centaurus and Leo with Hydra at its culmination Giza 9/21/10390 BC about 5:00 AM.

Because of the movement of the stars and planets, we can know accurately the date and time of this configuration.

From the Edgar Cayce readings:

> *"Yet, when the time draws nigh for the changes to come about, there will be the opening of the three places where the records are one, to those that are the initiates in the knowledge of the one god."* [446]

It seems that the knowledge of the knowledge of the One God is the knowledge of *"things that are large in the horizon"*... ASTRONOMY!

From the third hour of the Ancient Egyptian Book of Am Tuat:[447]

---
[446] ECRS 5750-1, #23
[447] From Chapter 3 of the Ancient Egyptian Book of Am Taut, line 185, as written in the tomb of Tuthmosis III, recorded by Paul Bucher.

Metu an neteru shetau kheft neter pen aa aq
Speech to gods hidden move about god this great enter in
Speech to hidden gods, move about this great god, he enters in

ef em ath tu nekht aa [448] *khenti ef net nu*
he upon seize this strong door travel by boat he of celestial water
to seize upon this strong door. He travels by the boat of celestial water.

neb ua neter khepert au tu aakhut em
lord one god things that are large give horizon in
Lord <u>One God gives things that are large in the horizons</u>

---

[448] Amenhotep II reads

Appendix 3: Three Measurements in the Text of Am Tuat: 480, 880, and 120

480 is a measurement of the length in minutes of the constellations of the double lion, from the appearance of the first star in the muzzle of Leo to the appearance of the last star of Centaurus on the horizon. The length of the two constellations is measured by time in minutes. (480 minutes = 8 hours)

880 is a measurement of the time of the journey of the constellation Leo, beginning with the appearance of the Iota Orionis (The Bright One of the sword). The appearance of this star heralds the appearance of the constellation Leo.

120 is a location, i.e.,
This is the location of the appearance of the great serpent: the constellation Hydra.

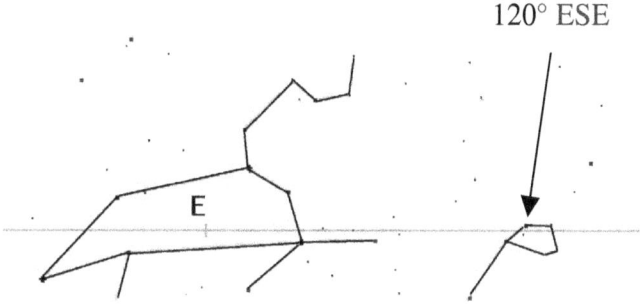

We used Sky-Globe software and found that these occurred 9/21/10390 BC.

250   APPENDIX 4

Appendix 4: The Significance of 220

The 'journey to the gateway' in the image below may refer to the transit time of the constellation of Leo. This picture is showing the twin goddesses (Gemini) in the sky, but the boat of the sun god (Leo) is behind the hidden gate of the horizon (the mat on the prow of the boat).

'The twin goddesses are not in the boat of the setting sun. He travels behind in the celestial water.'

'The journey by boat to the gateway of this place belongs to 220 degrees.'

When does the journey of the sun god begin, exactly? Using Sky-globe, it can be observed that the last star to appear on the horizon before Leo began to enter the sky in 10,390, was the star in the sword of Orion. This may have been when the ancient Egyptians began to count the beginning of the journey of the boat of the sun god.

Below, a circle has been placed over "the Bright One of the Sword," the last star to appear on the horizon before the transit of Leo begins.

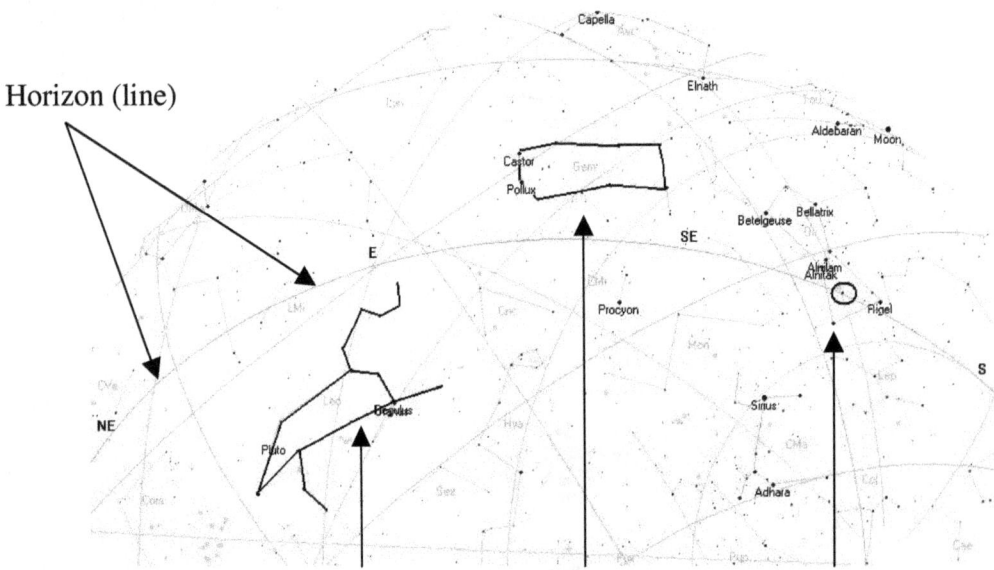

Horizon (line)

Leo just below the horizon in the East.   Gemini   The sword star of Orion

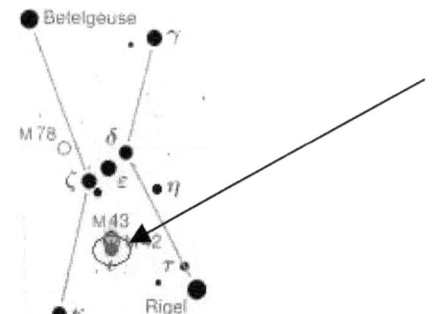

The arrow points to the star in the sword of Orion

Because of the rate of the spin of the earth, star constellations in the zodiac appear to move about 1 degree every 4 minutes. Therefore if we calculate 4 minutes per degree multiplied by 220 degrees, the product of this equation is 880 minutes. This is the length of the journey of the constellation Leo (the ram headed god in the boat) across the sky. This can be verified with Skyglobe. If we use the appearance of the sword star of Orion as the announcer of the journey of Leo, we notice the time it appears is 8:23 PM. Now we begin the count. He (Leo) travels behind the two goddesses (Gemini) in celestial water (sky). The horizontal line is the horizon of the Earth and the vertical line is the path of the ecliptic. The arrow points to the place on the horizon where the last star of Leo disappears below the horizon. The duration of the journey is 880 minutes!

252   APPENDIX 4

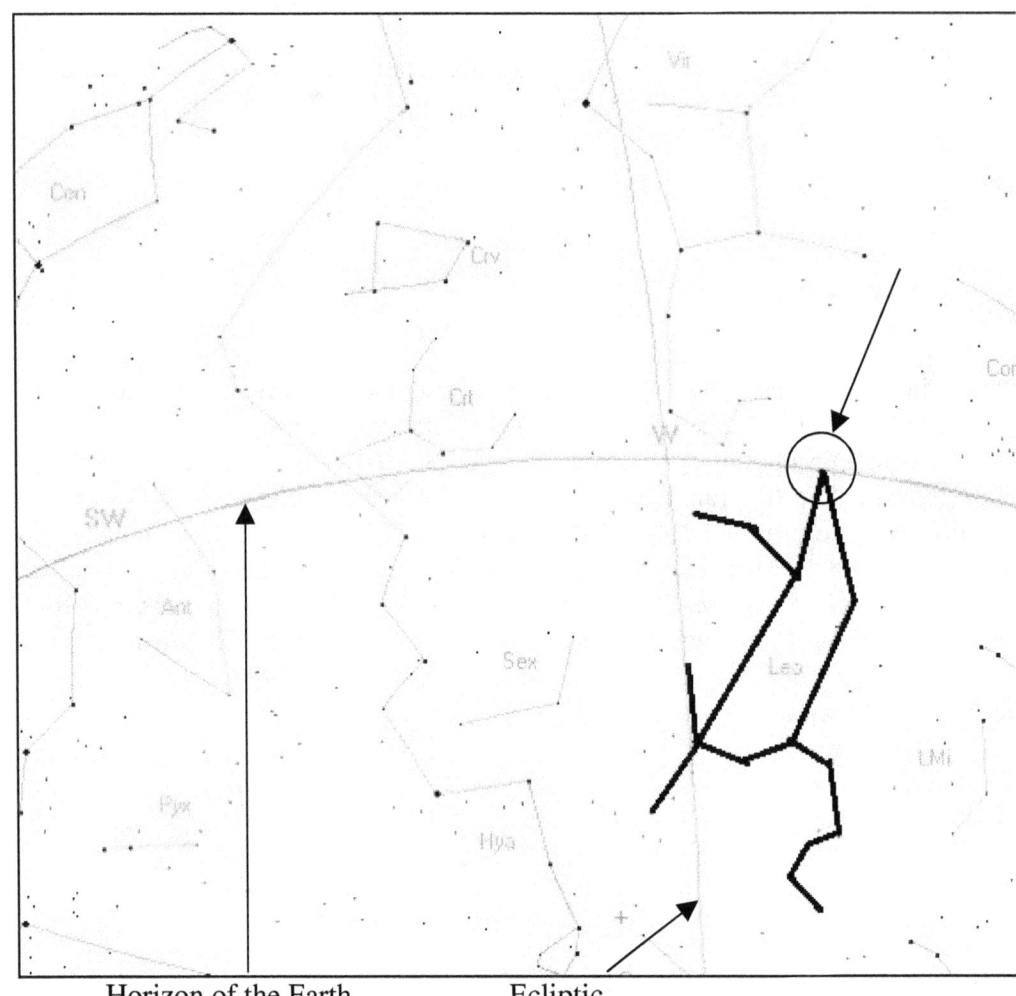

Horizon of the Earth   Ecliptic

Appendix 5: 300 Degrees – the 20th Hour

The spin of the earth makes the stars appear to move about 1 degree every 4 minutes. Therefore, 300 degrees multiplied by 4 minutes per degree results in a total of 1200 minutes.

Then, if 1200 minutes are divided by the number of minutes in an hour (60) the result is 20 hours.

Since the beginning of the day is midnight,[449] we are able to calculate the hour of the day from that point in time. 20 hours from midnight is the hour from 8:00 PM to 9:00 PM.

The 20th hour is the time of the entrance of Leo, the Lion god, from the entrance of the hidden gateway of the horizon into the celestial water of the sky.[450]

This is how the sky looked in 10,390 BC, on September 20th, during the 20th hour. (The lower curved line is the horizon of the Earth.) Leo is about to begin his appearance.

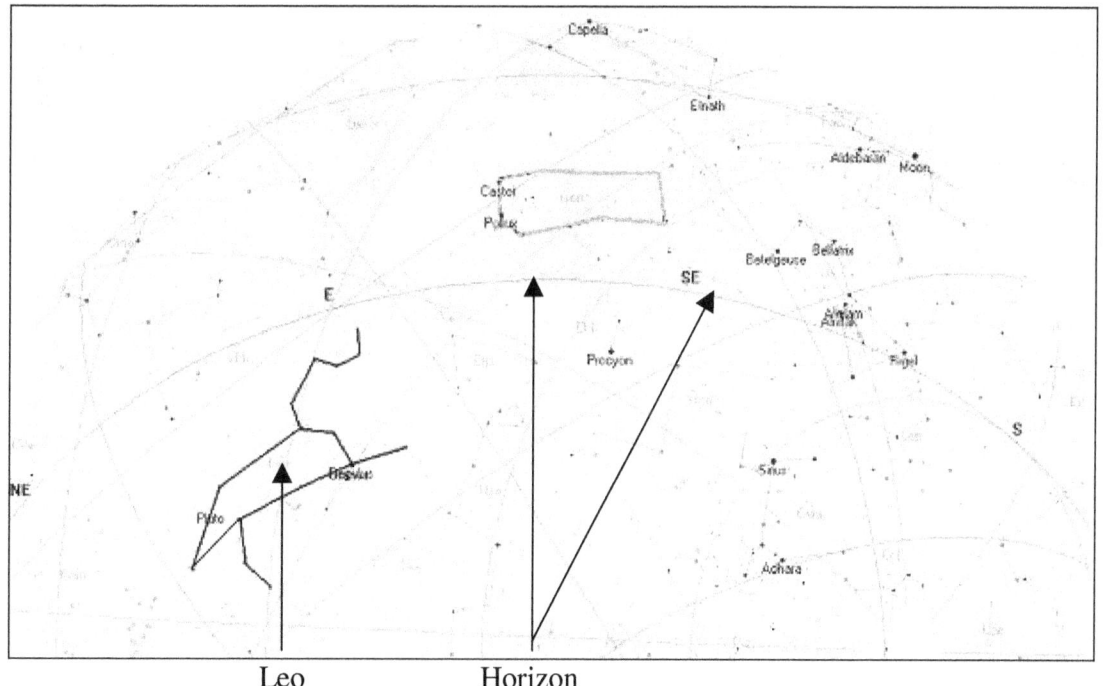

---

[449] Davidson & Aldersmith, *The Great Pyramid*, page 213: Pyramid's astronomical day defined as beginning at midnight and solar year beginning at the Autumnal Equinox
[450] As seen from Cairo, September 20, 10,390 BC, during the hour of 8:00 PM to 9:00 PM.

Appendix 6: The Sealed Room - The Hall of Records

(Q) Give in detail what the <u>sealed room</u> contains.
(A) <u>A record</u> of Atlantis from the beginnings of those periods when the Spirit took form or began the encasements in that land, and the developments of the peoples throughout their sojourn, with the record of the first destruction and the changes that took place in the land, with the record of the SOJOURNINGS of the peoples to the varied activities in other lands, and a record of the meetings of all the nations or lands for the activities in the destructions that became necessary with the final destruction of Atlantis and the buildings of the pyramid of initiation, with who, what, where, would come the opening of the records that are as copies from the sunken Atlantis; for with the change it must rise (the temple) again.[451]

This <u>in position lies</u>, as the sun rises from the waters,[452] *the line of the shadow (or light) falls between the paws of the Sphinx, that was **later**[453] set as the sentinel or guard,*

[454]

[455]

and <u>which may not be entered from the connecting chambers from the Sphinx's paw (right paw)</u>

---

[451] ECRS 378-16 Page 3, #11.
[452] The alignment of the sun with the paws of the Sphinx points to the pyramid of Khafra.
[453] *'The Sphinx that was later set as the sentinel or guard'* may indicate there was an earlier sphinx.
[454] From the Book of Aker, tomb of Ramesses VI
[455] Look at what lies just beyond the Sphinx!! *The temple of records that lie just beyond that enigma that still is the mystery of mysteries to those who seek to know what were the manners of thought of the ancient sons who made man - a beast - as a part of the consciousness.* 2402-2 Page 6, paragraph 38

This illustration is from the tomb of Tuthmosis III.

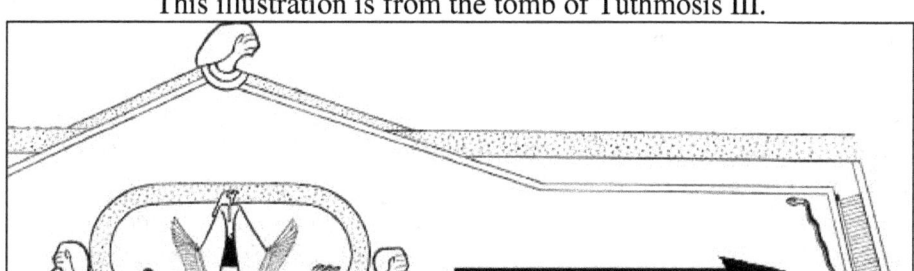

The head at the apex of the pyramid is the ancient Egyptian hieroglyphic word tep, which means "the top." We used a black arrow to show how the Sphinx's paw (right paw) points to a sealed door.

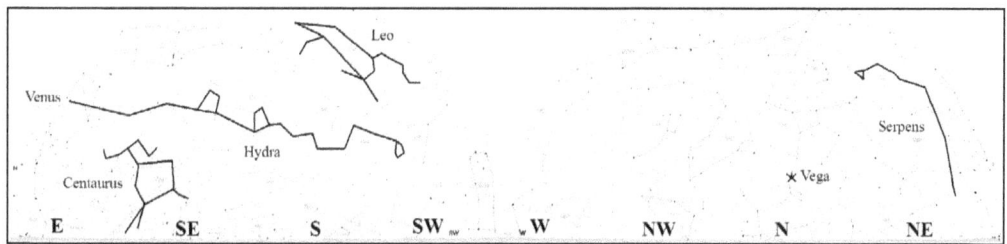

The date this star configuration takes place is September 21st, 10,390 BC at 4:45 AM.

The positions of the stars perfectly match the illustration from the tomb of Tuthmosis III.

...until the TIME[456] has been fulfilled when the changes must be active in this sphere of man's experience.

Between, then, the Sphinx and the river.[457]

The same reading expresses the need to realize the date and time at which those ancient astronomers *"preserved that record for the future entering souls, that will be physically known when time has set its mark."* [458] The mark of time is the date!

In another reading Cayce tells us:

> 5748-7, 17: *With the storehouse, or record house (where the records are still to be uncovered), there is a chamber or <u>passage from the right forepaw to this entrance of the record chamber, or record tomb</u>. This may not be entered without an understanding, for those that were left as guards may NOT be passed until after a period of their regeneration in the Mount.* [459]

Passage from the right paw to the tomb entrance is what we find painted in the tombs of the Pharaohs, pointing the way to the sealed entrance of the tomb on the Northeast corner of the

---

[456] TIME: September 21st, 10390 BC at 4:45 AM
[457] The alignment of the sun with the paws of the Sphinx points to the pyramid of Khafra. The observer would have been between the Sphinx and the river, to see the alignment with the pyramid as the sun rose.
[458] ECRS 378-16, #15
[459] ECRS 254-10, #22 clarifies this: *"in the mount of our own consciousness"*

pyramid[460]. This is the understanding that is needed. This awareness needs to be awakened in the *Mount* of our consciousness.

2329-3 Page 5, paragraph 36:
(Q) *Where are those records or tablets made of that Egyptian experience, which I might study?*
(A) *In the Tomb of Records, as indicated. For the entity's tomb then was a part of the Hall of Records, which has not yet been uncovered. It lies between - or along that entrance from the Sphinx to the temple - or the pyramid; in a pyramid, of course, of its own.*

"*It lies along that entrance from the Sphinx to the temple-or the pyramid; in a pyramid, of course, of its own.*"

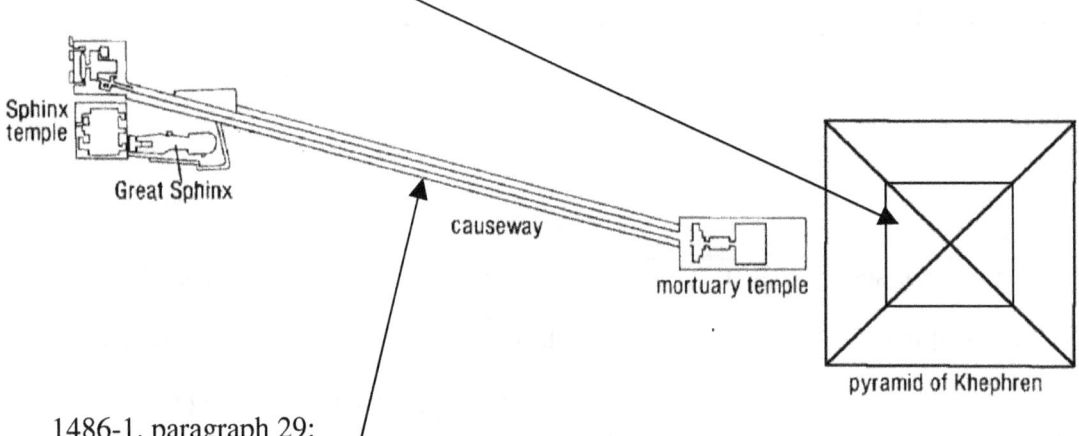

1486-1, paragraph 29:
*The chambers of the **way** between the Sphinx and the pyramid of records.*

2012-1, paragraph 31:
The place of records that leadeth from the Sphinx to the Hall of Records in the Egyptian land.

---

[460] ECRS 341-1 Page 3, #17: "*will be found in the North Corner of the second Pyramid,*" and, "*in the upper chamber of the northeast corner*"
ECRS 341-8, page 4, #17: "*The entity, then, in the upper chamber of the northeast corner of the first pyramid builded, there placed by the grandson, the king who afterward ascended to the throne in Egypt.*"

BIBLIOGRAPHY

Adams, W. Marsham, and E. J. Langford Garstin. 1933. *The Book of the Master of the Hidden Places*. London: Search Pub. Co.

Andrews, Carol, and Raymond O. Faulkner. 1990. *The Ancient Egyptian Book of the Dead*. Austin: University of Texas Press.

Aufrère, Sydney. 1995. *Description de l'Egypte: ou, Recueil des Observations et des Recherches qui ont été faites en Egypte pendant l'Expédition de l'Armée Française*. [Paris]: Inter-Livres.

Bucher, Paul. 1932. *Les Textes des Tombes de Thoutmosis III et d'Aménophis II*. Le Caire: Impr. de l'Institut français d'archéologie orientale.

Budge, E. A. Wallis. 1906. *The Egyptian Heaven and Hell*. Chicago: Open Court Pub. Co.

Budge, E. A. Wallis. 1978. *An Egyptian Hieroglyphic Dictionary: with an Index of English Words, King List, and Geographical List with Indexes, List of Hieroglyphic Characters, Coptic and Semitic alphabets, etc.* New York: Dover Publications.

Budge, E. A. Wallis. 1991. *A Hieroglyphic Vocabulary to the Book of the Dead*. New York: Dover Publications.

Budge, E. A. Wallis. 1973. *Osiris and the Egyptian Resurrection*. New York: Dover Publications.

Clark, Robert Thomas Rundle. 1978. *Myth and Symbol in Ancient Egypt*. London: Thames and Hudson.

Davidson, David, and Herbert Alder Smith. 1927. *The Great Pyramid. Its Divine Message. An Original Co-Ordination of Historical Documents and Archæological Evidences. By D. Davidson and H. Aldersmith*. 4th Rev. Ed. London: Williams and Norgate.

De Santillana, Giorgio, and Hertha von Dechend. 1969. *Hamlet's Mill; An Essay on Myth and the Frame of Time*. Boston: Gambit.

Egyptian Literature; Comprising Egyptian Tales, Hymns, Litanies, Invocations, The Book of the Dead, and Cuneiform Writings. 1901. New York: Collier.

Faulkner, Raymond O. 1977. *The Ancient Egyptian Coffin Texts*. Warminster: Aris and Phillips.

Gardiner, Alan H. 1976. *Egyptian Grammar: Being an Introduction to the Study of Hieroglyphs*. Oxford, [Eng.]: Griffith Institute, Ashmolean Museum.

Hancock, Graham, and Robert Bauval. 1996. *The Message of the Sphinx: A Quest for the Hidden Legacy of Mankind*. New York : Crown Publishers.

Haney, Mark A., creator. 1994. *Skyglobe for Windows* (astronomical software program).

Hawass, Zahi A., and Sandro Vannini. 2006. The royal tombs of Egypt: the art of Thebes, Erik. 1987. *Texte zum Amduat*. Genève: Editions de belles-lettres.

Lefébure, Eugène. *Mémoires publiés par les membres de la Mission archéologique française au Caire, 1882-1884*.

Lehner, Mark. 2008. *The Complete Pyramids*. London: Thames & Hudson.

Lockyer, Norman. 2006. *The Dawn of Astronomy: a Study of the Temple Worship and Mythology of the Ancient Egyptians*. Mineola, N.Y.: Dover Publications.

Mercer, Samuel A. B. 1993. *The Handbook of Egyptian Hieroglyphs: A Study of the Ancient Language*. New York: Hippocrene Books.

Mission archéologique française au Caire, Eugène Lefébure, U. Bouriant, Victor Loret, Edouard Naville, and Ernesto Schiaparelli. *Mémoires Publiés par les Membres de la Mission Archéologique Française au Caire, 1882-1884. Tome second-tome troisième, Les hypogées royaux de Thèbes*. Paris: E. Leroux.

Perrot, J. F. A. 1845. *Essai sur les Momies. A Monsieur le Ministre de l'Instruction Publique*. Nimes: Imprimerie veuve Gaude.

Piankoff, A. 1954. *The Tomb of Ramesses VI*. New York: Pantheon Books.

Reymond, Eve Anne Elisabeth. 1969. *The Mythical Origin of the Egyptian Temple*. (Manchester [usw.]): Manchester Univ. Pr. [usw.]

Clark, R. T. Rundle. 1978. *Myth and Symbol in Ancient Egypt*. London: Thames and Hudson.

Sharpe, Samuel, and Joseph Bonomi. 1864. *The Alabaster Sarcophagus of Oimenepthah I, King of Egypt, Now in Sir John Soane's Museum, Lincoln's Inn Fields*. London: Longman, Green, Longman, Roberts, and Green.

Smyth, C. Piazzi. 1978. *The Great Pyramid: Its Secrets and Mysteries Revealed*. New York: Bell Pub. Co.

Stewart, Basil. 1927. *The Witness of the Great Pyramid; An Exposition Concerning the Anglo-Saxon Race, Their Identity, History, and Destiny, As Revealed by Scripture and the Great Pyramid, with Special Reference to Current Events*. London: Covenant Pub. Co, Tompkins, Peter. 1971. *Secrets of the Great Pyramid*. New York: Harper & Row.

Universität (Basel). Ägyptologisches Seminar, and Université (Genève). 1974. Faculté des lettres. *Aegyptiaca Helvetica*. Basel: Schwabe.

INDEX

10,371 BC 4
10,390 BC 4, 14, 41, 49, 52, 64, 68, 73, 80, 85, 112, 113, 115, 139, 155, 176, 179, 192, 199, 200, 201, 223, 231, 232, 235, 239, 245, 246, 249, 250, 253
1137 BC, death of Ramesses VI 178
120..... .4, 41, 42, 45, 46, 47, 49, 52, 53, 54, 56, 62, 73, 76, 77, 78, 80, 83, 139, 200, 248, 249
2084 BC 67
220° 250, 251
480 .... 42, 53, 56, 62, 76, 83, 248
880 .... 248, 249, 251

A

Abode of the dead 3, 43, 45, 46, 63, 66, 73, 88, 96, 97, 110, 115, 120, 122, 123, 126, 129, 134, 145, 156, 157, 158, 241
Af 4, 43, 57, 66, 192
Aker 66, 85, 112, 220
Alpha Centauri 139, 140
Amenhotep Huy, pyramidion of 219
Amenhotep II, tomb of 49, 90, 91, 109, 124, 131, 132, 144, 145, 161, 163, 200, 211, 227, 247
Amilius
  creator of astronomical charts 49
Amon 104
Ani, papyrus of 235
Apep 42, 53, 58, 61, 80, 109, 111, 112, 115, 116, 117, 118, 152, 157, 200, 201, 202, 211, 212
Araaraart. 49, 114, 139, 207, 214, 230, 231, 232
Araart 49, 114, 139, 214, 230
Arura 148, 149–50, 202
Astronomy... 3, 4, 5, 13, 73, 112, 140, 204, 211
  celestial water..... ..42, 43, 44, 45, 47, 62, 63, 67, 68, 122, 124, 136, 146, 153, 193, 202, 247, 250, 251, 253
Atlan 226
Atlanteans 5, 49
Atlantis 49, 205, 210, 226, 230, 231
  record of 254
  submergence 254
Autumnal Equinox 49, 73, 232

B

Babylonians 67
Bellatrix (star) 41
Belzoni, Giovanni 7
  discovery of the tomb of Seti I 9–39
Boat
  as a solar vehicle . 22, 29, 42, 44, 46, 47, 58, 67, 68, 81, 95, 111, 132, 135, 144, 145, 146, 167, 172, 173, 189, 200, 247
  of the sun god 250
Book of the Dead 141, 222, 257
  Chapter of the Four Torches 223
Bright One of the Sword 250
Bucher, Paul...... 72, 80, 86, 87, 88, 89, 90, 91, 92, 93, 96, 97, 99, 100, 103, 104, 109, 121, 122, 124, 126, 134, 144, 211, 246

C

Calendars 49
Casing stone 206, 225
Castor 76
Causeway (as the way that leads to the Hall of Records) 205
Cayce, Edgar 113
  readings . 5, 6, 49, 99, 204–10, 211, 226, 230, 231, 232, 246
Celestial water....... 74, 83, 84, 94, 96, 117, 122. *See* astronomy
Centaurus .. 41, 51, 63, 75, 85, 88, 92, 112, 139, 200, 222, 226, 227, 232, 246, 248
Coffin texts 58, 222
Complete Pyramids, The 5, 225
Constellations 251
Construction
  change in 5
Cubits 4, 116, 148, 149
Culmination of stars 116, 151, 218, 236, 239, 246

D

Davidson, David
  Great Pyramid. It's Divine Message 253
Dawn 75, 112
Dawn of Astronomy, The 3, 5, 73, 140
Dennefeld, Canon 103
Deshret 223
Djedu 58, 212, 213
Double lion god 141, 227

E

Ecliptic 4, 63, 196, 251, 252
Edfu 5, 230
Egypt
  delta 234
  flood 5, 49, 210
  mapping of 234
Egyptian Hieroglyphic Dictionary (EHD)
  .... 6, 72, 216
Egyptian language 5, 51, 110
Eleventh division 127
El-Ka 226
Equinoctial orientation 5
Equinox, Autumnal 253
Equinoxes 219, 232
Esne 139
  zodiac of 226

F

Fifth division . 4, 51, 53, 54, 55, 78, 83, 85,
  111, 141, 144, 150, 155, 200, 202, 213,
  223, 232
  discussion 184–99
Fifth root race 207, 214
First division 4, 139, 144
Flood 49
Fourth and fifth divisions spread out 42,
  53, 56, 62, 77, 78, 83, 191
Fourth division 4, 50, 53, 54, 55, 76, 78,
  83, 139, 142, 155, 164, 190, 191, 202
French Institute of Oriental Archeology
  104

G

Gateway (of the horizon) 47, 250, 253

Gemini ... 4, 41, 42, 52, 58, 76, 80, 90, 144,
  145, 176, 177, 178, 200, 202, 232, 235,
  236, 238, 239, 241, 245, 250, 251
  goddesses of truth 139, 175, 181
  star of 52
Giza 209
Great House of Heaven 65
Great pyramid 209, 231
  construction of 209, 230, 232
Greeks 227
Greenfield papyrus 216, 240
Guardian lion gods 4

H

Hall of Records 256
  as secret house 211
  as storehouse 99, 109, 110, 113, 114,
    116, 139, 207, 211, 212, 214, 227
  contents 224, 254
  entrance 128, 189, 211, 226
  entrance location . 3, 110, 113, 139, 141,
    153, 205, 207, 214, 221, 222, 223,
    227
  guardians of 207, 214, 227, 228, 255
  location of 204, 207, 208, 210, 214, 224,
    225
    in a pyramid of its own 256
    misinterpreted 227
  not yet uncovered 206, 224, 225
  opening of 210
  sealed entrance 192, 227, 255
  sealing of 112, 226, 231, 232
  still to be uncovered 113, 206, 207,
    214, 221, 227, 255
  who will open? 226–28
Hamlet's Mill 233
Hedjet 223
Hept-supht 226
Hidden house 41, 43, 44, 51, 65, 66, 68,
  69, 75, 88, 91, 93, 97, 110, 112, 126,
  133, 144
Horizon 49, 121, 252, 253
  gateway of 73
  represented by oval 201
Hornung, Erik 219

Hydra.... ...4, 41, 49, 51, 52, 58, 63, 67, 73, 75, 76, 80, 84, 85, 88, 92, 112, 115, 116, 118, 139, 151, 156, 157, 175, 176, 177, 198, 200, 201, 202, 212, 218, 222, 232, 236, 238, 239, 246, 249
    as evil 115, 116, 118, 139
    as the enemy god..... 42, 53, 58, 80, 118, 131
    god of evil 4, 200, 202
    transit time of 4

I

I.F.A.O. (Institut Français d'Archéologie Orientale) 104
Iltar
    temple of 210
Inscription of Kasr es Saijad 104
Isis
    temple of 231

K

Khafra pyramid . 5, 75, 207, 220, 221, 222, 225, 226, 233
    apex of 44, 187, 218
    constuction of 201, 202, 210, 221, 226
    building of 232
    change in contruction 3, 5, 207, 225
Khemit... 44, 67, 93
Kheper 44, 48, 69, 98, 131, 197
Khepera 125, 129, 181, 183

L

Latitude 237, 238, 239
Leclant, Jean 103
Lefébure, Eugène....... 7, 17, 18, 21, 24, 72, 86, 90, 93, 95, 100, 103, 109, 161
Leo .. 4, 41, 47, 51, 63, 75, 85, 88, 92, 112, 144, 200, 222, 223, 227, 232, 246, 248, 249, 250, 251, 253
Libra 232, 235, 243, 244, 245
Life readings 209
    significance of 204
Littmann, Enno 103
Lockyer, Norman 3, 5, 49, 73, 140
Longitude 196, 238, 239

M

Mehen 217
Memphis 51, 65, 75, 88, 110, 192, 193, 234
Memphite necropolis 43, 65, 66
Menmenut 202
Meridian 196–97
Meridians 196, 222, 234, 239
    in Egyptian art 195, 221, 222, 236
    used surveying land 234
Miss 993 209
Montet , P. (Pierre) 104
Mound
    primeval .. 4, 5, 139, 201, 207, 214, 224, 225, 226
    trapezoidal..... 4, 201, 202, 203, 184–99, 226
Mount
    regeneration in the Mount (mind) ... 207, 214, 255
Mythical Origin of the Egyptian Temple 5, 83, 91, 95, 117, 121, 122, 127, 128, 129, 133, 193, 237

N

National University Library of Strasbourg 104
Nesi-ta-neb-ashru
    tomb of 240
Nesitanebetisheru (preistess) 232, 236
Newton, Isaac 73, 140
Nile region 5
Nile Valley
    submergence of 226
Ninth division 122
Noeldeke, Theodor 103
Nu 122, 124, 136
Nut 44, 90, 97

O

Og 209
Orion 4, 175, 176, 177, 178, 181, 250, 251
    Iota Orionis (sword star) 249
Osiris . 6, 27, 42, 43, 44, 48, 51, 58, 59, 61, 62, 63, 69, 83, 84, 98, 99, 110, 116, 146,

149, 151, 170, 191, 192, 193, 194, 211, 212, 213, 214, 217, 218, 219, 223, 225, 240, 242
- house of. 4, 44, 58, 60, 69, 88, 110, 116, 212, 213
- place of 4, 42, 63, 170, 191
- serpent guardian of 152, 217
- throne of 4, 194, 213, 216, 235, 236, 240–47
- tomb of 51, 211, 235

P

Pisces.. 234
Place of destruction.................... 43, 63, 86
Psusennes (Pharaoh) 104
Pyramid
- apex of.. 255
- first built............. 59, 209, 210, 215, 256

Pyramidion of Amenhotep Huy 219

R

Ramesses VI, tomb of. 49, 51, 66, 67, 111, 141, 175, 178, 200, 201, 220, 227, 246
Ra-Ta............. 49, 114, 209, 230, 231, 232
Restau.. 156, 170
Reymond, E.A.E. 5, 83, 91, 95, 96, 110, 117, 121, 122, 127, 128, 129, 133, 193, 230, 237
Ruins
- excavation of 5, 49, 139, 214, 230

S

Scorpio 158
Sealed door.......................... 192, 227, 255
Secret house 51, 110, 211
Seker. 41, 43, 44, 51, 65, 66, 67, 88, 90, 92, 93, 132, 143, 144, 145, 150, 171, 193, 203, 234
- and trapezoidal mound 184–99
- earth of 4
Sekhmet... 146
Sekri .... See Seker
Serpens.. 192, 223
Serpent 4, 17, 32, 42, 49, 52, 53, 54, 57, 58, 61, 62, 64, 80, 85, 109, 111, 112, 117, 118, 119, 141, 148, 149, 151, 152,

153, 154, 155, 156, 157, 162, 176, 177, 178, 182, 183, 186, 192, 198, 200, 201, 217, 218, 223, 225, 238, 240, 246, 249
- guardian of Osiris..................... 152, 217
- standing.. 223
- transit time of 179
- united with Venus 155
- winged...................................... 156, 222

Seti I
- death of.. 177
- tomb of 3, 6, 7, 9, 14, 40, 49, 54, 72, 86, 90, 91, 93, 95, 100, 104, 109, 111, 142, 160, 161, 162, 177, 178, 190, 195, 200, 227

Seventh division............ 61, 152, 217, 223
Shabaka Stone....................... 192, 193–94
Shefit... 223
Shuti 223
Sirius 4
sixth division.................... 44, 69, 94, 99
Skyglobe astronomical software 6, 14, 113, 139, 176, 179, 200, 202, 223, 251
Sokar .... See Seker
Solstices 219, 232
Solsticial orientation 5
Sothis.. 68
Sphinx . 114, 116, 139, 141, 204, 205, 208, 220, 222, 226, 230
- chronology 230–31
- constellation 226, 227
- ka of 223
- monument 227
- right forepaw ... 113, 139, 207, 214, 220, 221, 223, 227, 254, 255

Spiegelberg, Wilhelm 103
Square of Pegasus 233, 234
Star asterisms 74
Stecchini, Livio Catullo. 234, 237
Sunrise... 75

T

Tenth division 125, 127
Text
- red 72, 161, 211
Thebes 16, 109, 151, 178, 218, 236
Thoth 13, 169, 235, 243, 244

Three places where the records are one .. 6, 210, 246
Throne 4, 27, 29, 58, 59, 112, 123, 144, 145, 149, 150, 193, 194, 202, 212, 213, 216, 235, 236, 240–47
Time
    when time has set its mark 255
Tomb of Records 205
Torches 223
Torches, four 222, 223
Tuat .... .51, 57, 74, 75, 80, 85, 93, 97, 98, 115, 116, 120, 122, 123, 124, 125, 126, 127, 128, 129, 131, 132, 134, 135, 144, 156, 243
    canal of 4, 42, 47, 53, 54, 56, 76
    circle in 112, 118, 133
    daily journeys in 96
    god of 124
    goddess of 90
    gods and other beings of . 42, 44, 46, 58, 62, 67, 68, 69, 74, 77, 81, 82, 95, 97, 98, 99, 111, 120
    hidden house of 97, 112, 126, 133
    hour goddess in 82
    images in 81, 92
    meaning of 3
    river of 42, 80
    serpent in 117, 118, 119, 128, 217
Tuthmosis III, tomb of 3, 47, 49, 55, 76, 83, 84, 90, 91, 92, 145, 175, 200, 221, 227, 246, 255
Twin Goddesses of Truth 90
Two and a guide 226

U

Urnes 73, 76, 80
Utchat 172, 219

V

Vega 192, 223
Venus 85, 154, 155, 198, 232, 243, 244, 245, 246
    in Libra 232, 244

W

Winged disk 176, 181

About the Authors

John and Karen met in 1993, and immediately became involved in intense research that has continued to blossom and flourish to this day. What began as research into the authorship of an enigmatic book called *The Urantia Book* led to a study of the psychic and healer, Edgar Cayce, and the publication of their first book together, *Edgar Cayce and the Urantia Book*. During that process, Egyptian history and its unanswered questions began to surface through Cayce's intriguing 'life readings,' and ultimately led to their discovery of the location of the Hall of Records in Egypt, in a very unexpected location. They are in the process of laying the groundwork to prove their findings by translating and studying the ancient Egyptian funerary texts, some never before translated, and all interpreted from the perspective of astronomy in a way never before undertaken. So far their work includes *The Book of Aker, The Book of Am Tuat*, and their newest release, *The Abridgement of the Book of Am Tuat*. Once the translations are completed, they anticipate putting it all together to prove that the Hall of Records is in the top of the middle pyramid at Giza, known as Kahfre's, along with the tomb of Osiris.

John is the president of his company, Bunker Professional Telemarketing, and also works for Edgar Cayce's Association for Research and Enlightenment (A.R.E.) as their Membership Renewal Coordinator. Karen has worked more than 25 years at the Allen County Public Library in Fort Wayne, Indiana. They live in the country in Northeast Indiana with their three cats, Sasha, Kitten, and Mia.

Other Titles by Bunker Pressler Books

Edgar Cayce and The Urantia Book

by John M. Bunker and Karen L. Pressler

ISBN 978-0966977417

The Book of Aker

by John M. Bunker and Karen L. Pressler

ISBN 978-0966977431

A Sailor and his Ship: The Voyage of the USS Shoshone (AKA-65)

by D.D. Cayce

ISBN 978-0988500129

Rainwater: The Answer to the Pyramids

By Patrick Giles

ISBN 978-0966977448

The Am Tuat

By Paul Bucher

ISBN 978-0988500150

The Story of Zoo-Key-Knee and the Origin of Rute-of Bagas

By John Bunker

ISBN 978-0966977493

www.ingramcontent.com/pod-product-compliance
Lightning Source LLC
Chambersburg PA
CBHW080240170426
43192CB00014BA/2508